Thirteen hundred people crowded into a
plush and gilt theatre to watch an
American film-actress singing and
dancing in a musical; repertory actors in
Elizabethan costume performing in a
classroom; an agent and a producer
arguing about the size of an actor's name
on a poster; Arts Council officials in
Piccadilly planning how to spend three
million pounds; out-of-work actresses
queueing at a Labour Exchange . . .

These are a few of the component
elements of the English theatre which
Ronald Hayman takes into his sights in
The Set-Up. What makes the theatre tick
in the way it does ? This book
investigates the power and the pressures
behind it, analysing its structure and
systems, and the way that money and
motives flow through it.

On the one hand there are the
organisations: the big national
companies, the West End managements,
the regional repertory theatres, the
'fringe' groups, the trade unions, the Arts
Council. On the other are the individuals:
actors, directors, playwrights, agents,
administrators. Our theatre is what it is
partly because of the State, which
provides rather more money than do the
people who buy tickets at the box office;
partly because of the surrounding social
and cultural situation; partly because of
the individuals who run it and work in it,
their strengths and weaknesses, their
talents and working habits. Ronald
Hayman's challenging book illuminates
the conflicts and contradictions in the
set-up. It is a mine of information
about how theatres are run, what it costs
to put shows on, how they pay their way
and what happens when they don'

THE SET-UP

THE SET-UP

An Anatomy of the English Theatre Today

RONALD HAYMAN

Eyre Methuen London

FOR IMOGEN

First published in 1973
Copyright © Ronald Hayman 1973
Printed in Great Britain
for Eyre Methuen Ltd
11 New Fetter Lane, London EC4P 4EE
by Cox & Wyman Ltd
Fakenham, Norfolk

ISBN 0 413 29120 0

CONTENTS

	Acknowledgments	*page* 9
1	The Actor's Motives	11
2	The Actor's Relationships	22
3	The Actor Prepares—for What?	40
4	The Theatre and the Theatres	57
5	The National Theatre and the Royal Shakespeare Company	78
6	The West End	115
7	The Royal Court	147
8	The Mermaid	165
9	The Regions versus London	171
10	Repertory	182
11	The Fringe	207
12	Culture and the Arts Council	227
13	Equity and Democracy	249
14	The Actor's Agent	264
15	The Playwright and His Agent	275
16	Directors	288
17	The Audience and Its Motives	297
	Bibliography	311
	Index	313

FOREWORD

The word *anatomy* was the starting point for this book. Would it even be possible to write analytically about the English theatre today as if it were an organism? Certainly it was once, but today the component parts are scarcely holding together, let alone growing together. All those flaking rococo interiors in Shaftesbury Avenue, and all those eager young actors driving about the North of England in minibuses to put on one-night stands. Laurence Olivier in make-up and costume as Shylock at the Old Vic; muscular nudes swimming about the 'see thro pool' installed on the stage of the Whitehall for *Pyjama Tops*. Suave and soigné agents with three telephones on their desks; tense young drama students sweating in movement classes. Arts Council officials in Piccadilly apportioning a three-million-pound drama budget; militant radicals at Equity meetings agitating for a strike. Press agents buying journalists expensive lunches; out-of-work actors queueing at the Labour Exchange in Lisson Grove. Think about the disparate elements for long enough and all pattern disappears. You are left with a mass of jigsaw pieces that must surely belong to different puzzles. Maybe the English theatre exists only as an abstract concept. Generalisations about it can still sound convincing, but can any of them be relevant to more than part of such a complex and hetero-geneous whole?

This book is as specific as I can make it. The approach is anatomical rather than critical, historical or psychological, but some of the anomalies are so grotesque that an objective description of them constitutes a criticism. A few historical digressions are inevitable: the present situation cannot be detached from the past that led up to it. And I have to attempt an analysis of motives. Theatre can exist only if actors want to perform and audiences want to watch, but neither set of motives remains constant. In Ancient Greece, and even in eighteenth-century England, actors and audiences may have wanted something similar to what they want today, but we need to define where the similarity ends. I have started with the actor's motives because the more commercialised and industrialised our theatre becomes, the more it is subject to economic laws, and the current situation would be very different if the supply of actors did not vastly exceed the demand. Not that the actor's job is the only one in the theatre that seems glamorous and enviable. Even telephonists who work for theatrical agents tend to be less well paid than telephonists who work for mortgage brokers. Some of them may be frustrated actresses, just as impresarios may be frustrated directors or writers. Even inside the theatre hardly anyone is doing exactly what he wants to do at the time he wants to do it, but if nearly everyone settles for less money than he could earn in another trade or profession, what is the sacrifice for if not relative freedom from frustration? But, though most actors have to put up with the frustration of being out of work for most of the time, the pressure from outside the profession of people trying to get in is so enormous that it has created a counter-pressure to keep them out. So, alongside the question of training, it is necessary to consider the profession's methods of making itself more exclusive.

The playwright, the director and the actor all have to establish a relationship with an audience within a given space, but buildings, unfortunately, are much more durable than ideas about what the relationship ought to be, so I have considered how progress has been retarded by the necessity of working in old buildings. We have plenty of post-war theatres, but only two of the big ones are in London.

Any decision, in a book like this, about how space should be allocated between London and the regions is necessarily arbitrary. The chapters on the National and the Royal Shakespeare Company, the West End, the Royal Court and the Mermaid occupy more pages than the chapter on regional repertory; and in the chapter on the Fringe I have not been able to give a detailed account of the work being done by the groups which are not centred on London. But London is the main nerve-centre for both kinds of theatrical activity, though, as

I have suggested in the chapter on London versus the Regions, the relationship between the centre and the system is constantly changing. The Arts Council's policy of fair shares for the regions has greatly helped the reps, and, if commercial touring has suffered, the touring Fringe groups have benefited.

The role of the Arts Council is steadily increasing as the state becomes more committed to investing in the arts, but this development needs to be examined in a fairly wide cultural context, and it is possibly quite important that from time to time someone should challenge the assumptions about culture that underly official policy. The Arts Council's practice is not altogether in line with its own Charter, and its Charter is not very realistic. But the deviations between Charter and practice are not the ones that realistic considerations would seem to prompt.

No theatre can remain healthy without regular doses of innovation, and these shots in the arm are invariably administered by individuals, never committees. One of the troubles with committees is that they tend to put their trust in other committees and encourage their proliferation. The actor's relationships, as I argue in the second chapter, become depersonalised. He becomes uncertain who his boss is, who is responsible for the decisions that control his work. If the Arts Council's Drama Panel is one of the two most influential committees in the theatre, the Council of Equity is the other, though Equity is gradually becoming more democratic.

Moving rapidly, as most actors now do, between different engagements and different media, they do not stay in the same company for very long at a stretch, and the old feeling of solidarity with the group can only partially be replaced by a feeling of solidarity with members of the same union. And the relationship with the paternalistic old employer can only partially be replaced by the relationships with the agent and director, who now divide the role of father-figure. But this is not the only reason for their increased importance in the theatre of today, as I try to explain. Finally there is a chapter on the audience and its motives, which must interrelate with the actor's motives, completing the circle.

RONALD HAYMAN

ACKNOWLEDGMENTS

This book could not have been written but for the generosity of a very great many friends, acquaintances and strangers in and around the theatre who have taken time to talk to me about it. I have greatly enjoyed most of the conversations: they have affected – and sometimes reversed – the opinions I started with, but I must emphasise that the people who have helped me are not to be blamed either for the tenor of the book or for the arguments it advances.

I am most grateful to Richard Findlater for reading the book in galleys and commenting very usefully. Many other people read individual chapters and criticised constructively. Lore Schacht gave me professional advice on my amateur excursion into psychoanalysis in the first chapter, and Donald and Ian Albery both read the fourth and sixth, as well as providing a lot of valuable information. I am grateful to Trevor Nunn for corresponding with me while I was working on the fifth chapter, and I had useful conversations with Kenneth Tynan, Patrick Donnell, Michael Hallifax, David Brierley, Maurice Daniells and Peter Kemp. Patrick Donnell and David Brierley not only spared time for several discussions but provided figures and read the first draft of the chapter.

I had help on the sixth chapter from Hugh Beaumont, Oscar Lewenstein, Michael White, Bob Swash, Richard Pilbrow, John Gale, Toby Rowland, Martin Tickner and Alex Cohen; the chapter was read in draft by Hugh Beaumont, Michael White, Richard Pilbrow, John Gale and Toby Rowland. In the seventh chapter a meeting with Bill Gaskill, a telephone conversation with Jonathan Hales and the loan of balance sheets from Jon Catty were all helpful.

David Aukin and Nancy Meckler were kind enough to help with

information on the Fringe both before and after reading my draft chapter on it, and Malcolm Griffiths's reaction to it were very valuable. Sir Hugh Willatt, J. W. Lambert, N. V. Linklater, Dennis Andrews and Nick Barter all talked to me about the Arts Council, and the chapter was read by Sir Hugh, N. V. Linklater and Dennis Andrews, who also read most of the book in proof and provided a good many useful facts and statistics. Celia Palfrey, Hugh Manning and Steven Sylvester talked to me about Equity; Celia and Hugh read the chapter in draft and commented. Larry Dalzell, James Sharkey, Cary Ellison, Gordon Harbord and Margaret Ramsay talked to me about agents. Larry Dalzell and Cary Ellison read the chapter on actors' agents, Margaret Ramsay the chapter on authors' agents.

Earlier versions of three chapters appeared in *Drama*, and of two chapters in *Theatre Quarterly*: I am grateful to the Editors for permission to reprint this material. I am also grateful to John Higgins, Arts Editor of *The Times*, for commissioning me to do so many interviews with actors, directors and playwrights. Those on which I have drawn most in this book were (in chronological order) with Ian Richardson, Peter Brook, Ronald Eyre, Paul Scofield, Terry Hands, Peter Nichols, Joan Plowright, Frith Banbury, David Hare, Elizabeth Spriggs, Alec Guinness, Peter O'Toole, Michael Codron, Michael Hordern, David Warner, Robin Phillips, Ronald Pickup, John Neville, Ralph Richardson, John Barton, Maggie Smith and Robert Stephens, and John Dexter. I am also grateful to Walter Lucas, Executive Editor of *Drama*, who started me thinking about the pros and cons of permanent companies by commissioning a piece called 'The More We Are Together', and for that I talked to Donald Sinden, Judi Dench, Robert Lang, Jane Lapotaire and Clifford Williams.

1 THE ACTOR'S MOTIVES

*I exist only through those who are nothing apart
from the being they have through me.* GENET

Acting and playing – the words are synonymous, and the word *actor*
did not come into common use until the end of the sixteenth century.
The word *player* had been used since the middle of the fifteenth.
What actors do when they are working is what children do when
they are playing: they dress up, slip into other identities, mimic
other people's ways of talking and moving, all the time wanting to
be watched, and feeling more confident, more real, than when they
are merely being themselves. The pleasures of acting are usually more
apparent in a bad performance than in a good one. There are actors
whose relish for self-assertion is blatant. They listen to their own
voices, as if the auditorium had an echo. They occupy stage-space
like a liberating army. They dunk each gesture in the nectar of the
audience's silent attentiveness. For the good actor, too, there is pleasure in controlling the reaction of a large number of people, but there
is also a possibility of being buoyed up, stimulated by their concentration to a higher level of creativity. And when this happens it feels
very much like an upward escape from the confines of the everyday
personality. Aldous Huxley would have called it a form of self-
transcendence.

Dr D. W. Winnicott, a paediatrician who became a psychoanalyst,
has suggested that for the adult, as for the child, it is only in playing
that the individual can be creative and use the whole personality. If
this is true, it would follow that there are far too few situations in
our social life in which creative play is possible for adults, and this
would help to explain why so many people, so different from each
other in type, talent and background, are constantly and persistently

struggling to join a profession which is already overcrowded. It is not a cohesive profession. The word 'actor' is indiscriminately applied to people involved in a range of fairly diverse activities from street theatre to television commercials, from summer seasons on the Isle of Wight to two-year contracts with the Royal Shakespeare Company. The life of an actor who stays for three years at the repertory in Stoke-on-Trent is totally unlike the life of an actor in London whose agent gets him a succession of brief but highly paid jobs in films and television, with only a very occasional foray into the theatre when he can afford it. Working on the so-called 'Fringe' is a very different experience from working in the established theatre. And all this is to make no mention of the differences between being a star and being a small-part actor who is usually out of work.

While there are some actors who become addicted to high salaries, money is not usually a prime consideration. In 1972, when London Transport was advertising for bus conductors at £34 a week, Equity, the actors' trade union, was still fighting to raise the minimum for work in the West End to £30 and had only recently raised the national minimum to £20 for full members and £18 for provisional members. If the five thousand actors and actresses who replied to Equity's questionnaire are typical of the profession, about 70 per cent of it is out of work at any given time, and in the whole of 1971 six actors and actresses out of ten earned less than a thousand pounds. As an executive of American Equity put it, 'An actor is the only human being who will work for nothing, if you let him.' He will put up with long periods of unemployment, and long periods of waiting around in theatres, rehearsal-rooms, film-sets and cramped, shabby, ill-equipped dressing-rooms. He is also working with no prospect of a pension. The fact that so many actors tolerate such very daunting professional conditions indicates an extremely powerful drive to go on working in the theatre, a drive which has never properly been explained.

We cannot hope to understand the situation in the English theatre today without understanding the strength of the drive to join the profession. Most actors do not themselves understand why it is so important to them to be actors. If asked they will reply disarmingly,

'There's nothing else I could do.' But there is more to it than this. Psychoanalysts like Winnicott and Ronald Laing have shed so much light on identity delusions that it may be worth considering whether there is any underground connection between the actor and the schizophrenic. While the actor is not under the delusion that he is really Galileo or Julius Caesar, there may be unconscious processes at work which have little to do with schizophrenia but which can be understood better in the context of what has been discovered about it.

In *The Divided Self*[1] Laing describes the life of the schizophrenic as being torn between two contradictory desires: to reveal himself and to conceal himself. The sensation of being an object of other people's observation – whether based on fact or illusion – is a source of both pleasure and pain. The schizophrenic feels that he is more exposed and vulnerable than other people: their gaze is dangerous to him because it could penetrate to the core of his inner self. At the same time he feels isolated. Desperation at not occupying the first place in anyone's affections can lead to paranoiac delusions of persecution. An illusion of the enmity of all others is preferred to the realisation that they are indifferent.

The schizophrenic feels unreal, precariously differentiated from the rest of the world, uncertain of his identity. At the same time as dreading relationships with other people, who may rob him of his autonomy, he needs them because without them he has no sense of his own reality. 'I am only a response to other people,' one of Laing's patients said. 'I have no identity of my own.'

Against this background, exhibitionism can be seen as a desperate bid for attention. It seems possible to show oneself off at the same as holding one's real self back, to exhibit the body while inhibiting what goes on inside the mind. Or, as Laing puts it in *The Self and Others*,[2] 'The exhibitionist who shows off his body, or a part of the body, or some highly prized function or skill, may be despairingly trying to overcome that isolation and loneliness which tend to haunt the man who feels his "real" or "true" self has never been disclosed to, and/or confirmed by others.'

[1] Tavistock, 1960.
[2] Tavistock, 1961.

This splitting of what feels like the real self from what feels like the unreal self is characteristic of schizophrenic behaviour. Another patient of Laing's felt 'as though somebody was trying to rise up inside and was trying to get out of me'. This is very much like what the actor feels when the character seems to be taking over. The split, for the schizophrenic, can come to feel like a separation between the self and the body. The real self is held back so much that it comes to feel disembodied, while the body becomes the centre of what Winnicott calls 'the false self'. The disembodied self is then withdrawn from contact with other people, confined to purely mental activity, while the body feels as though it is capable of acting independently, without compromising the integrity of the real self. It is only the body that is exhibiting itself or dressing up in women's clothes or pretending to be Napoleon. The real self remains detached, elusive, uncommitted, and the schizophrenic may well be priding himself on the absolute honesty he is maintaining in communing with it. The persona assumed by the false self is an amalgam of part-selves, collected from different sources and undeveloped or only partially developed. Deliberate mimicry of other people's ways of walking and talking is a form of defence against the impression that one's own existence is unreal. By resembling other people one can participate in their reality. The alternative is to behave so outrageously that they will be embarrassed or offended. If the effect you produce on them is real you must be real too. It is only their indifference which is intolerable.

So the desire for reciprocity in relationships with other people has been first subordinated and then sacrificed to the compulsion to get through to them, at whatever cost, to be certain that they are receptive to what is being transmitted. But to expose oneself to what they might want to transmit would be too dangerous: it could lead to a dependence on them in a way they might exploit. Underneath all this, of course, is a loss of faith in one's own capacity to give or to receive love. Other people are made into an audience and whatever is going out to them is given out by the false self, so the real self is safe.

Anyone who has worn a mask, whether as an actor or at a fancy dress party, can understand something of the relief that the schizo-phrenic experiences when, without realising that he is acting, he assumes a false self. The face reflected in the looking glass is someone else's; the feelings behind the eyes are still one's own, but different. The iceberg has shifted, and something that was laboriously sub-merged has floated effortlessly to the surface. There is a new freedom, a release from the self-imposed restrictions that have become too familiar to be observable, an almost intoxicated sensation of privileged irresponsibility. Self-confidence mounts to the point where it seems almost possible to do anything and get away with it. Physically the mask is restricting: voice and movements need to conform to the new persona. But this sense of being circumscribed by someone else's physical characteristics is precisely what produces the feeling of libera-tion. There is no reason to be shy. If you go too far it will be this other person, not yourself, who has to take the rap.

This is only an intensification of what the actor always feels when he is 'in character'. Wearing make-up and a costume can be almost like wearing a mask, and without wearing either, the actor can still have the feeling that he is and is not himself, that some of the puppet strings are in somebody else's hands. He is concealing himself behind the character but simultaneously revealing more of himself than he could normally reveal in his off-stage life. There may be things about him-self that he dislikes – physical characteristics, personality traits. These can be made to disappear. When Alec Guinness started to work in the theatre in the early thirties, he had to play a lot of character parts. 'And I suppose I got into that sort of habit. And it amused me. And I was very happy to disguise myself. I was always rather embarrassed with me, personally, so to speak. I didn't quite know what all that was about and I was glad to go into a thin cardboard disguise. Later I tried to make it a bit rounder.'[1]

The actor can enjoy the fact of being observed by other people but without letting their gaze penetrate to what he thinks of as the weak spots in his private identity. He is palpably making an impact on an audience. If he cannot hear its reaction to him he can at least sense it.

[1] Interview in *The Times*, 7 August 1971.

Other people are reaffirming the reality of his existence and showing their attitude towards him, but, hiding behind the shell of an *alter ego*, he does not have to reveal his attitude towards them. He may think they are a rotten audience compared with last night's, but this will not show in his behaviour. The controlling intelligence remains detached, uncommitted, while the voice and the body do what the character has to do.

No one will be able to judge how much satisfaction the real self is getting from dressing up in a fine costume and putting make-up on and impressing an audience. Nor will anyone know what went on in the actor's mind when he was auditioning for the part or how much gratification he felt at being wanted for it. He may have been waiting in suspense for a cast list to go up on a notice board, announcing whether he was to have a big part or a minute cameo, to appear as a romantic juvenile or a coachman with bad breath. However shy he is in his private life, however much reassurance he needs about the management's or the director's regard for him, the audience will never find out. The time and the space that he fills in the play have been carved out for him by other people. It will be the production, not his own self-assertiveness, that will push him into the foreground; the only rebuffs he can receive on stage are rebuffs for the character he is playing. The relationship with the audience is the only one that cannot be predetermined, and this cannot possibly be reciprocal. Nor was there ever less danger of rebuff from that quarter than in England today, when audiences hardly ever show any displeasure at a bad performance. So he may appear three times as self-possessed as he ever does in private.

Consider a young Wagnerian soprano. She may be plump and nervous. The week before she makes her début as Isolde it may seem terrifying that she has to make a huge audience accept her as a romantic heroine; on the actual night it feels as though she is being carried along by the music and the movements she has rehearsed. There is a tiny corner of her mind in which she is excited by the sense of being in control of a voice that is exciting the audience, but it feels more as if her voice and her body are being controlled by something bigger than herself which is making her feel and seem bigger than she is, or as though she is handing herself over to something which is using her as its medium. If the thought suddenly struck her in the middle of a high C how dependent the whole performance was on her own will-power, her throat muscles might contract so much that the sound would be strangled. And in fact her willpower is not involved at all in any conquest of new territory: the space she is to occupy has been mapped out for her in advance. All she has to do is fill it out. The analogy is not totally misleading: the actor has no orchestra to buoy him up, but for him too the territorial battles have already been won, the script is a score which has been developed in rehearsal into a series of interdependencies involving not just the cast but the people operating the lighting board and the sound effects. The actor's responsibility to everyone whose performance slots in with his own is not merely a pressure that weighs him down, it also holds him up, provides him with a sense of duty that distracts him from the function-ing of his own willpower, just as a soldier shooting at the enemy can be distracted by a sense of duty and loyalty to his fellow-soldiers from any private desire to kill a man.

This is not to suggest that the aggressions involved in acting are murderous or that actors, any more than the rest of us, are potential schizophrenics, or that they are incapable of reciprocal emotional relationships. But obviously the libidinal discharge they can achieve through performance is profoundly satisfying, and obviously there is an element of exhibitionism in it, together perhaps with a bigger appetite for admiration than can be satisfied privately. There is also, probably, an element of voyeurism, as Edmund Bergler has suggested[1]: the actor is narcissistically peeping at himself through the audience's approving eyes.

The actor's actions are also effective only in appearance. There are no real bullets in the revolver, no desire to kill in the duel or seduce in the love scene. The display of virility is an end in itself. The actor is choosing to realise himself by making himself into an object of other people's observation, and in Sartre's terms[2] this is more passive than active, more female than male. Not everyone today would

[1] *Psychiatric Quarterly Supplement* XXIII, 1949.
[2] See Sartre's *Saint Genet*. W. H. Allen, 1963.

accept this conventional equation of activity with the male principle and passivity with the female. There is also a danger that this approach to the actor's unconscious reasons for wanting to act could be abused by the people who jump all too readily at any opportunity to tell you that theatre is essentially camp, acting essentially a homosexual pursuit, that only 'queers' enjoy making up their faces and dressing up in showy costumes.

It would be hard though to find any indications of effeminacy or homosexuality in the dances out of which drama originated. They seem to have been primarily acts of dedication to the invisible powers that were believed to control the workings of nature. As the dancer gave himself up to the spirit, the gods became a felt presence in the rites. In Bacchic revels, for instance, they were believed to participate personally, joining in the orgies of drinking and sexuality. With the normal human restraints thrown aside, the divine and the animal elements could enter in. This objective of self-abandonment is less remote from modern acting than it sounds. Nineteenth-century romantic actors believed themselves to be at their best only when in a state of 'frenzy' and when 'inspired'. Sarah Bernhardt said that the actor should 'forget himself and divest himself of his proper attributes in order to attain those of the part . . . Hamlet's frenzy will make the spectators shudder if he really believes he is Hamlet'. Today we no longer want 'frenzy', but the word *inspiration* is still used, and there is even an explicit suggestion of its divine source in the phrase that old actors still use for moments of apparent self-transcendence: 'The god descends,' they say. The assumption is that the performance reaches the heights only when the actor partially loses control of himself, abandons himself to something external which is waiting to take possession of him.

But of course it is not really external; it has been inside him all the time, waiting to get out. The relevance of Euripides' play *The Bacchae* and of the appeal it still has will be obvious. In forbidding the worship of Dionysus, the austere King Pentheus is inhibiting a part of his nature at the same time as inflicting repressive laws on his subjects. Dionysus himself, disguised as a priest, encourages Pentheus to dress in female clothes so that he can spy on the women who are breaking the law by worshipping the god on Mount Cithaeron. But then the god drives his worshippers into a frenzy. The disguised king is mistaken for a lion and torn to pieces by the women who are led on by his own mother, Agave. He had denied part of the nature she gave him.

But is there any relevance in the behaviour of the psychotic who puts on female clothes and tries to mimic female behaviour in order to protect himself from the woman that he feels is there inside him, struggling to get out? His schizophrenic subterfuge is to put on an act of submitting to her as a defence against really having to submit.

One possible cause of schizophrenia is parental treatment of a baby as if it were of the opposite sex. The father and especially the mother, having had two sons already, badly want the third child to be a girl and they damage his psyche for life by handling him, talking to him and dealing with him physically as if he actually were a girl. The growing child, confused but eager to please, tries to adapt himself to what seems to be required of him. Already he is playing a role. Perhaps he will grow up to be an actor. One of our greatest living actors started life in this way. Or perhaps he will grow up to be neurotic, or even psychotic. Dr Winnicott describes[1] how he helped one of his patients by talking to him as if he were a girl. The man, who was married and had two children, was eventually able to reply, 'I could never have said "I am a girl". But you said it and you have spoken to both parts of me.'

One of the qualities that the neurotic and the artist have in common, then, can be described as a feeling of having more parts to the self than can safely be brought into play in the normal relationships that society permits. While a man who is mentally ill may have a distorted notion of what is safe, society can also be sick and do a lot of distorting. In England industrialisation produced a social morality which is still with us. The spirit of Mr Gradgrind and Mr Podsnap is not dead. The virtues of early rising and regular hours for work are still religiously cultivated, and one attraction of a theatrical career

[1] In *Playing and Reality*.

is the refuge it offers from a nine-to-five day of boring repetitive work.

In the twentieth century, as in the sixteenth, Puritanism flourishes more in some climates than in others. In the Mediterranean countries the regime of office and factory work breeds less Puritanic values than in England, while the church, which is more theatrical than ours – not only in its rituals but in its colours, costumes and décors – bulks larger in the community's life. Both the professional theatre and the amateur are correspondingly less active, but there are more outlets for histrionic impulses in everyday life. A conversation in a shop or a café is patently more demonstrative and more physical: there is more movement of the body and of the adrenalin inside it. Africans are still more extrovert and uninhibited in their natural speech and movement. When the Zulu version of *Macbeth* was brought to the Aldwych in 1972, the director had to tone down behaviour which was quite unexaggerated, because to an English audience it would have looked too theatrical.

Mechanisation of a society also tends to make song and dance less available as means of self-expression. We listen to records instead of performing, whereas Zulus break into song or dance spontaneously and unselfconsciously both individually and in groups. In many of the less industrialised areas of Europe song and dance arise more naturally than they do here. There are still folk singing and dancing which belong to a tradition that goes back almost as far as the Greek tragedies and tell us something about the way their choruses may have been a formalised theatrical coefficient of the singing and dancing that went on spontaneously in Greek society. In our society, there is relatively little ritual and theatre in everyday life. The aggressions which, in a primitive society, each adult male could release in a series of activities like hunting, fishing and fighting, or in ritual dances that represented fights, can hardly ever be released except vicariously, in watching football matches, for instance. And industrial society inevitably casts most of its members in roles which engage only a fraction of their potential. The endemic fear of automation is pathetic: men are fearful of losing jobs which could be done better by machines.

There are still societies where it would be inaccurate to suggest that the adult, like the child, can be creative and use the whole of his personality only when he is playing. But if it is true of England, it must be the basic reason so many thousands of would-be actors feel that, riddled as it is with unemployment, the profession still provides the best available life.

2 THE ACTOR'S RELATIONSHIPS

Drama is an art but theatre is an industry.
HARLEY GRANVILLE-BARKER

Theatre is an industry which ideally would produce good plays and good acting, together with good direction and good design (both of theatres and sets), while attracting a good audience representative of the whole community – the consumer being an integral part of the system. This combination of conditions has existed only once in the history of our theatre: for about thirty years, long before the Industrial Revolution, and long before the theatre itself became industrialised. The achievement of Marlowe, Shakespeare, Jonson and their contemporaries would have been impossible but for the theatres which were being built from 1576 onwards and but for the society which, from Queen to groundlings, responded actively and excitedly to the new drama. But the middle stratum of the audience soon began to crumble away, while the court masques, with their amateur actors and their spectacular scenic effects, became a serious rival to the professional theatre, which depended more on good scripts and good performances.

After the Puritan Interregnum had withered our sapling theatrical tradition, the drama that revived under Charles II generated a different kind of excitement. To a public that consisted largely of the upper crust and the lower dregs, the visual appeal of the scenery was eclipsed by that of the actresses. Recruited to the profession as replacements for the boy actors, they rapidly became the main attraction to a disorderly and predominantly male audience. They appeared in low-cut dresses or sometimes in breeches, as when Peg Woffington played Sir Harry Wildair in Farquhar's *The Constant Couple* or when whole plays were cast with women, mainly for the sake of showing off the shape of their calves and ankles to a public which otherwise saw little of the female body except the face and hands. Respectable ladies and respectable merchants stayed away from the theatres. Prostitutes used them as a hunting ground for clients, and managers added to their profits by charging the gallants for admission to the actresses' dressing-room. Listening to the actors was therefore only one of the pleasures of theatre-going and, in any case, it became increasingly difficult to hear them as the audiences grew larger and rowdier, and as the theatres at Covent Garden and Drury Lane also grew larger. Each time they were burnt down they were replaced by bigger buildings. Long before the end of the seventeenth century, when William Davenant's lavish scenery had more audience appeal than Thomas Betterton's acting, the spoken word had already lost its dominance.

Throughout the eighteenth and nineteenth centuries the theatre went on growing more commercial and more industrial. The early Victorian theatre was primarily a popular theatre which did not appeal to either the social or the intellectual *élite*. In the eighteen-nineties, thanks mainly to the impulse given by Ibsen, some intellectual agitation began to make itself felt, and in 1891 the Independent Theatre was founded, the first non-commercial theatre in our history. In 1895 Shaw wrote that it was

> ... an excellent institution, simply because it is independent. The disparagers ask what it is independent of ... It is, of course, independent of commercial success ... If Mr Grein had not taken the dramatic critics of London and put them in a row before *Ghosts* and *The Wild Duck*, with a certain small but inquisitive and influential body of enthusiasts behind them, we should be far less advanced today than we are. The real history of the drama for the last ten years is not the history of the prosperous enterprises of Mr Hare, Mr Irving, and the established West-end theatres, but of the forlorn hopes led by Mr Vernon, Mr Charrington, Mr Grein, Messrs Henly and Stevenson, Miss Achurch, Miss Robins and Miss Lea, Miss Farr and the rest of the Impossibilists.

If this is true, the reason is that since 1660 the appeal of theatre had been more visual than verbal. The poetic plays of Wordsworth,

Coleridge, Byron, Shelley, Keats, Browning and Tennyson do not have an important place in the history of our drama; they have no place at all in the history of our theatre.

By the eighteen-nineties it had acquired a middle-class orientation, and though the actor flourished, it was within the limiting tradition, of middle-class gentility. Earlier actors had been judged in relation to current conceptions of 'nature'. 'Always as deep in Nature as the Poet,' was the Earl of Chatham's description of Garrick's Shakespearean performances, 'but never (what the Poet is too often) out of it.' Victorian actors came to be judged according to current standards of good taste, and the theatre went on either failing to attract the best writers or seducing them – as T. S. Eliot was later seduced – into producing work well below their best level. Eliot's most dramatic piece, *Sweeney Agonistes*, was not written for performance, and his best play, *Murder in the Cathedral*, was written to be performed in a cathedral, not a theatre. The later plays steadily become less dramatic as they become less literary: and they become more theatrical only in the most superficial way.

It was only in the nineteen-fifties that our theatre suddenly became more verbal and less visual, and it is no accident that this happened at the moment when the working-class elements, which had been shut out for so long, were finally re-admitted. The Music Hall, which had entertained working-class men and women since the middle of the nineteenth century, was dying, but as working-class playwrights, directors and actors swarmed into the middle-class theatre, they brought music-hall techniques with them. It suddenly became possible for actors, like comedians, to talk straight out to the audience, and the new kind of relationship that this created immediately made the words matter more and scenery matter less.

Coward and Maugham, Priestley and Rattigan had depended very much less on language for their theatrical effects than Pinter and Osborne, Arden and Orton. The new audience had to use its ears, and the epicentre of the new working-class movement was the Royal Court Theatre, where George Devine had launched a policy of giving more prominence to the writer. Suddenly it looked as though, for the first time in nearly four hundred years, we had a chance of developing a situation in which good actors could be presented in well-written plays to an audience in which factory-workers would soon be rubbing shoulders with intellectuals.

If we really had that chance, we missed it. If, as I believe, we never really had it, one of the main reasons was that our theatre was becoming more like an industry, with a complex economic structure and much greater social mobility for employees. The profession became less like a hierarchy posing as a fraternity, more like a pool of labour. The evil of the old system was that the small-part actor was almost bound to remain a small-part actor all his life. Today we have equality of opportunity, but working relationships have been depersonalised. The actor's basic relationships are with his fellow-actors, his employer and his audience: at one time all three were likely to be steady relationships. Today there are few companies in which the same actors go on working together for more than a few weeks or at most a few months; meanwhile the profession has grown so large and so heterogeneous that actors can think of themselves corporately only as members of a trade union. The employer is usually a board of management which seldom if ever meets the actors. In most theatre buildings the audience is invisible in the dark and, except in some regional repertory theatres, has little to do with any coherent community.

The theatre is not even an industry which can provide its workers with enough work. The most successful actors can afford to appear on the stage only in between bouts of better-paid employment in television and films, while the less successful are out of work most of the time. One of the basic problems in an industrial economy is that there is a limit beyond which theatre, by its very nature, cannot be industrialised. An actor can give only a limited number of performances in a week and the theatre can be only of a limited size. The output can be increased only by introducing the eye of the camera. By multiplying the actor into an almost unlimited number of images, this multiplies the size of his audience, but it subtracts the element of live contact which is the essence of theatre. Theatre has been raped by the camera and given birth to two new industries, which are nearly separate, but not quite. Cinema and television have both grown into parasitic and unembarrassed monsters which go on eating at the parental table, consuming the same acting talent and even some of the same writing and directing talent. For twenty-five centuries acting had been impossible without an immediate and living relationship with an audience. Suddenly, in our century, the cold eye of the camera has made that optional, multiplying not only the size of the audience but with it, proportionally, the actor's power. For the leaders of the profession, whose charisma is carried electronically and cinematically all over the world, the rewards are bigger and brighter than ever – not only the money but the prestige and the power, the fame and the fun. Compare Richard Burbage and Richard Burton. To an Elizabethan, the perquisites of Burton's success would have seemed more like the prerogatives of a sultan than of an actor.

It is not only the size of the star actor's fame which is new, but the ease and speed with which it can be achieved. Henry Irving had to spend ten years working extremely hard in provincial stock companies. In Sunderland he had to work without pay; in two and a half years at Edinburgh he played over four hundred roles; towards the end of his provincial career, at the age of twenty-eight, he could command a salary of three pounds a week. He was thirty-three when he made his famous breakthrough in *The Bells*. Gielgud was twenty-five when he made something of a breakthrough with an Old Vic *Hamlet* which transferred to the West End, but before he secured his position as a star and his first three-figure salary – three years later with *Richard of Bordeaux* – he had played seventy-eight parts in the theatre. Richard Burton played only seven parts in his first three years and was already a star. Gielgud has never deserted the theatre for more than a few months at a stretch, and even Olivier never ceased to be oriented primarily towards the theatre, though he has given a far larger slice of his career than Gielgud to the cinema, spending several years in Hollywood, later directing six films and altogether appearing in over forty. But Peter O'Toole and Albert Finney, having once made their name in the theatre, have both devoted most of their time to films. O'Toole became a co-director of a film company in 1959, and since 1965 Finney has had a company which produces both plays and films.

Except in the nineteen-twenties, when Sir Gerald du Maurier was acknowledged as the leader of the profession, all the great actors in the English tradition had founded their careers and built up their reputations mainly on Shakespearean roles. With Paul Scofield this tradition has come to an end. Where Sir Cedric Hardwicke, Robert Donat, Charles Laughton, Trevor Howard, Richard Burton and Dirk Bogarde were regarded as renegades for preferring to spend most of their working lives in the cinema, this preference has become the norm. When our National Theatre was founded in 1963, Peter O'Toole, who was still younger than Irving was when he graduated out of rep, was too busy filming to give more than twenty-seven performances as Hamlet in the opening production.

A film star can now earn £3,000 for a day's work, and in the priorities of the actor and his agent the stage is naturally secondary to the screen. The whole of the money that pours into London theatre box offices during the year would serve to finance only about five large-budget films. A great many actors – perhaps most – prefer working in the theatre. There is direct contact with the audience and obviously technique can be developed and range extended far better on the stage than in television or films, where actors are cast more according to physical type. Talent can be stretched most of all by the experience of playing a mixture of parts, classical and modern, old and young, character and straight. When they left drama school, O'Toole and Finney both worked in repertory for several years, as most recruits to the profession did at that time. But the generations of young actors that have emerged since then are much more resigned to spending most of their working lives being type-cast, and speaking mediocre dialogue manufactured for mass-consumption.

For Stanislavski the actor's belief in his material was the foundation for the performance; most actors in England today spend only a minute proportion of their time working on scripts in which this sort of belief is possible. Generally they are less willing to work in the provinces and altogether they do not plan their careers so far ahead as actors used to. Many are aiming frankly at the biggest financial prizes their faces and their personalities can win for them. Peter O'Toole is not just joking when he says, 'I'm coining it in before my teeth drop out. It's as simple as that.'[1] Not that screen acting bulks any larger in the average actor's life than it did fifteen years ago. The British film industry has declined and the television companies have reacted to higher pay levels by opting for plays with smaller casts. Nevertheless, experience, versatility and voice have come to count for less, personality, face and reputation for more. Actors have merely adjusted their sights to the profession's new horizons.

While the advent of cinema and television multiplied the identifiable audience into an unknown number of separate audiences, invisible and unreachable, the development of air travel brought an ever-increasing element of international tourists into the audience of every theatrical metropolis, lowering the proportion of regulars. But by then two important milestones in the London actor's relation with his audience had already been passed. The first was early in the nineteenth century, when the custom grew of extinguishing the house-lights during the performance. The second was when it became impossible for the actor to think of his audience as a single entity. In Restoration London the two theatres shared an audience which consisted largely of the same people: that was the only audience there was. With nineteenth-century industrialism the population of London grew vastly, and with the improvement of public transport the audience became more mobile. But the actor–managers each gave their theatre its distinctive character, and audiences would go on patronising it because they liked him and expected to find his personality reflected in everything they saw, from the front-of-house décor to the style of the staging.

First nights at the St James's Theatre were great events . . . I sat in my box sick with anxiety, and between the acts I used to put on an apron and go behind the scenes and place all the little things on the stage myself until the men got used to it. I arranged the flowers;

[1] Interview in *The Times*, 7 September 1971.

in those days we had so much detail, and I loved to make things look real, I ordered gowns to suit the decorations of the scene so that nothing clashed or was ugly ... Our first nights at the St James's Theatre were like brilliant parties. Everybody knew everybody, everybody put on their best clothes, everybody wished us success.

This is George Alexander's wife, Florence, writing in the eighteen-nineties.[1] Her description pinpoints something which has completely disappeared.

The whole history of theatrical organisation in England can be seen in terms of a see-saw between employers who were themselves actors and employers who were not. Now one was in the ascendant, now the other. Before the first Elizabethan theatre was built in 1576, wandering groups of actors would perform in the open air, collecting pennies from the spectators by rattling money-boxes at them. They also performed in inn-yards, charging everyone a penny at the entrance. The money would be divided daily between the actors and the landlord.

When the early theatres were built, conditions of employment remained simple. The actor would be either a 'sharer' or a 'hired man'. There would usually be between four and eight sharers who had invested their savings to pay for the costumes, the scenery, the plays and perhaps the theatre buildings. They then shared the profits in proportion to what they had contributed, and if enough money was coming in they could hire additional men for six shillings a week. Soon business was brisk enough to attract speculators. Philip Henslowe, who had started life as a servant and made a fortune by marrying his widowed mistress, became first a money-lender and then the first commercial manager in the history of the English theatre. He bought up scenery left over from medieval miracle plays, invested money in building the Rose Theatre, which was started about 1587, had the Fortune built in 1602 with a stage modelled on that of the Globe, and went on in 1614 to build the Hope. He loaned money to Ben Jonson, who needed it to buy a share in a company of actors,

[1] Quoted in *Nineteenth Century British Theatre*. Methuen 1971.

and to other playwrights who were then obliged to go on writing exclusively for his theatres until they were out of debt. He married his step-daughter to Edward Alleyn, the actor who created the roles of Orlando, Tamburlaine, Faustus, Barabas in *The Jew of Malta*, Hieronimo in Kyd's *The Spanish Tragedy*, and he made many other actors dependent on him by lending money, sometimes for bail. He had a controlling financial interest in two companies of actors – Worcester's Men and the Admiral's Men. He died in 1616, the same year as Shakespeare.

When the London theatre was revived after the Cromwellian Interregnum, Charles II issued Letters Patent (or charters) to two playwrights, Thomas Killigrew and Sir William Davenant, giving them a monopoly of the London theatre. Killigrew's company, The King's Servants, was technically part of the Royal Household and it appeared in the theatre at Drury Lane. Davenant's company, the Duke of York's Servants, appeared at the theatre in Lincoln's Inn Fields, and the charter descended first to Dorset Garden and then to Covent Garden. The monopoly was reinforced by the Theatres Act of 1737 but the law was often broken and Samuel Foote successfully evaded it at the Haymarket by inviting his friends to a dish of chocolate or tea, sending out invitation cards which also gave them admission to an entertainment. Eventually the Duke of York, who had played a practical joke on him – mounting him on an unmanageable horse which broke his leg – made amends (after the leg had been amputated) by procuring him a Royal Patent for summer seasons at the Haymarket. These continued after he sold the theatre ten years later, in 1776, to the elder George Colman, author of *The Clandestine Marriage*.

But the Patent system was not changed until 1843, and for the most part it was not playwrights but actors like Garrick and Macready who were effectively to control what happened at both Covent Garden and Drury Lane throughout most of the eighteenth and nineteenth centuries. The Victorian theatre was dominated by the actor–manager, but during the 1914–18 war the possibility of making huge profits out of star names and long runs attracted the entrepreneurs. Actor–managers like Fred Terry and Sir John Martin-

Harvey went on touring the provinces but became less important in London, though it was only in the fifties and sixties of the present century that the actor–manager disappeared altogether. Lord Olivier and Sir John Clements, before they became the salaried directors of the National Theatre and Chichester Festival Theatre, were both financially involved in presenting plays in which they starred themselves and their wives. Today a number of actors own film companies, and one of these, Albert Finney's Memorial Enterprises, has also put on plays, in a few of which he has appeared himself.

Given a large enough theatre, it is possible for a star to pull in over a million pounds with a single show, as Danny la Rue did at the Palace in 1970. But a legitimate actor who wanted to base his whole career on the theatre would have often to take bigger risks in smaller buildings. Even without his own production company, a star can make more money out of the cinema and can live free from the tedium of long runs. So when he appears in the theatre it is invariably as a salary earner, and with a clause in the contract limiting his commitment to a few months. If his name is valuable enough at the box-office, the salary may be supplemented very substantially by a percentage of the gross takings – sometimes as much as 10 per cent – but he is no longer risking his own capital, no longer working for himself.

While the actor–manager was in the ascendant, relationships generally were much more personal. When one man's name was linked to each theatre, the whole working lives of his actors would revolve around his. Today, of all the theatres in England, the one most dominated by a single personality is the Mermaid, but there is no permanent company and even Sir Bernard Miles cannot be the boss in the same sense that a Victorian actor–manager could: a large proportion of the money in the pay packets at the Mermaid comes out of the Arts Council's subsidy. Both the National Theatre and the Royal Shakespeare Company are too large for the director to have a close working relationship with all the actors, and it is impossible for them to know who is making the decisions that govern their lives. There are invisible committees which stop Olivier from letting Kenneth Tynan include Hochhuth's *The Soldiers* in the National's repertoire and tell Trevor Nunn how much he can spend on new hydraulic lifts for the Stratford-on-Avon stage. Financial policy affects not only artistic policy but the size of a company. An actor-manager would sack a small-part actor if he got angry with him; an actor in the RSC or the National might lose his job because an Arts Council grant is not increased sufficiently from one year to the next to maintain the company at the same strength. And who really makes the decisions about policy, programmes and casting? The Artistic Director or a meeting of directors at which his voice is only one of several? The larger the set-up and the more associate directors there are involved, the more the actor–employer relationship is de-personalised.

Government by committee has become dangerously prevalent in our theatre during the last fifteen years. It is probably an inevitable concomitant of state subsidy – the feeling being that public money is safer in the hands of a well-balanced committee than of a brilliant individual. But in the theatre committees are dangerous. People who enjoy sitting on them and who master the techniques of persuasion involved are not always the right people to control the destiny of a theatre. Bernard Shaw was an exception: he gave up a good deal of time to serve on committees of the Society of Authors, the Shakespeare Memorial National Theatre, the London Shakespeare League, the Academy of Dramatic Art and the Stage Society, as well as of the Fabian Society and the St Pancras Borough Council. But the people who could contribute most to the theatre do not always have the mentality or personality that can thrive under the conditions that committee discussion creates. To be a good committeeman, according to Shaw, you must 'spend precious working hours in drafting documents and then see your work wasted and spoiled without turning an outward hair ... [and] use your wit to prevent the idle people from squabbling and then let all the bad blood pass off as being your fault'.

Committee discussion usually ends in compromise, and compromise always tends towards a preservation of the *status quo*. If it is hard to find an individual prepared to take the kind of risk involved in staging the work of a really original playwright like Beckett or Pinter for the first time, it would be impossible to get a committee to agree on it.

Granted, nearly every theatre has some kind of council or board or committee governing it. What varies is the division of power between it and the individual at the artistic helm. Considerable risks have been taken at the Royal Court, particularly when George Devine was Artistic Director, but since he resigned in 1965 the overall structure of the English theatre has altered considerably: nearly five times as much public money is put into it, which ought to make it far easier to take artistic risks, and if less risks have in fact been taken, the reason is partly that the balance of power between committees and individuals throughout our theatre has been readjusted. The two most important committees, the Drama Panel of the Arts Council and the Council of Equity, have both become demonstrably far more powerful; the degree of autonomy allowed to an Artistic Director still varies from theatre to theatre, but the tendency is for it to be reduced. It is Arts Council policy not to interfere in the affairs of the theatres it supports, but local borough councils seldom subsidise their theatres without wanting representation on the board of management. This is making it more necessary than ever before for a good artistic director in rep to be a good committeeman.

Another danger is that the artistic director is tending to be put more in the position of a middleman between the actors and the committee. It hardly ever happens that a representative of the actors is elected to sit on the governing committee, though in theory probably no one would deny that the viewpoint of the company which actually appears in front of the audience ought to be represented at discussions of policy. But the structure of our theatre reflects the structure of our society, and if during the next few years the practice grows in industry of inviting a representative of the workers on to the board of management, perhaps it will also spread to our theatre. Meanwhile some initiatives have been taken by actors to form groups which they themselves control co-operatively. But even the most important of these, the Actors' Company, has had relatively little publicity, mainly because it has been operating outside London. So has Paradise Foundry, in which the actors are directors of the company. Everyone is paid £30 a week and no one can be sacked.

Nearly all the working relationships inside the theatre have been affected by the enlargement of its component units. The Royal Shakespeare Company and the National Theatre are both enormous organisations, each with a big company and a big staff, and the large regional reps are larger than they have ever been before. Many of them have big new buildings with a large catering and administrative staff and three separate companies of actors – one for the main theatre, one for the experimental theatre and one for 'theatre-in-education'. The bigger the organisation, the less the individual member of it sees of the artistic director.

In the West End, too, relationships between actors and commercial managers are also becoming less personal and less long-lasting. From 1931 to 1936 all John Gielgud's appearances in London were for Sir Bronson Albery, who had put him under contract for three plays. And for the next thirty years almost all his work in the theatre was for the Tennent management. Albert Finney at first had a long association with Oscar Lewenstein, making his West End début in Jane Arden's play *The Party* in 1958, and, after signing a three-play contract, he went on working for Lewenstein till 1964, when he was in Osborne's *Luther* on Broadway. Today long-term contracts with commercial managers are almost extinct, and even Gielgud works for different managements, both subsidised and commercial. Actors hardly ever have direct contact with their employer. The negotiations that have to take place – about the actor's salary, billing, length of commitment, conditions, holidays and so on – are all taken over by the agent, and most actors hardly ever meet the man who is employing them – even at parties.

The only way to induce a star actor to remain with a particular management or a particular theatre on a long-term basis is by inviting him to become an associate director of it, as Scofield was of the Royal Shakespeare Company from 1966 to 1968; but his appointment as Associate Director of the National Theatre in 1970 failed to keep him with the company for more than two productions. In 1972 Albert Finney was made an Associate Director of the English Stage Company at the Royal Court, when Oscar Lewenstein took over as Artistic Director.

The only long-term contracts that actors now sign are with the National Theatre or the Royal Shakespeare Company or one of the regional reps. These provide the only possibilities of a continuous relationship with the same management and (roughly) the same ensemble, while it is only in the regions that there can be any continuous relationship with the same audience. Not all repertory theatres have permanent companies and, even with those that do, the degree of permanence varies. It is noticeable that the few theatres with actors who have been in the company for several years are those, like Stoke-on-Trent, which have a deep-rooted relationship with a local community. This is unattainable in London and the big provincial cities, simply because of the size of the population. In the Greek city-states, theatre was a forum and a focus for community-consciousness. Though our theatre is largely deprived of this function and this means of recharging its own batteries, there is at least a growing awareness of what is missing without it.

The acting profession, as it has become more organised, has also become more exclusive, and while it would be pleasant to think that the 'Fringe' to our theatre had grown in reaction to the impersonality of Establishment theatre, the truth is that it also represents an over-flow system, an arena for those who are unable to join Equity or, having joined, to find enough work at the regularised salary levels. But this arena is also open to those who want to opt out of the existing system. Apart from actors, there are playwrights and directors who find it impossible, inside Establishment theatre, to make the relationships they want either with an audience or with the workers whose collaboration is going to culminate in a performance.

A London theatre is a tremendously complex machine, which needs to be staffed with managers, secretaries, book-keepers, usher-ettes, box-office managers and assistants, barmaids, electricians, car-penters and stage-hands. Many of these individuals may never even meet the actor, but the fact that they have to be there affects both his relationship with the audience and the conditions of his employment. Any performance needs publicity if an audience is to be attracted; at one time this could be achieved by parading through the streets in costume, beating a drum, cutting capers, doing somersaults and cartwheels and exchanging banter with the passers-by. The modern publicity machine involves photographs, posters, newspaper advertising and press officers whose full-time job it is to promote the interests of companies, productions and performers by arranging appearances on television, interviews on the radio, mentions in gossip columns and anything else that can be contrived. The actor is involved in procedures which will sometimes gratify his ego and sometimes bore him, as the publicity machine claws into the mass audience for the show's potential public.

In the smaller reps and in Fringe groups both the public and the social unit involved directly in the production are small enough for everyone to know everyone else. There is much less money involved but there is also less pressure and less formality. On the Fringe there are no limitations on the length of a rehearsal. Not that Establishment theatre could have continued without a system of regulations. The pressure from outside the theatre of people trying to get in meant that newcomers were especially vulnerable to exploitation. Youngsters were often delighted to be taken on as 'students' and to be paid a couple of pounds a week to assist the overworked assistant stage managers and occasionally to appear in one-line parts. Without unionisation there is no way of controlling abuses like this, but with the comprehensive regulations that Equity and the National Association of Theatrical and Kine Employees have introduced, there is often too little freedom of manoeuvre at moments when valuable creative work is being done. A director and a group of actors may be just on the point of solving a problem which has been causing a stalemate for days when the rehearsal has to be stopped because of union regulations. It is only by breaking right away from the Establishment theatre that directors, writers and actors can find freedom to collaborate on a more friendly basis within a less rigid framework.

But while there are highly talented directors (like Peter Cheeseman and Michael Elliott) and highly talented writers (like John McGrath and Alan Plater) who prefer to base their activities away from the London theatre, it is hard to think of any actors of comparable talent or comparable reputation who choose to give the bulk of their time to rep or Fringe theatre.[1] There are not many actors who would turn down all other offers in order to stay at the same theatre or with the same company; often, when they do that, it is because no other offers are coming in. Most of them, in any event, keep moving from one audience to another, and the more successful they are, the more freedom of choice they have at each point.

The more impermanent and impersonal an actor's relationships become with his audiences, his employers and his fellow-actors, the more dependent he becomes on his relationship with his agents. It is not merely that he needs someone to take care of the business arrangements involved in contracts or to advise him about which job to accept when several are offered at the same time. He needs a feeling of continuity in his career and it is very hard to get this from a part in a West End play which rehearses for four weeks and runs for six, followed by ten days out of work, followed by three days of filming, followed by a voice-over for a television commercial, followed by a week out of work, followed by three weeks of rehearsal and three of playing in a rep, followed by four days out of work before rehearsals start for two episodes of a television serial. The greater the discontinuity of the work, the greater the need for a 'father-figure'. Formerly, when there was more direct and more continuous contact with the employer, whether actor–manager or commercial manager, it was he who assumed this role. Now it is largely the agent, who, though he will not provide the next job himself, may be the means of securing it. Since he takes 10 per cent of his client's earnings, he appears to have his interests at heart, and it is part of his business to be available whenever his client needs him – for a late-night chat, for a meeting at the week-end, for telephone calls at any time and to go along to auditions or dress-rehearsals whenever the client is under

---

[1] In general actors tend to be more conservative and less non-conformist than writers or directors. This is hard to prove, but a revealing survey of reading habits in which Equity members replied to a questionnaire issued by Casting Report, the newsletter, in 1971, showed that 38 per cent of them read the *Daily Telegraph* and 62 per cent the *Sunday Telegraph*. *The Observer* polled 57 per cent. Eighty-four per cent read *What's On in London* and under 2 per cent *Time Out*.

emotional stress. There is nothing practical the agent can do in these situations but if the actor feels a need for him to be there, he goes – assuming the actor is earning enough money to justify the investment of this amount of time. The less successful actor is more liable to find that his agent is too busy with other clients to be available as a private audience.

Theatrical agents existed, of course, long before cinema and television came to bulk so large in the actor's life, but there were not nearly so many of them. The year 1927 was one in which their professional organisation, the Agents' Association, was formed, and at that time 10 per cent of the total earnings of all actors in England would not have supported a tenth of the number of agents who are thriving today. It is especially in the last fifteen years or so that they have multiplied. Excluding variety agencies, a hundred are listed in the June 1957 issue of 'Contacts'; in the Spring 1972 issue there were 263 —whereas in New York (where agents are franchised by Equity) there were only ninety-two at the beginning of the seventies.

At the moment of performance, of course, the only relationships that matter to an actor are those with the other actors and with the audience, but emotionally and financially the sense of dependence on the employer has largely been replaced by a sense of dependence on the agent. Which means a shift of orientation in the direction of commercialism. The employer may have been an entrepreneur but he was also concerned with standards of performance: his livelihood depended on them. The agent is more of a businessman: his livelihood depends on how much his clients earn. There are a few agents who care genuinely about the development of their actors as artists, who take pride and pleasure in picking a promising beginner and helping to develop his talent by advising him and promoting him simultaneously, trying to get him the jobs he needs to stretch him but advising him to turn down a part for which he isn't ready, fighting on his behalf against the sclerosis of type-casting, encouraging him to follow a balanced diet of classical and modern work, helping him to get experience of the different media, boosting his morale when he is depressed, criticising constructively when he is becoming over-confident or mannered, and protecting him from the pitfalls of lucrative jobs in long-running television serials (which would make it hard for him to get other jobs afterwards because people would go on identifying him with the character). But the unscrupulous agent is an exploiter of a situation in which most actors have only one agent and all agents have more than one actor. Actors are expendable. While drama schools are producing large crops of fresh young faces every summer, agents can always take on new clients, either discarding a few middle-aged ones whose earnings are falling off or keeping them on the books to be fobbed off with honeyed regrets over the telephone while little or no time is spent on trying to get work for them.

Most actors read most scripts which are offered to them, but when they have to choose between a good play in the theatre and a bad play on television, the agent's influence could be decisive, and a great many agents are more interested in milking talents than in developing them. In most ways the actor has never been able to feel so protected as he does today, but in some ways he has never been so vulnerable.

3 THE ACTOR PREPARES – FOR WHAT?

Ralph Richardson got his first job in the theatre by offering to pay ten shillings a week to a man called Growcott, who ran a small company, half amateur, half professional, in a theatre made out of a disused bacon factory near Brighton Station. They arranged to go on like this for twenty weeks, and then if Growcott wanted to keep him on, he would pay Richardson ten shillings a week. There are still people who are so keen to get into the theatre that they would gladly pay for an apprenticeship or work long hours doing routine stage management jobs for very little money: 'studentships' were not abolished until the late sixties. Since the 1939 war more and more people from outside the profession have been trying to get in, but the pressure has been countered, if not quite balanced, by the rapidly growing pressure from inside to keep them out.

Equity became a closed-shop in 1933 – members had to refuse to work with non-members – but by 1935 membership was still only 4,000. At the beginning of 1948 it was 9,904 and 1,910 new members joined during the year. In 1961 it had risen to 14,206 and by 1969 to 19,584. (This figure is swollen by the 1967 amalgamation with the Variety Artistes' Federation, but that made a difference of only 1,637). In the middle of 1972 there were about 19,500 members in full benefit and about 23,000 on the mailing list. About 12,000 of these would be actors, the remainder being dancers, singers, stage managers and variety artists. Meanwhile the number of provincial theatres was rapidly dwindling. In March 1948 there were 232 repertory companies[1] and ninety-eight productions were touring the provinces; in

---

[1] About 40 per cent performed all through the year, the rest mounting only summer seasons.

March 1968 only eighty-four reps and twenty-two productions on tour. In 1952 there were 2,477 jobs for actors in British feature films; in 1968, 1,888. The additional work to be had from television came nowhere near to compensating for what had been lost. As one sad old actor put it, television had 'opened up a vast new field of unemployment'.

Not that there had ever been enough work for the number of people who wanted to do it. The profession was in danger of being overcrowded almost before it was constituted as a profession and before there was any clear separation between amateur and professional. Protective barriers date back to 1469, when Edward IV founded the Guild of Minstrels in an attempt to illegalise competition from peasants and craftsmen. But minstrelsy was by then in decline, while folk drama was thriving and pagan elements from the seasonal rituals that flourished in the country were filtering into performances of religious plays. When a play was successful in one town, the actors would take it on tour around the district, and the nascent profession rapidly attracted recruits. The servant who after two years of employment left Sir John Paston to play in *St George* and *Robin Hood and the Sheriff of Nottingham* must have been one defector among a great many.

Some of the Guilds producing cycles of miracle plays employed professional actors and others boycotted them, but amateur actors were paid for their performances. At Coventry one earned $\frac{3}{4}d$. 'for playing God' while another received $4d$. for hanging Judas, and the same amount for cock-crowing. There was obviously considerable competition for the parts. In York a fine of forty shillings was imposed for taking more than one. But while the religious plays had an audience far more representative of the whole community than the entertainments in noblemen's castles had, it was mainly to the castles that professional actors gravitated, employment being so much more regular. Nevertheless, as Glynne Wickham has demonstrated,[1] it was the amateur religious stage that not only prepared the ground for the popular audience of the Elizabethan theatre but also gave professional players the cue to start performing in ensembles,

[1] *Early English Stages 1300–1600.* Volume Two 1576–1660 Part 1, Routledge, 1963.

with scripted dialogue, instead of working as solo reciters, singers, dancers, acrobats.

By the end of the sixteenth century the semi-professional productions which had been so popular in the country towns had been killed off by the Tudor government, with its fear of the Catholic orientation of the old religious plays, and of polemical plays which might work subversively on the population. But the history of the Elizabethan theatre shows that the restrictive practices which drove many actors out of the profession also contributed to the growth of professionalism. In 1572 Parliament passed the first bill designed to reduce the number of strolling players. Previously there had been no strict licensing system, though wandering groups were liable to be treated as vagabonds unless they could prove that they were in the service of some nobleman connected with a nearby town. The new law stipulated that no gentleman below the rank of Baron could retain a private company of players. All other troupes had to be licensed by two Justices of the Peace, one of whom was local to the shire where they were performing. This immediately cut down on touring, and when the licensing power of J.P.s was withdrawn by the legislation of 1597-98, many more companies had to be disbanded. A good deal of talent, no doubt, went to waste, but the profession was stabilised.

It is often said that there was no organised training for actors until the Academy of Acting (later RADA, the Royal Academy of Dramatic Art) was founded by Beerbohm Tree in 1904. This is not true. In Restoration London both the Patent Theatres had 'nurseries' where apprentice actors were tutored by their seniors. Betterton received fifty guineas a year for teaching. But in the eighteenth and nineteenth centuries, the easiest way for an actor to learn his trade was as an amateur, and there was nothing to stop the amateur from breaking into the professional theatre. Garrick made an anonymous début in the East End of London at Goodman's Fields in 1741, playing Richard III and billed as 'A gentleman (Who never appeared on any stage)'. A twenty-four-year-old wine merchant, he had never been taught how to act but, although the play was being presented in the elongated interval of a concert – to evade the law which gave the two Patent Theatres a monopoly of 'legitimate' drama – he scored such a success that he could turn professional immediately.

Throughout most of the nineteenth century the barrier between amateur and professional theatre remained fairly easy to cross. *The Actors' Handbook* published by Dicks was a 'Guide to the Stage for Amateurs' but obviously not aimed primarily at those who intended to remain amateurs. 'A good stock of tights, boots, hats, swords, etc. etc.,' it advised, 'often procures a young man an engagement when he could not obtain one on his merits.' Amateur acting was very much more than a hobby. There were even amateur tours like the one Dickens encouraged in 1851 to take Lytton's play *Not So Bad As We Seem* to the provinces. This was rather in the tradition of the medieval tours by groups of town players.

The amateur theatre often served as a stepping-stone to employment in one of the provincial stock companies, where it was common for the apprentice actor to work for nothing, as the young Irving did. In the last thirty years of the century, when the theatre was becoming socially respectable and the possibility of founding a National Theatre was already being debated, there was an influx of young men who, as Henry James observed in 1880, 'had gone on to the stage after being educated for something very different'. This was the beginning of the trend that was to lead to the overcrowding of today.

By now several attempts had been made to organise a proper training for the profession. The first Musical and Dramatic Academy was started by a Mr Glover and his wife in 1848 at 21a Soho Square. This was small and short-lived, but the need for properly organised training was becoming obvious, and in 1859, when a meeting was held at the Adelphi to discuss the establishment of a Royal Dramatic College, Charles Kean, Ben Webster, Charles Dickens and William Thackeray were appointed as trustees. In 1876 a foundation stone was laid by the Prince of Wales, and in 1882 the academy was opened, with Matthew Arnold and Wilkie Collins on the committee, but three years later it was forced to close.

In 1890 B. W. Findon, who maintained that a drama school financed by the state would produce 'nothing but dramatic dummies', emphasised the value of the amateur movement to professionals in the making. 'The future School of Dramatic Art,' he urged, 'is the amateur dramatic club.' What he proposed was 'the formation of a Grand Central Club' to which all amateur societies could be affiliated, while the movement would be controlled by professionals, so that the theatrical manager 'will regard it as his recruiting ground and that it shall be to the stage what our great military schools are to the army'.[1] This line of thinking led to the foundation of the British Drama League in 1919. Meanwhile the first meeting of the Actors' Association had been held in 1891, and this was to lead, eventually, to the foundation of Equity in 1929. Efforts were made within the Actors' Association to take the initiative in founding a drama school, but though these prepared the ground for what was later to be RADA, it was not opened until 1904.

If the profession was bothered at the turn of the century by not having any drama schools, the trouble now is that there are far too many. With so many young people so eager to become actors, a great deal of money can be made out of offering to train them, especially when teachers encourage beginners to believe they have a reasonable chance of surviving in the profession. It is not even possible to say how many drama schools there are: the number can be given as 40 or 140, according to how you define what a drama school is. In Equity's November 1971 analysis of newcomers into the profession, there was a list of 'principal' drama schools in Britain. Ten of these are in England: the Birmingham School of Speech Training and Dramatic Art, the Bristol Old Vic Theatre School, the Central School of Speech and Drama, the Drama Centre, the East 15 Acting School, the Guildhall School of Music and Drama, the London Academy of Music and Dramatic Art, the Rose Bruford College, the Royal Academy of Dramatic Art (RADA), and the Webber Douglas Academy of Dramatic Art. Eighty-three per cent of the students leaving these schools obtained jobs. Then there are nine 'other' drama schools: the Birmingham Theatre School, the Brighton School of Music and Drama, the Coventry Centre for Speech and Drama, the Guildford School of Acting, the Mountview Theatre School, the New

[1] *The Theatre*, August 1890, cited by Allardyce Nicoll.

Era Academy, the New College of Speech and Drama, the Northern College of Speech and Drama, and Studio '68 of Theatre Arts London. In addition there are university drama departments, colleges of further education, teacher-training colleges, private coaches, and stage schools in which children are taught acting alongside the normal educational curriculum.

The ten 'principal'[1] schools turn out about 275 students annually – about fifty-nine graduate from RADA; forty-five from the Rose Bruford; sixteen each from the Drama Centre and the E 15; between twenty and thirty-six from each of the others. There are no statistics for the total annual output of England's drama schools. In a letter to *The Times* (19 June 1972) the President of Equity, Ernest Clark, estimated that it was not less than three thousand.

Not everyone, of course, who succeeds in getting into the profession is a drama school graduate. In the year October 1970–September 1971 there were 1,428 new members of Equity (including 19 stage management staff and 127 opera singers and ballet dancers). Of those admitted as actors 21·5 per cent had had no training at all. Only 24·5 per cent had been to drama schools and 13 per cent to stage schools.[2] Ninety per cent had had private tuition and 45 per cent had been either to university or to teacher training colleges. Of those who became actors in films or television 31 per cent had been at one of the principal drama schools, and 32 per cent of those who joined reps or children's theatres had been at one of these drama schools. Only 14 per cent had had no training.

Getting into the profession, though harder than it used to be, is much easier than surviving in it. According to the Equity survey based on replies from 4,819 members to a questionnaire sent out to about 23,000, the average amount of work obtained by English actors during 1971 was 14½ weeks in the theatre and 21 days in television and films, while actresses were averaging 11½ weeks in the theatre and 7½ days in other media. Sixty per cent of the profession

[1] There are 16 schools in the country that are 'recognised as efficient' by the Department of Education and Science, which sends an inspector to visit them regularly.

[2] I.e. the schools at which children are given acting lessons alongside their normal education.

earned less than a thousand pounds during the year; 20 per cent earned less than £250; 14½ per cent between £250 and £500; 12½ per cent between £500 and £750, and 13 per cent between £750 and £1,000. Twenty-five per cent earned more than £1,000 but less than £2,000; 8 per cent between £2,000 and £3,000; 3½ per cent between £3,000 and £5,000 and only 3½ per cent more than £5,000. The median weekly wage for men was under £20 and for women under £12.[1] In April 1972 (according to the Department of Employment) the national weekly average for men was £36 and for women £20.

Comparing these figures for actors with the 1966 figures, the medians are slightly higher for both men and women, because the level of minimum salaries was higher. But in real money terms, both medians are considerably lower, because of inflation. There was also less work available. In 1966 the average for an actor had been seventeen weeks in the theatre and nineteen days in other media; for an actress fourteen weeks in the theatre and eleven days in other media. The cutback in employment was due partly to the raising of minimum salary levels.

The *Morning Star* for 17 November 1971 analysed the income of a twenty-eight-year-old actor, married with two children, during the eight months March to October. He appeared in two London shows and in a play on television, but these were his earnings:

3 weeks of rehearsal at £12 per week	£36
3 weeks of performances at £18 per week	54
Television fee for 2 weeks of rehearsal and performance	143
4 weeks of rehearsal at £18 per week	72
9 weeks of performances at £30 per week	270
	£575

Ten per cent of this had to go to his agent and he had to pay contributions towards the cost of his National Insurance Stamps for the twenty-three weeks he worked. And to get a television job and two London shows within eight months is, of course, to be very much more successful than the average actor.

[1] This excludes earnings from repeat fees, but these add less than a pound a week to median figures.

According to Equity, the amount of work to be had today is enough to provide about 6,500 actors and actresses with a reasonable living. Restrictions on entry are having some effect: there were 1,750 new Equity members in 1969, about 1,900 in 1970 and only 1,492 in 1971. But if over five thousand have joined in three years, the fact that less than 20,000 are in full benefit is a reminder of the number who are admitting defeat. Between 1946 and 1953, though Equity enrolled an average of 1,850 new members each year, the total membership increased by only about 9,000. Between 1959 and 1969 there was an annual average loss of 1,482 members and of course there is no knowing how many people resign themselves to the reality of having been crowded out of the profession without resigning their membership. There are also many who work sporadically as actors but earn more money each year from a variety of part-time or semi-permanent jobs, either enrolling with one of the agencies that provide domestic cleaners and baby-sitters, or working as bunnies, telephone operators, shop assistants, secretaries, clerks or receptionists or doing door-to-door selling or market research. The Equity survey for 1971 revealed that 39 per cent of the women and 27 per cent of the men had to do temporary work, but their earnings from it were surprisingly low, the median being only £210. There are many actors and actresses who divide their lives for years in this unsatisfying way and end up reluctantly taking a permanent job outside the theatre.

It may seem incredible in this situation that nothing is being done to stop the drama schools and drama coaches from puffing up so many students each year with false hopes. But, like Parliament, local councils are very much more willing to subsidise anything which can be categorised as educational than to subsidise the practice of the arts or help people to earn a living once their education or training is complete. And the system by which local education authorities make grants for drama students has both encouraged the proliferation of second-rate drama schools and their expansion. It is hard to run a school economically with less than a hundred students, and if local education authorities are making money available for each student taken, it is understandable that principals of institutions should be eager to scoop it up. Competition for places at the best schools is extremely high; at LAMDA there have been as many as 750 candidates in one year for 24 places. But most of the grants from local education authorities are available only for students to be trained locally, so it sometimes happens that a highly talented student who wins, or could win, a place at one of the good schools ends up with an inferior local training because his parents cannot afford to support him without a grant.

The price that an actor's services command is obviously affected by the ratio of supply to demand. Until 1970 an actor in the West End could be earning as little as £12 a week for the first four weeks of the rehearsal period and then £18 a week for the remainder – if it went on longer – and for the run of the play. The practice of paying actors less for rehearsing than for performing dates from the time of the Victorian actor–managers who often had no money for salaries until it started coming in at the box office. Actors obviously work both harder and longer when they are rehearsing and learning lines than when the play is on and all they have to do is give performances; but in the theatre illogical habits tend to survive for a very long time. It was only recently that some theatres, like the Royal Court, raised rehearsal salaries to the level of playing salaries. In most theatres they are still lower.

In regional repertory the same actors are usually rehearsing every day and performing every evening, but until 1970 a probationary member of Equity – an actor with less than forty weeks professional experience – might have been earning only £7·75 a week and a full member only £9·50 a week. Obviously salaries on this level are acceptable only to people – probably without family commitments – who are willing to put up with almost anything in order to work in the theatre. And unlike the old apprenticeships, it is not even a means of acquiring a skill that can be counted on to provide a livelihood. A talented graduate of a good drama school might spend fifteen months of his first two years in rep, with perhaps a few days of well-paid filming and a few weeks of fairly well-paid television, only to find that in the third year of his career, things become not better but worse, with over 3,000 new members of the profession competing for the same jobs and quite happy to accept ten pounds a week where he would have hoped to stick out for fourteen. In 1966, when the Arts Council drama budget jumped from £766,066 to £1,352,224, it was hoped that part of the money would go to raising the general level of actors' salaries, but it was all absorbed by rising costs, and salaries remained virtually unchanged. Perhaps there is an element of unacknowledged envy in the way most people think about the income of actors, if they think about it at all: they're doing work they enjoy so why should they be paid properly?

In 1970 Equity launched a 'Living Wage' campaign, which has been successful in raising minimum salaries to £18 a week for provisional members (they are no longer called 'probationary') and £20 a week for full members. In relation to the dwindling value of the pound and to salaries earned in other jobs, these rises were very modest and long overdue. Miners' salaries had been raised from £18 to £23 for surface workers, from £19 to £25 for underground men, and from £30 to £34·50 for coalface workers.

Many theatres are run on such tight margins that the new salary levels could have caused bankruptcy. Equity, therefore, set up a joint committee with the Council of Repertory Theatres and the Theatrical Managers' Association to consider applications for exemption from the new rates. The theatres at Farnham and Westcliff were both given temporary dispensation to go on paying salaries below the new levels. But for the vast majority of the subsidised reps all over England, actors were suddenly very much more expensive. The natural reaction was to use less of them.

For Nottingham Playhouse, where an average of thirty actors used to be employed regularly, the weekly wage bill had varied between £600 and £1,000. The minimum salary had been £12 and actors in the permanent company had received between £18 and £50 a week. The immediate reaction to the new wage scale was to reduce the average strength. At Oldham it would have cost an extra £10,000 annually to go on giving jobs to the same number of actors. At Bolton, where the top salary was £20, the extra expense would have been between £5,000 and £10,000 a year, and the immediate reaction was to consider keeping the theatre closed for three months out of twelve. The Theatre Royal at Lincoln had to sack three actors, three technicians and eleven members of the administrative staff, including all the usherettes. At Northampton, where a deficit of £6,600 was incurred during 1970, £5,000 had been added to the annual wage bill. At Richmond, faced with increased expenses of £6,000 a year, the company announced that it would have to depend more on the box-office appeal of star names. The Yvonne Arnaud Theatre, Guildford, affected to the tune of £21,000 a year by the new wage scale, reacted by adding between five and fifteen pence to the price of each ticket, and at Leatherhead the Thorndike Theatre responded in the same way.

If economies had not been made by cutting down on the employment of actors, between £750,000 and £1,000,000 would have been added to the annual wage bills of regional repertories in 1971–72, and at a time when the Arts Council subsidies for the year had already been fixed. In many theatres, boards of management reacted by imposing restrictions on artistic directors. In some of the less well subsidised theatres, the new minimum became the effective maximum, the director being instructed never to offer more than £20 a week without special permission from the board. Economies were also imposed by banning large-cast plays altogether, and limiting the number of sets.

The new salary scales alone would have had a big effect, but part of Equity's 'Living Wage' campaign was directed at restricting entry into the profession. Ever since the fifties there had been agitation for action to be taken against the annual flood of new members who were making it harder for the old members to survive in their highly competitive profession. At first the Council of Equity was opposed to the idea of imposing rigid controls, but overcrowding was becoming so endemic towards the end of the sixties that something had to be done. The method employed was to make 'casting agreements' with organisations representing the employers, limiting the number of newcomers they could take on. In this way a 'post-entry closed shop' in which employees had to become members (or provisional members) of Equity as soon as they got work in the theatre, was transformed into a 'pre-entry closed shop'. In other words they now had to become members of Equity before they could be employed.

The first casting agreement came into operation in the West End in 1964, when it effectively halved the number of actors who won their union cards by walking straight on to a West End stage. The casting agreement with commercial television became effective during 1969, so its results can best be seen by comparing the number of new entrants in 1968 (278) with the 1970 figure (38). The BBC was unwilling to enter into casting agreements, but they became effective in regional repertories during 1971. In 1970 there were 1,324 new entrants through regional theatres, and in 1972 only 840. The situation was complicated by the Industrial Relations Act which made 'pre-entry closed shop' agreements void. Approved closed shops are allowed when there is a joint application by a union and an employer to the National Industrial Relations Court. The employers' associations agreed to co-operate with Equity and the casting agreements have been amended to cut out all reference to union membership as such. But employers are allowed under the Act to give preference to Equity members and possession of a full (or provisional) Equity card can be used as a proof of experience, so the new Act makes no real difference to the effectiveness of the casting agreements.

Undoubtedly, overcrowding is being reduced, however marginally. But the citadel could only be protected against the invaders from the drama schools by erecting fortifications on which some of the defenders were bound to be impaled. The actors who have suffered most are those who used to scrape a living out of the commercial reps and the touring companies, which had been surviving without subsidy by operating on very narrow financial margins and by paying salaries well below the level which has now been established as minimal. These theatres can hope for no help from the Arts Council or from the municipal authorities, though the ratepayers' money would be better spent on subsidising commercial companies which at least provide entertainment for residents and work for actors, than on subsidising the inferior drama schools which only manufacture frustration.

The rise in property values was already making it extremely difficult for commercial theatre to survive in the regions. The space that a theatre occupies could be exploited more profitably in almost any other way, and town councils mostly showed little interest in protecting theatres from the developer. The few that survived were hit badly by the new salary levels. Many people are glad to see these companies die. They say that low salaries lead to low artistic standards, that the companies which are being forced out of business are not really in the business, that the profession will be better off without them. But no one was ever forced either to work for them or to buy tickets for their productions, and if people did both, there must have been some need for them. By killing them Equity is reducing the amount of live entertainment available in the country and raising its more successful members' standard of living by depriving some of their less successful colleagues of the chance to work at all. If a theatre subsidised by the Arts Council gets into financial difficulties, the Council will usually plough more money in rather than let it close. But unsubsidised theatres were allowed to go quietly bankrupt.

The relationship between London theatre and regional theatre has been profoundly altered: only a very small proportion of the bigger theatres in London are subsidised; only a very small proportion of the bigger theatres outside it are not. The growing power of Equity is working together with the growing involvement of the state in the theatre to push the profession in the direction of tighter organisation and greater exclusivity.

Already there are embarrassing anomalies between the earnings of actors and those of backstage workers. Stage managers, deputy stage managers, assistant stage managers, lighting operators, stage-hands – are all unionised. Since the jobs of these invisible workers are less glamorous than the actors', the relation between supply and demand is different. The current minimum for a stage manager in a subsidised rep is £25 a week, which often means that he is earning more than any of the actors and possibly more than the director. Meanwhile an out-of-work actor, who may never have earned more than £20 a week, can sign on as a stage-hand in a West End theatre and – especially during the pantomime season, when there is plenty of overtime – earn £45 for his week's work. In the United States the disparities are even greater. In 1972, at the new John F. Kennedy Center for the Performing Arts in Washington, stage-hands were earning 1500 dollars a week and actors about 175.

Unfortunately, the profession is bound to make itself smaller in the process of getting itself organised. Only an enormous infusion of state money could provide our impoverished theatre with the means to pay reasonable salaries to the same number of actors who somehow or other survived in the profession on the old salaries. Already many actors, and not necessarily the least talented, have been forced into other jobs. But at the same time as producing a new professional exclusiveness, the dialectic of the theatre's progress has produced a Fringe. This strong counter-movement tending towards a more casual theatre has gained a good deal of momentum since the middle sixties, and once again the frontier between professional and amateur has become hard to define, though not in the same way that it was in the nineteenth century. Just as the 'Fringe' of satellite events organised during the fifties to coincide with the Edinburgh Festival but staged in church halls, basements, attics and any other available spaces eventually became almost integral to the Festival, what we now have all over the country is a vigorous Fringe Theatre which is still less integral to the Establishment theatre than it will eventually become. Pubs, clubs, cellars, miscellaneous halls and even streets have become arenas for an enormous variety of theatrical performances ranging from the gauchely amateurish to the highly accomplished, from hide-bound conventionality to daring avant-gardism, from light-hearted pub entertainment to serious experiment which tests and reopens the frontiers dividing drama from painting, sculpture and music.

At the end of the fifties it was being said that one of the worst things about the London theatre was the absence of any equivalent to Off-Broadway. Since then the Off-Broadway theatre has become more of an Establishment, and a second layer of fringe activity has crystallised in 'Off-Off-Broadway'. It is still true that one of the worst things about the London theatre is the lack of any equivalent to Off-Broadway. Experiment is all the rage, in theory, though in practice the label is often stretched to provide an excuse for work which could hardly be less experimental or less interesting to anyone except the performers. But if a climate exists in which a certain amount of good work can be done, a huge amount of bad work is bound to accompany it.

Meanwhile training in acting techniques, after being virtually unavailable in the nineteenth century, even for the profession, is now freely available all over the country, not just in drama schools but in evening institutes and in ordinary schools. Thanks to the drama-in-education movement, schoolchildren are being taught how to express themselves through acting and improvisation. Formerly stage schools (like the Italia Conti and the Corona) were the only places at which children could gain experience and skill in acting while still so young. Most drama students arriving at RADA or the Central School were initiated into techniques that were quite new to them. Now these techniques are being taught and being used in different ways by many sections of the community. There are groups, both inside hospitals and outside, which use improvisation and drama as a means to acquiring greater freedom of self-expression, whether or not this is regarded as part of a mental therapy programme. There are classes and workshops in drama – some attached to adult education colleges, some independent – all open to anyone who wants to come along.

Not that all the training on offer is of a high standard. Obviously most of the voice and movement training cannot be as good as at the better drama schools, where classes are frequent and attendances regular. But the desire to act is obviously being stimulated in more people than ever before. In the past the Amateur Dramatic Club at Cambridge and the Oxford University Dramatic Society have been important as nurseries for professional talent. No doubt they will go on being important, but now they are only two of many playgrounds where young men and women who want to act can acquire skill and experience. The mere fact that there are so many new universities creates a huge pool of young people to whom the leisure and the opportunity to act is guaranteed for at least three years. But there are also much more leisure and much more drama outside universities. In technical colleges, youth clubs and in other institutions where young men and women are brought together, drama groups are often formed, and people whose parents had no chance to savour the pleasures of acting develop such a taste for it that they become determined not to give it up. No professional organisation and no way of organising the profession could force them to.

For Equity the existence of fringe groups poses a formidable problem. Some of them are based in pubs, some have small theatres improvised out of buildings intended for other uses, some tour the country, putting on their productions anywhere they can. Most of the actors involved are professional in the sense that there is nothing else they are doing or want to do with their working lives, but many have no formal training and no professional qualifications that a union can recognise, while the money they are earning is well below the levels that Equity has established. Equity members, though, unable to find any better-paid work, have often worked on the Fringe, sometimes temporarily, sometimes permanently. Until the Industrial Relations Act became law in February 1972, Equity could have stopped its members from working with non-members, but this would have been very unpopular when work was so scarce. It is obviously inconsistent to give more latitude to Fringe groups than to commercial reps, which may have equal difficulty in finding the money to pay Equity salaries. Here Equity may have been swayed by the Arts Council's recognition of some of the Fringe companies, though, even when subsidised, they have still been unable to pay their actors more than twelve or fifteen pounds a week. Nor is Equity, apparently, basing its discrimination between Fringe companies and commercial reps on an assessment of the artistic value of the work done. But this is just one of several anomalies which may or may not be adjusted as the dialectic of the profession's progress continues. At the moment Equity is deliberately ignoring what happens outside conventional theatre buildings, but insisting that normal salaries are paid when a Fringe production transfers to a normal theatre. At the Open Space Theatre, for instance, a basement in the Tottenham Court Road, Charles Marowitz was not given Equity dispensation to pay his actors as little as £12 a week,[1] but though they were nearly always members, the union held back from intervening, on the grounds that it did not regard the theatre as 'conventional'. It would have interfered only if he had transferred a production to

[1] He now pays considerably more.

the West End without raising salaries to the normal level. But provisional members who worked at cut rates would be penalised in that the work done would not count towards the forty weeks of professional experience they need to become full members. In fact, of course, experience in an experimental production can be more valuable than experience in a commercial thriller or farce for raising an actor's standard of professional competence, but this is only one of many ways in which Establishment theatre still treats the Fringe in the way that the United Nations used to treat China. It cannot be denied that it exists, but it is more convenient to behave as though it does not.

This kind of behaviour is damaging to our theatre. The more highly organised and the more exclusive Establishment theatre becomes, the more it needs to come to terms with its large, unwieldy and unorganised Fringe, which is going to become increasingly large and unwieldy until it is organised. Equity and the Arts Council are already involved: if they do not take the organising initiative now, they will have to adjust to it when it is taken. Already there is too much interchange between the two theatres for them to separate, but it is still very hard to see how they can integrate.

4 THE THEATRE AND THE THEATRES

Nowhere in the English theatre is history more damagingly present than in the buildings, especially in London. In the provinces over twenty new theatres have been built since 1958 and more than a dozen others drastically modernised. In Coventry, in Nottingham, in Sheffield, the word 'theatre' hardly has the same meaning that it still has in London. It makes people think of bright modern buildings, clean-looking, well-lit, airy and attractive, with restaurants, roomy bars and car-parks. In London the word calls up a picture of a Victorian or Edwardian building with a picture-frame stage, a heavy curtain and a three or four-tiered auditorium full of plush and gilt, baroque curlicues and cupids in half-relief with the paint chipping off.

London has only two large new theatres, the Mermaid, which opened in 1959, and the New London Theatre (1973). Of the other post-war buildings, the Mayfair is a small theatre inside a hotel, the Royalty, which opened in 1960, became a cinema in 1961 and was not reclaimed as a theatre till *Oh! Calcutta!* opened there in 1970, the Prince Charles opened at the end of 1962 and became a cinema in 1964. The Young Vic was opened in 1970 with the knowledge that a new site would have to be found at the end of five years. The Shaw and the Hampstead Theatre Club are useful but small theatres built by Camden Council. The Queen's, which was hit by a bomb in 1940, was reconstructed in the old style, with a proscenium stage and an Edwardian-style auditorium, though the exterior, the foyer and the bars are modern. The Roundhouse is a converted engine shed. Twelve of our theatres are Victorian and seven Edwardian. Of the remainder, three opened between 1911 and 1916, one in 1924 and five between 1928 and 1930. The only one to open later, in 1937, the newly rebuilt Prince of Wales, was designed – like several of the earlier theatres – primarily for musicals. In New York the situation is quite different: not a single nineteenth-century theatre survives.

Today society is far less hierarchical than it was for our Victorian and Edwardian ancestors and the experience of theatre-going is very different. Even the Victorians were apt to complain about the interior decorations of their theatre. 'In the house itself,' Henry James wrote in 1877, 'everything seems to contribute to ... the impression that the theatre in England is a social luxury and not an artistic necessity.' Twenty years later Shaw was to congratulate Beerbohm Tree on his restraint in decorating Her Majesty's. 'He has had the good sense – a very rare quality in England where artistic matters are in question – to see that a theatre which is panelled, and mirrored, and mantel-pieced like the first-class saloon of a Peninsular and Oriental liner or a Pullman drawing room car, is no place for *Julius Caesar*, or indeed for anything except tailor-made drama and farcical comedy.'

The décor contributes a lot to audience expectations and to the atmosphere for the rapport that develops between actor and audience. This is also influenced greatly by the actual shape of the theatre, the spatial relationships between the stage and the various sections of the auditorium. Unfortunately the shape which is still dominant was evolved for a very different kind of actor–audience relationship from the one we want today. Ideas of what this relationship ought to be can change fairly quickly; buildings are more durable. What is happening now, I think, is that many of our best playwrights and directors are moving towards a conception of that relationship which is not so far removed from that of the Elizabethan theatre. But in London nearly all the large-scale productions have to be done in buildings that belong to a tradition of theatre which did not grow from Elizabethan roots.

In an Elizabethan theatre, an actor standing at the front of the forestage was largely encircled by his public. In spite of being split into four levels, the whole of the audience concentrated on the actor, the words he was speaking and the way he was speaking them. His costume, his gestures, his movements *vis-à-vis* the other actors were all more prominent than they can be if they are merely part of a larger picture which fills a frame the size of a proscenium arch. The actor was then a fully three-dimensional figure, palpably present among the public that was watching him. But in our Victorian and Edwardian buildings the audience sits in darkness, not encircling the actor with its collective attention but staring into an illuminated space in which the natural centre of focus is several yards above the actors' heads.

In Shakespeare's Globe Theatre, a spectator sitting in the back row of the top gallery was not so very much farther away from the stage than the front row of the groundlings or the courtiers sitting on the side of the stage itself. In the back row of the gallery at the Apollo Theatre (1901) you are nearly thirty yards away from the stage – looking down at an angle of nearly forty-five degrees at the tops of actors' heads. At the Chichester Festival Theatre (1961–2) the highest seat has an angle of sixteen degrees to the stage and is only 5·8 metres higher, while at the Apollo it is 15·2 metres higher. This affects the fortunate people in the stalls as well as the unfortunates in the gallery. As Tyrone Guthrie said, 'The rapport between the stage and the audience is tremendously conditioned by the amount of cubic space that is empty.'[1] His theatre at Stratford, Ontario, contains 2,225 seats packed into thirteen rows. It is planned on a circle of which just less than half is backstage. Afterwards he wished there had only been ten or eleven rows. Similarly, Peter Hall, in briefing the architects for the new Royal Shakespeare Company Theatre in the Barbican, insisted that no one should be more than sixty-five feet away from the actors. 'Even if you are in the fifth or sixth row and know there are people far behind you, it dilutes the experience for you.'[2] There are to be three galleries in the Barbican Theatre but, without being stacked vertically above each other, as at the Globe, they are to be brought in much closer to the stage than at Stratford-on-Avon or the Aldwych or most English theatres, which fall a long way short of Guthrie's or Hall's ideal.

[1] *The Actor and the Architect.* Edited by Stephen Joseph. Manchester University Press, 1964.
[2] Quoted by Forbes Bramble in 'The Barbican Theatre', *Theatre Quarterly* No. 1.

Because the monopoly system that Charles II inaugurated lasted for nearly two hundred years, few theatres were built in London between 1660 and 1850. Two of the surviving theatres which have their origin in the seventeenth century are Drury Lane and Sadler's Wells, and there were four – Her Majesty's, the Haymarket, the Royal Opera House and the Lyceum – which were first built in the eighteenth. Of our surviving nineteenth-century theatres only two, the Adelphi and the Old Vic, date from before 1850. If more theatres had been built during the eighteenth and early nineteenth centuries it is possible that a stronger architectural tradition would have developed, and it might have produced a more satisfactory compromise than we now have between the Elizabethan type of theatre, in which the forestage jutted out into the centre of the wooden O, and the late nineteenth-century picture-frame theatres.

These were built for an audience that needed rather the same sort of entertainment as television and the popular cinema now provide. Rapid industrialisation had brought a huge inflow of population into the towns, while improvement of public transport had increased the audience's mobility. The aristocracy patronised the theatre less than in the eighteenth century, and the new middle-class audience could be satisfied most effectively with a readily digestible diet of melodrama, comedy and spectacle. Unadventurous and commercially minded, most managers mounted only the plays that would be sure to command silence in the pit, where the audience readily became vociferous. In 1906, when Max Beerbohm (for once) watched a play from the pit – at the Garrick, where the pit was a comparatively good one – he found himself resolving to be more tolerant about public taste. 'Twaddle and vulgarity always will have the upper hand,' he wrote. 'The marvel to me is not that the public cares so little for dramatic truth but that it can sometimes tolerate a play which is not either the wildest melodrama or the wildest farce. Where low tones and fine shades are practically invisible, one would expect an exclusive insistence on splodges of garish colour.'[1]

The rigid separation between stage and auditorium was necessary

[1] Quoted in *Victorian Dramatic Criticism*. Edited by George Rowell. Methuen, 1971.

because the scenery was so important and the machinery controlling it had to be hidden: the stage had to be vertically below a tower containing the grid from which it was flown. The sets were so important to the Victorians that they figure prominently on the playbills. 'Realistic scenery' was often promised, and with revivals of old tragedies the public was frequently assured that the scenery would be new. Locales of different scenes were listed, and where unusual pieces of stage machinery or spectacular visual effects were to be featured, they would be advertised. In productions of Shakespeare plays the script was far from being sacrosanct, but immense ingenuity and a lot of money were expended on the sets. Telbin's setting for the final scene in *Romeo and Juliet* in Irving's production at the Lyceum looked like something out of Piranesi, and his design for Charles Kean's *Merchant of Venice* had practical bridges and boats moving on the canal. Architectural detail was reproduced two-dimensionally with painstaking accuracy by highly skilled scene-painters, even in quite unrealistic plays like *A Winter's Tale*. Kean had a reputation for introducing the most new-fangled scenic devices in his Shakespeare productions, and the lovers in his version of *A Midsummer Night's Dream* wandered through the woods against a background produced by a moving diorama. (A diorama consisted of two panoramic cloths on rollers with holes cut in the front one to reveal sections of the rear one.) Even Beerbohm Tree introduced a spectacular Magna Carta tableau into *King John*, and a vision of the Sphinx into *Antony and Cleopatra*.

This sort of visual theatre can be seen as a continuation of the tradition that started in England with the court masques of James I, which introduced the proscenium arch. But even in the Restoration and eighteenth-century theatre, which made abundant use of the backcloths, borders, wings and all the visual trappings that the proscenium encourages, the actor had much more contact with the audience than in the nineteenth-century theatre. The Restoration stage projected beyond the proscenium arch with doors on either side of this apron projection. When Drury Lane was rebuilt without them in 1812, the actors asked for them to be put back: without them they felt cut off from the audience. Later, in the Georgian theatre, there was only one door. The apron was still the main acting area until it was removed at the beginning of the nineteenth century and the actors played in a confined area representing the locale speci-fied by the surrounding scenery. When the Bancrofts took over the Haymarket in 1880 they had a gilt picture frame painted around the proscenium arch. In *The World Behind the Scenes* (1881) Percy Fitz-gerald commented:

> A rich and elaborate gold border, about two feet broad, after the pattern of a picture frame, is continued all round the proscenium, and carried even below the actors' feet – There can be no doubt the sense of illusion is increased, and for the reason just given – the actors seem cut off from the domain of prose; there is no border-land or platform in front; and, stranger still, the whole has the air of a picture projected on a surface.

This was setting the seal on the development that was making the space inside the proscenium frame into an invisible wall. The phrase 'fourth wall' dates back to the beginning of the nineteenth century. Leigh Hunt used it in describing the actor John Bannister.

> The stage appears to be his own room, of which the audience compose the fourth wall – if they clap him, he does not stand still to enjoy the applause.

This was a healthy step towards realism in acting but today we are on the other side of the naturalism that culminated at the end of the nineteenth century. The theatre cannot compete with the cinema in creating the illusion of real life being lived out in front of us.

Of all the influences currently at work on our theatre, that of Brecht is still the strongest – not the influence of his plays but the influence of the production style he evolved in theory during the late twenties and early thirties, and in practice between 1949 and 1956, when he was directing his own actors in the Berliner Ensemble. In spite of – and partly because of – having to work in a proscenium theatre, his characteristic stylistic devices (like the famous 'alienation effects') were all aimed at smashing the illusion of the fourth wall, and his productions were the main source of a movement which has largely freed directors of the old dependence on backcloths and painted flats. There is no knowing what Brecht's productions would have been like if the East German government had built a new theatre for him to work in. Certainly the audience would have needed fewer reminders that what they were watching was a performance.

Following Brecht, the playwrights, directors and designers of today all tend to make a point of reminding audiences that they are sitting in a theatre watching a play. But the illusion of the invisible wall is still very much with us, even at the Royal Court, which has been the most important cockpit of experiment for English playwrights since 1956, when the English Stage Company took over with George Devine as Artistic Director. This 1888 theatre was not changed very substantially by the structural alterations of 1903, the improvements of 1921, the renovations of 1952 or the extension of the stage in 1956. It still has the shape of a Victorian theatre.

Had it been a post-war building, John Osborne's development might have been very different. Although he never had the post of Resident Dramatist (which was not introduced until the late sixties), all his plays since *Look Back in Anger*, except the musical *The World of Paul Slickey* and *A Bond Honoured* (which is a translation), have been created there: from *The Entertainer* onwards he was writing with the Royal Court stage and auditorium in mind. So it is no accident that after *The Entertainer* and *Luther*, which are both Brechtian in construction and in their alienation effects, he reverted more and more to the structure of the well-made play. In *The Entertainer* he makes the auditorium into an old Music Hall when Archie Rice talks directly to the audience: 'Don't clap too loud – it's a very old building.' In *Luther* the auditorium becomes a market-place when Tetzel tries to sell Indulgences, and the audience becomes a congregation when Luther preaches from the steps of the Castle Church at Wittenberg. But the later plays – *Time Present, Hotel in Amsterdam* and *West of Suez* – fall back behind an invisible fourth wall. One of the reasons his 1972 play *A Sense of Detachment* is more interesting is that it faces up to the fact that it consists of a performance inside a theatre.

Most dramatists conceive their plays partly in terms of a shape. David Hare, who was Resident Dramatist at the Court until July 1971, wrote his first and third plays for Portable Theatre, a group which needs only a space, not a theatre. His second play was written for production on a proscenium stage in the West End, though it was actually presented at the Hampstead Theatre Club and revived at the Royal Court; his fourth, *The Great Exhibition*, was written for the Royal Court, though it, too, was put on, instead, at Hampstead. 'That's the only way I can do it – to think of environments and know exactly what you're aiming for.'[1] For his proscenium plays he thinks more pictorially, more in flat images, he says.

The fact of writing for a proscenium theatre makes the set bulk far larger in the playwright's mind than it would otherwise, and the more he thinks of scenery, the less free he feels to move his action from one locale to another. Unity of place was once an artistic necessity; today it is as out of date and as restricting as a ball and chain. Oddly enough it is the example of two much more visual media, films and television, which has gradually had the effect of liberating our playwrights. In John Whiting's first four plays there is no change of scene. In his fifth, *The Gates of Summer*, the action shifts from a room to a terrace outside the house and back to another room inside it. It was only after eight years of writing for the cinema that he experimented, in *The Devils*, in stringing together short sequences in different locales without feeling obliged to make changes in the setting that filled the proscenium frame. But playwrights like David Mercer, Charles Wood, and Peter Nichols, scoring their first successes on television, got into the habit of constructing in smaller units, and it was natural for them to arrogate more freedom of movement.

Experience of television has also tended to encourage the playwright to develop more flexibility in letting characters strike up direct relationships with the audience. An illuminated realistic set and a darkened auditorium encourage the pretence that the audience is not really there, but the playwright who, while writing for the screen, has been deprived of a live audience, is more likely to respond directly to its presence in the theatre. Once he lets a character talk

[1] Interview in *The Times*, 22 May 1971.

straight out to it, a whole new vista of possibilities opens out, as it did for Peter Nichols in *A Day in the Death of Joe Egg*. Of course there are precedents for this kind of direct relationship between actor and audience in Elizabethan drama, in music hall (which functioned well in proscenium theatres) and in the work of iconoclastic directors like Joan Littlewood, but it is generally harder for a playwright to explore these possibilities in theatres that tend to push the actor back into a picture inside a frame.

Modern directors are equally cramped by having to work in old buildings. The shapes of the acting area and the auditorium – and above all the rigid separation between them – reduce the possibilities of developing a free-flowing relationship between actor and audience. Struggling to break beyond these limitations, even Peter Brook may be driven to devices which are clumsy and embarrassing. In his production of Seneca's *Oedipus* for the National Theatre at the Old Vic, he wanted to merge the chorus into the audience and to produce choric sounds that would come from all over the theatre. The best method he could devise was to dot actors about at strategic points in the auditorium. They had to sit or stand on specially constructed perches and some were strapped to pillars. Spectators arriving at near-by seats had either to ignore them or try to involve them in conversation, which was embarrassing for the actors, who had been instructed not to respond.

In his production of *A Midsummer Night's Dream* for the Royal Shakespeare Theatre at Stratford-on-Avon, which even managed to make the fairies meaningful to a sceptical seventies audience, Brook was handicapped by having to devise the production for a badly designed theatre with poor acoustics, appalling sight-lines and, of course, an uncompromising separation of stage and auditorium. When he had the opportunity of bringing the production to the Roundhouse for a single night (4 December 1970) staging it with no set, no costumes, no make-up and no rehearsals to familiarise the cast with the new building, he was determined to mix the actors up with the spectators and he had all the seats removed. By moving in and out of the audience, the actors were able to make much of the play into a game which everyone could join in.

c

If we had more theatres in which performances like this could be given every night, a new discipline would evolve with the new freedom.

We are also far too ready to take it for granted that it is natural for a stage to be about twice as wide as it is deep. This is natural only for the picture-frame stage. Different shapes like the square thrust of the University Theatre at Manchester or the hexagonal stage at Greenwich, with three of its sides projecting into the auditorium, can make it easier to get the actor's relationships with the audience on to quite a different footing and for the director to build moving pictures with the actors instead of using them to fill out a static picture created by the scenery. At a theatre like Chichester, where the open stage brings the action out into the auditorium, it is natural for much more to be spent on costumes. Good costumes help to keep the audience's eye on the actors who are wearing them, whereas spectacular scenery keeps pulling the eye away from the actor. In any case, naturalistic scenery encourages naturalistic acting, and the public of today, which has been thoroughly familiarised with impressionistic techniques of story-telling, no longer needs an actor – any more than a painter – to fill in all the details of what he is portraying. Old age can be suggested without a realistic make-up or a meticulous imitation of every vocal quaver, every physical sign of senescence. But while actors and directors are belatedly growing more aware of the possibilities of the new vocabulary, the buildings are still pressuring them back to naturalism. Describing what he wanted in the Barbican, Peter Hall said, 'It should be a theatre where it is possible to create a background which is a total void. Absolutely nothing.'

Certainly there is now a strong, if tardy, reaction against the flat-fronted proscenium stage. The new National Theatre building is to have two theatres, one of which is conventional in structure, but the larger of the two will have an open stage, as will the RSC's new theatre in the Barbican. But even when these theatres are ready, they and the Mermaid will be the only large non-proscenium theatres in London. It looks extremely improbable that it will ever have as many new theatres as old ones. In the regions, where space is less expensive, there has been a theatre-building boom, and even in the theatres built with prosceniums there is at least a degree of flexibility – more flexibility than can be achieved at a theatre like the Aldwych by removing a few rows of front stalls and building the stage forwards. At the Nottingham Playhouse a thrust can be added to the basic proscenium, and as the architect, Peter Moro, puts it, 'the cylindrical form of the auditorium clearly envelops the audience and the performance in one architectural space when the forestage is in use. Alternatively, it is possible to take the action out of the auditorium and place it in a different space, which is seen through a wide gap in the wall of the cylinder.'[1]

Many of the theatres built in the last twelve years have been designed for flexibility. At the Billingham Forum, the Chester Gateway, the Leatherhead Thorndike and the Leicester Phoenix, the basic proscenium can be adapted by adding aprons to the front of the stage. The Bolton Octagon takes its name from its octagonal auditorium, and five of the eight sections of tiered seats can be taken out to accommodate open stage, thrust or in-the-round productions. The Northcott Theatre at Exeter has an open stage at floor level and for thrust or in-the-round productions the shape can be changed by putting seats on the stage area. Not all these compromises are successful. A picture-frame stage with a removable proscenium arch and an apron attachment is not the same as an open stage. Much depends on the angles of the stage walls and the extent to which the focus is on the actor rather than on the background.

Of the Victorian and Edwardian theatres in the provinces, relatively few are still in use. A few, like the Birmingham Alexandra, the Oxford New and the Wolverhampton Grand, are municipally owned and used either for tours or repertory. Others like the Theatre Royal at Brighton and the Bristol Hippodrome are still important as touring dates. But of the forty-five repertory companies outside London which the Arts Council was supporting in 1970–71 with a grant of five thousand pounds or more, twenty-six are in new

[1] Quoted in *The Mermaid 10*. Edited by Gerald Frow. Published by Mermaid Theatre.

buildings or old buildings improved by major conversions or are about to move into new theatres. Only nineteen are continuing in old buildings which are still much as they were.

Land values in central London are so disproportionately high that it would be virtually impossible ever to achieve the same ratio of new theatres to old theatres. It would make a huge difference if we could have four or five theatres built on roughly the same lines as the Mermaid, but with its 498 seats it occupies a site in the city one and a half times as large as that of Wyndham's, which contains over one and a half times as many seats. Without a gigantic subsidy any new West End theatre will inevitably be cramped for space. To buy a West End site and build a theatre of the same size as the Queen's (which has not quite a thousand seats) would cost about two million pounds. Up to three companies can be involved in the use of a West End theatre – one owns the freehold, one runs the building and another presents the plays. All three are aiming, naturally, to make a profit. To get a mere 10 per cent of his investment of two million pounds, the freeholder of our hypothetical new theatre would have to charge the leaseholder a rent of about £200,000 a year, as well as passing on responsibility for rates and maintenance of the building. The leaseholder, who also has his own administrative expenses, cannot think of charging the producing management less than £4,500 a week for the theatre, whereas, at present, the rent for an old theatre of this size would be only about £900 a week on account of 20 per cent of the gross box office takings.

Theatres incorporated in giant office blocks are likely to be inferior theatres because the architect has less freedom in his use of space, and though this is obviously a more economical way of building theatres, it still fails to make them economically viable. The leaseholder of the site on which the Criterion stands is the company which was formed by the merger between Trust Houses and Fortes. A theatre cannot be demolished without incorporating a substitute 'place of entertainment' into the new block, and in 1972 the company was promising to replace the 598-seat Criterion with an 800-seat theatre in the 246-foot tower it proposed to erect. Building costs, of course, would be enormous and would have to be recovered through rent charged on the offices, shops and theatre in the new block. But since a theatre can be used for only two or three hours at a stretch and only eight times a week, it cannot easily be run on the same level of profitability as the offices and shops. The *Evening Standard* of 10 May 1972 calculated that the management responsible for rent and replacements would be paying out £100,000 a year. In other words the theatre could be viable only if capacity were maintained at about 60 per cent, with tickets about three times as expensive as they are today. In fact, it would be hard to make this projected auditorium profitable even as a cinema.

The New London Theatre, which opened in January 1973 with 911 seats, is the only large unsubsidised theatre to have been built in London since the war – a very belated replacement for the Winter Garden, which was demolished in 1965. The theatre is part of a complex which contains shops, flats, a restaurant, showrooms and a heavy goods lift, with a car-park outside. The cost was at least £2,500,000. Nearly a third of the theatre's floor area is on a sixty foot revolve which can move not only the stage and the orchestra pit but also the front eight rows of the stalls. The stage can be brought into the centre and the shape of the auditorium can be changed – the walls are movable. The stage is suspiciously shallow, but it will be a great pity if yet another 'place of entertainment', built dutifully to compensate for the disappearance of a theatre, is transformed into a cinema.

It is clear that unless or until the state involves itself on a massive scale in London theatre building, we are not going to get a reasonable ratio of new theatres to old, so meanwhile we need to hold on very carefully to the theatres we have. The only protection the law gives at present is to buildings which are intrinsically of historic interest, and even from that point of view the present law is inadequate. By the end of the fifties we had less than half as many theatres in England as before the war – not because they had been destroyed by bombs but because so many had been converted into cinemas or bingo halls or demolished by developers. Brighton had eight theatres in 1938; now there is only one open all the year round. The Town

and Country Planning Act of 1947 (which was replaced by the Act
of 1971) had given local planning authorities power to issue building
preservation orders to prohibit any interference with buildings of
special interest, historical or architectural. The Minister of Housing
and Local Government compiled a schedule, but only fifteen theatres
were listed and only three (Drury Lane, Covent Garden and the
Haymarket) were given the grading that made their preservation a
matter of national concern. Theatres in the second grade could
unceremoniously be struck off the protected list, as the Criterion was
in 1970–71, and in any case the only protection afforded by this
grading was that no one could redevelop the site without giving the
local authority two months' notice. But the local authority would
often fail to intervene, and the Theatre Royal, Leicester, was lost in
this way. In London we have lost the St James's, the Stoll and the
Scala, and we are about to lose the Lyric, Hammersmith.

Under the 1971 Act, the responsibility for scheduling lies with the
Secretary of State for the Environment, who still has the same three
theatres graded as national monuments, and only twelve theatres
currently in use are listed under Grade II: the Aldwych, the Coliseum,
the Criterion, the Duke of York's, the Garrick, Her Majesty's,
the Albery, the Old Vic, the Palace, Sadler's Wells, the Strand and
Wyndham's. Recently the Historic Buildings Board of the GLC
made a survey of our unlisted theatres and music halls, concentrating
on the period 1890–1910, when most of them were built, and it has
now recommended five theatres in central London as having a
particularly urgent claim for inclusion in the statutory list – the
Apollo, the Comedy, the Globe, the Lyric and the Palladium. Four
others were also recommended less urgently – the Ambassadors, the
Queen's, the Royal Court and the St Martin's.

The theatre as a whole always suffers when official responsibility
is divided, as it is here, between the government and the local council.
In the West End two local authorities are involved – the Greater
London Council and Westminster City Council. But they did a deal,
giving Westminster total planning control over the Piccadilly area,
leaving the GLC in command of Covent Garden's redevelopment.
It is the duty of both councils to protect the interests of the public,

but every institution tends to put its own interests first, and it is in the interest of both councils to increase the rateable value of the properties in their area. The 1972 plans for the redevelopment of Piccadilly Circus and Covent Garden could have involved the demolition of the Criterion, the Duchess, the Adelphi, the Vaudeville, the Garrick and the Arts. In their dealings with property developers, the two local authorities have been bartering the right to build higher blocks in return for the right to widen roads. This has been done without public consultation. (The Piccadilly plans were exhibited in New Zealand House but without any attempt to find out what Londoners wanted). Fortunately there was a loud public outcry and the original plan was dropped. The Arts Council commissioned Sir James Richards to produce a report on the situation of the West End Theatre, but without expecting either council to wait for it. At a meeting with representatives of the Theatres Advisory Council in the autumn of 1972, the GLC maintained that the area had to be developed and that the only alternatives lay between piecemeal development and planned development. The only promises they were prepared to make were that not more than four theatres were endangered, that there would be a replacement for each one demolished and that there would be no reduction in the total number of theatre seats.

At the moment rents and rates being paid on theatres are low in relation to those of surrounding properties. As soon as the first theatre is sacrificed on the altar of redevelopment, a precedent will be created which will encourage freeholders to make proposals to the council for redeveloping other theatre sites more profitably. Even if replacements are provided, they cannot be designed as well as the best regional, theatres, when architects will be so restricted by the cost of space; and so long as the only legal requirement is for a new 'place of entertainment' to be incorporated in the redevelopment, the landlords can deliberately build something which will be so awkward and expensive to run as a theatre that it is bound to be converted into a cinema or a conference hall. Or they can entrust the running of it to a puppet manager who has privately been instructed to fail. A year of failures prepares the ground unimpeachably for a change of use. This has happened at least once and may well happen again unless the law is changed to give the theatre more protection.

Other theatres are in danger too. The lease of Wyndham's runs out in 1977 and that of the Albery (formerly the New) two years later. Both these theatres were built by Charles Wyndham at the turn of the century on ground leased from the Gascoyne Cecil estate, which belongs to Lord Salisbury's family. Donald Albery, the Managing Director of the company which runs both theatres and also the Criterion, spent £45,000 on improvements to the Criterion in 1971 – a gamble on the possibility that the plans to demolish the theatre would not go ahead. He would also like to invest money in making improvements to both Wyndham's and the Albery, where a bigger bar could be built underneath the stalls, but this would be worth while only if he could be sure of renewing the leases.

Clearly a theatre-operating management needs longer notice of a landlord's intentions than a company which can find alternative accommodation for its business, but both are treated in the same way by the law. According to the Landlord and Tenant Act, the tenant must give the landlord nine months' notice if he wishes to renew the lease and the landlord then has six months to make up his mind. In 1967 Donald Albery was told of a possible redevelopment: whether, in fact, either or both the Wyndham's and Albery's survive, will depend on whether an effective policy is evolved by the Government, the GLC and Westminster City Council, during the next few years to defend theatres against commercial exploitation of the space they occupy.

The constellation of theatres that we have in the West End is greater than that of any other European capital and it is worth protecting. A theatre packed into the bowels of an office block cannot advertise itself as a theatre should with lights and pictures and a large welcoming foyer. Passers-by should be aware that it is a theatre they are passing. Ideally, though, we should not only keep all the theatres we have in the West End: we should also acquire new ones in office blocks. The plan that Mayor Lindsay introduced to New York in 1967, when midtown land values were rising steeply, could be applied to London, where office space is equally valuable. In return for including a new theatre in their buildings, developers in the theatre zone were allowed an extra 20 per cent of rentable office space. By the beginning of 1972 New York had its first new theatre since 1928, the American Place, and three other theatres were under way. The new 347-seat theatre cost about 1,800,000 dollars to build and the rent charged was only five dollars a year, but the three extra floors of office space, when fully rented, would bring in between 600 and 750 thousand dollars a year.[1] The new theatre was cleverly designed, with a large movable thrust stage, a rehearsal space of the same size directly underneath it, good backstage amenities, and space above for a café, a cabaret–theatre, and a studio.

None of the theatres which have been built into London office blocks can even begin to compare with this. Clearly, it is not enough to stipulate that the developer provides a 'place of entertainment' with a certain seating capacity. The Arts Council or the Theatres Advisory Council should be given a say in the design, provision should be made in advance for a low rental, and the leaseholder should not be allowed to turn it into a cinema or a bingo hall.

A theatre owner or leaseholder can make as much as a million pounds out of his cut from one show, but only with a big theatre and a huge success. A profit of £80,000 before tax would not be extraordinary, but the annual net profit produced by a theatre worth £5,000,000 is often less than £25,000, which is only 5 per cent. In 1971 the Piccadilly Theatre paid a dividend of 37½ per cent, but this represents a return of only 2·8 per cent on the capital raised in 1928 – or 0·7 per cent if allowance is made for the reduced value of the pound. In nearly all the West End theatres, bars are extremely cramped. They were designed for unaccompanied gentlemen: when they were built ladies would not be seen drinking in public. More important, side seats give only a restricted view of the stage in many of the West End theatres, which were designed before structural steel was in use. And most of our Victorian theatres were designed for gas lighting: electricity was not introduced until late in the last century. In a new theatre the siting of the front-of-house spotlights is integral

[1] *Saturday Review*, 20 January 1972.

to the planning of the auditorium; in an old theatre they have to be fitted in wherever they will not obstruct the audience's view, and often this mars the appearance of the auditorium. But given enough money for restructuring, big improvements could be made.

Lighting conditions are usually unsatisfactory. Seventy thousand pounds was recently spent on the Haymarket, which is secure as a National Monument; and the Vaudeville has been lavishly modernised by Peter Saunders, who owns the freehold. But most theatre operators do not have the funds either to buy the best available lighting equipment – a switchboard can cost £40,000 – or the security of tenure that would encourage them to invest money in making the theatres as attractive to visitors as they could be. The seats are nearly always less comfortable than cinema seats, and theatregoers may have to climb up uncarpeted stone steps with bare lightbulbs and flaking paint.

A strong case could be made for help from the Government. The buildings are intrinsically as well worth preserving as those in which subsidised companies are spending a substantial part of their grants on maintenance. In 1971–72 the Royal Opera Company at Covent Garden received a grant of £1,420,000. The Theatre Royal, Drury Lane, the Haymarket, Her Majesty's and the Palace cannot be very much cheaper to maintain, but the companies which ran them had no subsidy at all. The Government should also consider the value of the London theatres to the tourist trade. Figures released by the Tourist Board show that in 1971 tourists brought £469,000,000 of foreign currency into the country; 58 per cent of a sample that was questioned listed live entertainment among their main incentives for coming to England. A great deal of government money has been paid out on helping hoteliers to provide extra accommodation for them, but neither the Labour nor the Conservative governments have done anything to help theatre owners in London, though both governments have funded the Arts Council's generous contributions towards the cost of the new buildings in the regions.

Sustained over twenty-seven years, the Arts Council's habit of limiting its help to non-profit-distributing companies has created a strange imbalance between London and the regions. The feeling behind it is that public money must be kept away from managements that are interested in profit. Consequently, the West End Theatre is treated as if it were valueless as a social or cultural amenity, though, in reality, the value of a site within the Shaftesbury Avenue area reduces the chances of making a theatre commercially viable over a long term, because this is where other commercial pressures on space are at their highest. Official policy will, no doubt, be reversed eventually, but help will probably come only when the theatre-owning and producing managements have been weakened irreversibly and the standards lowered so much that many Londoners lose the theatre-going habit altogether.

Outside London the theatre has never been better off so far as buildings are concerned – qualitatively if not quantitatively. We still have no purpose-built theatre-in-the-round, and Peter Cheeseman's company at Stoke-on-Trent is still working in a converted cinema, but there is an impressive preponderance of good new buildings. We are lucky to have them, but the disequilibrium they create is bad for our theatre as a whole. In spite of everything that is so often said in favour of decentralisation, a comparison with Germany would suggest that no network of provincial centres, however good, can make up for the absence of a single centre in the capital. For a country's theatre to be healthy, the capital has to exercise a powerful magnetic pull on all the available talent. The best directors, designers and actors need to be working in the same place, exchanging influences, and not scattered all over England. London needs at least a dozen big new theatres to keep pace with the regions. Good work will no doubt be done at the new National, the new Barbican, and, sometimes, at the Mermaid. Good work will still be done in the old theatres, which are ideal for many of the plays that will remain in the repertoire. But the only other new theatres we can hope for under the present subsidy system are small theatres like Hampstead Theatre Club, the Shaw and the Almost Free Theatre, which will not fill the need for contemporary buildings in which a contemporary play can have an open-ended run limited only by the size of the audience that wants to see it. However successful productions are in these small spaces, they often fail to survive when transferred to a West End theatre, in which the production has to be adapted to fit a different space, a different atmosphere, and different audience expectations.

It is partly because we are so short of new buildings that the movement to take theatre outside theatres has become so strong. It is not new, of course. Early in the century Max Reinhardt made several spectacular experiments, including a production of *Oedipus Rex* in a Viennese circus and a religious mime at the Olympia in London. The Bauhaus lent powerful support to the idea that theatre ought to move away from theatres. Jacques Copeau was a great advocate of performing on a bare platform. But the main impetus to the current movement came from Grotowski, whose starting point was an urge to rediscover what theatre can do that films and television cannot. What can be eliminated without interfering with the essence of what the act of theatre is? Make-up, changes of lighting, sound effects, changes of costume can all be scrapped, as can the theatre itself. All that is indispensable is the living relationship between actor and audience. But this relationship cannot be created in a void. Some kind of environment is necessary, and Grotowski soon arrived at the idea of devising a different environment for each production, giving the audiences different spatial relationships with the action.

Something of this thinking has penetrated a good many Off-Off-Broadway productions and has infiltrated the London 'Fringe'. Ten years ago, after the disappearance of all the 'little' theatres like the Watergate, the New Lindsay and the Embassy, there was almost nowhere for small-scale productions of non-commercial plays. If there are many more Fringe productions now, it is not so much because there are more theatres as because the movement to carry theatre outside theatres has gone so much further. With lunchtime productions in pubs and basements, groups which perform in the streets and others which tour the country fitting their productions into any available space, it is easier than ever before for a theatre company to survive without having a theatre. This is one healthy consequence of the inadequacy of our theatres.

Not all these groups are hostile to the idea of normal theatre buildings, but it is symptomatic of the situation that the architect Sean Kenny should have made statements like 'The ideal theatre is no kind of theatre. That is, no theatre in the sense of architectural or physical definitions ... I think that to design a theatre today is simply to allow a space big enough for something to take place in . . . I think the ideal theatre would be as big as you can get – cover the whole site with an aircraft hangar, as tall as you can afford, as wide as you can afford, as strong as you can afford. And inside that you allow theatre to happen.' Like Grotowski, he now believes that 'the building has got to be free and flexible enough so that . . . the designer will become more and more involved in the arrangement of the house; the relationship of actor to spectator.'[1]

'Happenings' are already becoming less important as a phenomenon than they were in the mid-sixties, but the importance they had must be seen in the perspective of the reaction against the assumption that theatre is an activity that can only be carried on inside theatres. Peter Brook has written, 'A happening is a powerful invention. It destroys at one blow many deadly forms, like the dreariness of theatre buildings and the charmless trappings of curtain, usherette, cloakroom, programme, bar.' At the same time, Happenings have been knocking against the convention that a theatrical entertainment must take a particular form, involving actors, and that it must last between two and three hours. Happenings also represent an exploration by painters and sculptors of the combination of movement and three-dimensionality, formerly monopolised by the theatre. But while it is a thoroughly good thing that the barriers between theatre and the plastic arts should be broken down, it is not at all a good thing that there should be such a barrier as there is between the two 'theatres' we have now, the one inside the conventional buildings and the one outside. There are some playwrights, like Tom Stoppard, who write for both, and there are some directors and actors who work in both, consciously profiting by applying to one what they have learnt from the other. But the majority of those who work in either have very little interest even in going to see what is happening in the other. And this is wasteful. Few of the people who work in one of the two unequal halves of our theatre are willing to admit that their half does not have a monopoly of the vital juices. If we cannot yet have integration, we should at least have a degree of interpenetration.

[1] *The Mermaid 10.*

5 THE NATIONAL THEATRE AND THE ROYAL SHAKESPEARE COMPANY

No men can act with effect who do not act in concert; no men can act in concert who do not act with confidence; no men act in confidence who are not bound together with common opinions, common affections and common interests. EDMUND BURKE

It is now quite hard to remember the early fifties, when a poverty-stricken Old Vic and Joan Littlewood's even poorer Theatre Workshop were the only London theatres where an actor could get a job without the prospect of being out of work again immediately the production folded. Actors in the fifties had to start rehearsing – for £7 a week if their performance fees were less than £50 a week, for nothing if they were more – with no guarantee that the production would ever open in the West End. If it collapsed during the provincial tour they would receive four weeks' salary; if it flopped in the West End without a preliminary tour they would receive only two weeks' salary.

There were relatively few classical parts to be played in the provinces, while in London the Old Vic and Theatre Workshop provided the only opportunities to go on working with the same company for longer than the run of a single play. In the West End there were few seasons of plays in repertoire, and commercial revivals of the classics depended very much on stars who would usually commit themselves only for a limited season. Although the dichotomy we have today between subsidised and unsubsidised theatre is damaging and wasteful, the infusion of government money through the Arts Council has been extremely valuable.

It is easy to get the impression that the structural changes which have made our theatre so different from what it was at the end of the fifties were initiated by the government's decision to subsidise the arts on a bigger scale. In the financial year 1958–59 four London theatres were receiving Arts Council grants. The Old Vic's was £20,000, the Mermaid (which opened in May 1959) had £5,000, the Royal Court £5,500 and Joan Littlewood's Theatre Workshop £1,000. So the total subsidy to the London theatre was £31,500. Ten years later the National Theatre had £342,000 from the Arts Council, plus £90,000 from the Greater London Council, while the Arts Council contributed £221,308 to the Royal Shakespeare Company, £98,300 to the Royal Court, £28,000 to the Mermaid and £11,015 to the 157-seat Hampstead Theatre Club. These last two theatres both received substantial grants from local authorities, and the Arts Council also subsidised seven other theatre companies in London, paying out a total of £737,439 (including the grant to the Royal Shakespeare Company, which divided the money between its theatres in London and Stratford-on-Avon).

Without official help the RSC could never have maintained its London base at the Aldwych, and the National Theatre could never have opened. But the decision which started the chain reaction was a private one, taken by the governors of the Shakespeare Memorial Theatre at Stratford-on-Avon. In the middle of the fifties they were already considering the possibility of opening a London base, and in 1960, when they appointed Peter Hall as Artistic Director, he went into immediate action to translate the idea into reality – partly so as to be able to offer his actors continuity of employment throughout the year instead of engaging a new company for each summer season. He opened the first Aldwych season in the winter of the same year, 1960. The governors financed the venture out of the reserves that had been accumulated from endowments, bequests and gifts, including gifts of land. In 1962 the Royal Shakespeare Company – which is the name it had acquired in 1961 – was given £5,000 by the Gulbenkian Foundation, but this did little to offset the year's deficit of £40,000. The Arts Council was approached for help, but the possibility was being officially discussed of amalgamating the Old Vic and the RSC companies at Stratford and the Aldwych into a new, subsidised, National Theatre. Peter Hall was at first in favour of this plan, and it was not abandoned until December 1961. By then the Arts Council had already prepared its estimates for 1962–63, and nothing was voted to the RSC except £10,000 for touring. But the initiative of the Shakespeare Memorial Theatre's governors and Peter Hall's efficiency in launching an all-the-year-round season catalysed the slow processes that were working towards the formation of a National Theatre, and in 1963 it opened at the Old Vic under the leadership of Sir Laurence Olivier.

As so often when a worthwhile theatrical enterprise has insufficient funds, the actors in Peter Hall's company effectively became patrons, by virtue of working for very little money. Anyone who has to cast plays becomes all too familiar with the way actors' agents talk about clients who 'cannot afford to work in the theatre at the moment'. A single play is a self-indulgence that can be permitted between a fat film part and a long stint of television; a whole season at the National or the RSC is financially a very big sacrifice for an actor of high earning power. Peter Hall was asking actors to commit themselves for periods of up to three years, during which they would mostly be too busy in the theatre to appear in front of the cameras, and the highest salary he could offer was £60 a week; the majority of his actors committed themselves for very much less. In 1970 the top salary at the RSC was still only £80 a week, while the minimum was £18.

To move into the Aldwych the RSC had to engage new actors, but to administer two theatres instead of one it was only a matter of extending an existing organisation. The National Theatre was a new organisation. The two summer seasons Olivier had directed at Chichester in 1962 and 1963 turned out to have worked as a trial run for it. In forming the new company he used many of the same actors, the same directors, the same stage management and the same administrators. He even brought two of the Chichester productions, the 1962 *Uncle Vanya* and the 1963 *St Joan*, into the National's repertoire.

The success that Olivier made of the National in its first few years depended very much on surrounding himself first with the right advisers and directors, then with the right actors. He was 56 in 1963 and felt he needed adjutants who were younger and more intellectual, The three he chose were John Dexter, William Gaskill, who were made Associate Directors, and Kenneth Tynan, who was appointd 'Literary Manager'. It might have been expected that they would try to pull him in three different directions. Tynan was a drama critic with almost contradictory interests in heroic acting and in Brecht. Gaskill had in common with him an Oxford education and a devotion to Brecht; Dexter, like Gaskill, had worked a great deal for George Devine at the Royal Court, where Dexter had been very conscious of being the only non-graduate in Devine's entourage of young directors.

The differences of attitude between the four of them were reflected in the mixture of actors in the company. There was a strong contingent from the Royal Court. Frank Finlay had done no Shakespeare since drama school, and the choice of him and Colin Blakely for a company that would be concerned largely with classical work is representative of an important departure from the conventional view of what a classical actor should be. And neither Joan Plowright nor Robert Stephens would have seemed such obvious choices but for the leading parts they had played at the Court. There were also West End stars like Michael Redgrave, Diana Wynyard and Joyce Redman, who had classical experience in the traditional style, gained at the Old Vic or Stratford or both, while actors like Max Adrian and Maggie Smith had made their reputations in revue and comedy. But the company worked well together, and though it did not become an ensemble in the sense that Brecht's Berliner Ensemble was, the Brechtian ideal, which also exercised a powerful pull on the RSC, was one of the forces that helped to unify the National. Not that either company aspired towards political activism, and both worked from a premise of very much more respect for the text and the writer's original intentions than Brecht did. Neither Peter Hall nor Laurence Olivier was interested in didactic theatre, and Hall emphasised that there was nothing of the propagandist in Shakespeare. But both directors were aiming to create companies of a sort that was totally new in the West End theatre – anti-authoritarian, anti-heroic, anti-illusionist, and in so far as they had a model it was the Berliner Ensemble.

There are actors who thrive on independence and uncertainty about where the next job is going to come from, but there are others who do much better work when they have a feeling of solidarity with a group that is not going to disintegrate as soon as a notice goes up on a board announcing that the management is about to take the play off. Peter Hall and Laurence Olivier could now offer actors conditions of working which compensated for low salaries by introducing something that was almost unprecedented in the London theatre – the possibility of evolving a company style which would have nothing to do with stylishness and very little to do with the semblance of consistency an efficient director can impose on a disparate group of actors, each of which approaches his own character in his own way.

The process of forming a company is different when it is for more than a single play. There is no question of type-casting for one part, and it is not merely a matter of trying to pick the eighty most talented actors in the country who are available and willing to work for the salaries you can pay them. You gravitate towards choosing the people who will fit easily into the kind of group you want, or the kind of group you had the previous year. The disadvantage is that you tend to exclude the talented individualists who might turn out to be trouble-makers. The advantage is that you develop a group in which actors can communicate with each other about the way they are working. The process of rehearsal becomes one in which they will collaborate not just in going through the scenes together but in pooling ideas. It is easy for one actor to notice how another, playing a scene with him, may be muffing a climax or getting a smaller laugh one night than another by some very slight variation of timing, a line spoken a fraction too slowly or too loudly, or a movement of the hands made an instant too late. Even if the director is present in the theatre (which he usually isn't) he is more likely to miss minutiae like this than another actor involved in playing the scene. But the reserve prevalent among English actors is so great that unless they know each other very well, one will be too nervous of upsetting another to run the risk of helping him by pointing out a mistake.

Partly because of the greater security of the long-term contract, partly because of solidarity with the group, actors in a permanent company also tend to compete with each other less. An actor who is uncertain of his future is under pressure to go all out to make a good impression on management, critics and audiences. There will be moments when, consciously or unconsciously, he has to make a choice between winning the audience's attention and sympathy away from his partner in the scene or supporting him by adapting to his strengths and weaknesses – doing what is best for the scene and the play as a whole. Audiences are mostly unaware of how selfish or unselfish actors are being, but it can make an enormous difference to a production's impact.

How actors behave depends partly on how strong the feeling of ensemble is. This varies with the morale and mood of the company and with inter-relationships between the actors. The feeling of community that the RSC enjoys at Stratford is inevitably diluted when the actors who have been working there together for one season come to the Aldwych for the next. They are no longer together in the same sense. In London they see less of each other when they are not actually working. But even at the National, where company members have never had the advantage of alternate years in the country and no longer have the advantage of summer seasons at Chichester, there can be a solid identity of interest. At times when morale is high, it feels almost like having a common cause to fight for.

The directors' relations with the actors are also different: they are not merely interested in co-ordinating them in a single production but in developing them over a long term. This also affects casting. To develop your actors you have to keep giving them parts which are slightly beyond what they have played before, though it is dangerous to overdo this merely in order to encourage them or to reward them for long service. An actor's view of his own potential is liable to be more optimistic than that of the directors, and in a big company it is inevitable that most actors are playing smaller parts than they think they deserve. But resentment can be alleviated by a paternalistic concern on the part of directors who do genuinely care about the future of their actors. The Artistic Director can spend only a limited amount of time discussing actors' individual problems, but other directors can partly compensate for this.

When Peter Hall took over at Stratford-on-Avon he found that current practice had not altogether rescued Shakespeare's plays from the damage the Victorians had done in imposing a phoney tradition of gentility on the heroes, and in overstressing the music of the poetry. He was acutely aware of stage habits which tended to make the plays less Elizabethan. As he said, 'Audiences expect Shakespeare to be noble, classical, sentimental, decent, British, patriotic . . . The *Henry VI* plays as we did them in *The Wars of the Roses* emerged I think not as a great kind of celebration of England moving towards the nineteenth century empire, but as a really horrific analysis of power politics and violence'.[1] Similarly, the 1963 production of *Julius Caesar* outraged some of the audience. 'How dare you reduce great noble Romans to the size of Nazis?' But there were others for whom it was a revelation to see a clear focus on the statement about power politics that the play contains.

The reaction against the 'Gielgud' approach to verse speaking at first swung the pendulum too far in the opposite direction. Actors were encouraged to wrestle with the sense of a speech in ways that sometimes did damage to the rhythm, which, properly handled, supports the sense. But if there was a temporary loss here, there was an immediate gain with plays like *Troilus and Cressida*, which had seemed unattractive to audiences and now regained their relevance.

The debt to Brecht was particularly apparent in *The Wars of the Roses*, but it was a healthy debt: the lesson was well digested and every aspect of the production, from casting to costuming, was affected equally. In the nineteen fifties much of the Berliner Ensemble's casting looked rabidly anti-romantic and anti-aristocratic to

[1] *Plays and Players*, May 1964.

English eyes. If there were any physical equivalents amongst English actors to Heinz Schubert and Angelika Hurwicz (the 'Swiss Cheese' and the Dumb Kattrin in Brecht's production of *Mother Courage*) they would have found it very hard to get work at all, and certainly they would never have been cast in romantic or royal parts. But at Stratford in the sixties Peter Hall soon changed the mould of casting for Shakespearean heroic parts, while at the National, the influence of William Gaskill and John Dexter and the enlistment of Royal Court actors into the permanent company had a very similar effect.

The attitude of David Warner, Peter Hall's 1965 Hamlet, was typical of the new approach. 'So far as I'm concerned, there's no such thing as a king. King is just a title given by other people. How the hell do I know what being princely is? You can be a prince and you can pick your nose, because the prince has the freedom to do whatever he wants. My first objective is to make people who are bored with Shakespeare try and understand. If I cut under the verse, give the wrong inflections or pause in the wrong place or mess up the iambic pentameters, I don't care.'[1] Quite a lot clearly could be lost, but among the gains was the possibility of creating a more united and democratic feeling among the company than would have been possible when there was a more hierarchic division between the star actors, who gave heroic performances in the leading parts and the 'supporting' actors who were made to feel that their main job was to give support.

At the same time, new waves of visual *verismo* were spreading from Stratford East and the Royal Court to Stratford-on-Avon and the National, to engulf sets, costumes and accessories as well as the physical aspect of the actors. Traditional stage glamour was washed away. Costumes no longer looked as though an efficient wardrobe mistress had been protecting them from any sign of having been worn before, while trucks, council tables, ammunition boxes were presented in a way that reminded the audience realistically of what they were used for. With *The Wars of the Roses* at Stratford and with Gaskill's production of *The Recruiting Officer* at the National, we saw

[1] *The Times*, 4 March 1972.

what was not so much a new style as a revelation of how stylishness could be stripped away to reveal the social reality of what a play was about.

The actors themselves were fired by the new adjustment of focus, which brought the life of the common soldier and the ordinary people into the foreground. For the first three years in the existence of the new-born RSC, very few actors quitted, and this must have been at least partly because crowds were being given a realistic life of their own instead of merely being used to create a picturesque grouping around the better-lit leading characters. Life for the supporting actor had become very much more purposeful and interesting. But it was soon to become clear that neither Peter Hall's company nor the National stood any chance of growing into an ensemble in the Brechtian sense. In 1937 it had been possible for John Gielgud to plan a nine-month season in the West End with a permanent company that included Peggy Ashcroft, Alec Guinness, Michael Redgrave, Glen Byan Shaw, Dennis Price, Leon Quartermaine, Harcourt Williams, George Howe, George Devine and Frederick Lloyd. Of these he lost only Michael Redgrave, after three of the season's four productions, when a film contract was offered to him. Even in 1944 it was possible for Olivier and Ralph Richardson to collect round them at the Old Vic a company which included Sybil Thorndike, Margaret Leighton, George Relph, Joyce Redman, Nicholas Hannen, Harcourt Williams and Michael Warre. But today this kind of company strength is unattainable because our best actors are in much greater demand, receiving offers of theatre, film and television work in English-speaking countries all over the world.

As Kenneth Tynan has said, it is much easier to keep a permanent company together in Germany because the alternative offers that actors receive from film and television companies are so much less attractive, while there is much less demand for German-speaking actors on the international market. In France the situation is similar, and it seems strange to actors in the Comédie Française that our National Theatre actors would think nothing of uprooting themselves after a stay of only three years. Of the thirty-four actors who were originally contracted by Peter Hall for the RSC in 1960, Peggy

Ashcroft and Tony Church were the only two who were still in the company at the end of 1971. Peggy Ashcroft is a director of it and Tony Church had had several years' leave of absence to become Artistic Director of the new Northcott Theatre in Exeter. In fact Ian Richardson, who put in ten years' work from 1960 to 1970, was acting more continuously with the company than either of them. Of the sixty-three actors in Olivier's original company at the National, apart from himself and Joan Plowright, only three actors were still there eight years later – Kenneth Mackintosh, Louise Purnell and Maggie Riley.

Because both companies suffer from inadequate subsidies, they have difficulty in finding good supporting actors for the salaries available. 'You can always get Richard III for £60 a week,' Peter Hall said, 'but try and get Hastings for £30.' Even at the National it is hard to enlist enough good character actors, although salaries are higher than at the RSC (in spite of the fact that RSC actors have the added expense of accommodation in Stratford-on-Avon every alternate year). An actor joining the RSC has to sign on for two years. Even at the National it creates administrative problems to take an actor into the company for less than one. But a successful character actor will not commit himself for so long unless some of the parts he is offered are more rewarding than Hastings. In any case, if new actors are brought into the company to play these middle-range parts, it causes frustration among the lower echelons who have been working for years towards just such rewards as these. Often the experience they gain really does equip them to play better parts, but there is no certainty that the company will be able to keep the best of the rising stars it produces from its own ranks. When the National Theatre started in 1963, Robert Stephens, Frank Finlay and Colin Blakely were relatively unknown; now all three of them are in such demand that if they make return visits to their parent company they can dictate their own terms.

One of the main disadvantages of permanent companies is that it rapidly becomes too easy for each actor to know exactly what to expect from everyone else, both in rehearsal and in performance, so the stimulus to be had from them becomes blunted. It is hard enough in any event to avoid anticipating. A really good actor is constantly able to listen and react as if everything in the play were happening for the first time. But the more familiar he is with the inflexions, gestures, mannerisms and timing of everyone else in the company, the harder it is to stop staleness from corroding concentration and spontaneity. There are even disadvantages in the unselfishness that company life breeds. A gladiatorial competitiveness can add edge and tension: a genuine conflict between two actors can serve the conflict between their characters.

Probably the advantages of the permanent company outweigh the disadvantages. Without one it is impossible to build up a repertoire of plays which can be performed on different nights of the same week. Nearly all actors find it easier to give of their best when they are avoiding the deadly monotony of having to repeat the same lines, the same series of moves, gestures, glances, every night of the week and twice on matinée days. The conscious fear of growing stale pushes an actor into gravitating slowly away from what he started with. To varying degrees each actor in the company is subject to the same pressure, and gradually, as pauses are shortened or lengthened and motivational drives are deflected, however slightly, the shape of each sequence can be altered. With fewer performances of each play in any one week, the urge to change is not so strong: the production can be kept alive without it, and the fact that the lines themselves do not come so pat on the tongue – it can be quite a strain to remember them – makes for a tension which is on the whole more useful than dangerous.

On the other hand, the energy of each actor is divided between several parts, whereas an actor rehearsing for a continuous run of a single play is putting all his creativity into the one part, which is all he will have to work on until the play comes off. If he is playing four or five parts in the same repertoire, he may conceive his character-isations partly in terms of the differences between them, wanting to be as different as possible both in appearance and manner. There are some advantages in this: one part can give a stimulus which helps an actor to go on exploring another instead of letting it go stale. But there are also serious dangers in the diffusion of mental and physical energy. The actor who is rehearsing one part while playing four or five others knows he will need stamina for what may be a strenuous part in the evening performance, which may be of a play he has not done for two or three weeks. If so, anxiety about lines cannot but distract him from the new play he is rehearsing. The RSC has less actors than ever before, and in the spring, at the beginning of the Stratford season, the strain is enormous. Many of them are working a seventy-two hour week, not counting time for learning lines, and, besides giving performances, are rehearsing two plays at the same time.

Whereas few plays stay in the RSC repertoire for more than two seasons – one at Stratford and one at the Aldwych – the National is aiming to build up a cumulative repertoire in which half the productions are kept on for a second year and one-third for a third year. This produces problems, both artistic and administrative, when actors leave the company and their parts have to be taken over. *A Flea in Her Ear* played less than 200 performances, but by the end of the run only two of the cast, Geraldine McEwan and Edward Hardwicke, were still in their original parts. So time and energy which ideally would be spent on preparing new productions is in fact spent on re-rehearsing old ones for the benefit of actors taking over from those who are leaving. Not only is this tedious and demoralising, it is frightening for the actors who keep having to modify their original performance with each influx of cast changes. As Robert Lang put it, 'You've destroyed the basic roots that you built in during rehearsal. You've had to adjust to so many new people coming in, that you've almost wrecked what you depended on for supplying the energy, the basic reminder about things. And then in the take-over problem, you feel like saying "This fellow did this and you've got to do exactly the same or we shall all be thrown." Which just doesn't work out. You're ruining him. But if you let him go too free – and it happens too often – you've removed yourself away from what you started with.'

The anxieties of recasting are formidable. An actor engaged on a three-year contract may have had parts in five plays which are going to stay in the repertoire after his contract ends. He may quite legitimately feel, after giving three years of his life and his career to the company, that it is not worth his while to stay on for a fourth unless he is offered at least one much bigger part than he has so far had. The directors then have to discuss the question at one of their regular meetings and decide what to do. To replace this actor in five productions costs a great deal of re-rehearsal time. The alternative of offering him a new part which may be beyond him might seem the lesser evil.

This is only one example of the compromises a theatre like the National is constantly having to make in order to get or to keep the actors it wants. One of its functions must be to act as a showcase for the best actors in England, and Tyrone Guthrie once attacked Kenneth Tynan for failing to realise this.[1] 'You've got a lovely company, dear, for a civic theatre in Germany somewhere; but if you call yourself a National Theatre, you must engage, for no matter how short periods, the greatest national star actors. Where's your Wolfit, your Richardson and your Gielgud?' It is a pity that Richardson and Guinness have never played with the company and that Redgrave (who played in four of the productions), Finney (five), Gielgud (two) and Scofield (two) were not persuaded to stay on longer.[2] Quite apart from any duty a National Theatre has to display its country's best talents, actors of this calibre can contribute substantially to both morale and continuity. If there is a tradition of great acting, the National is where it should be nurtured and cultivated, where the stardust should be encouraged to rub off on the shoulders of the younger actors.

In any case, even the basic decisions about which plays to bring into the repertoire can be made only in relation to the actors who are available and willing to play the leading parts. The National depends more than the RSC on actors of established reputations, and these, because they are in such demand, may accept two parts they are being offered only on condition that a particular play is brought into the repertoire to give them a third part that they want. It has happened that the directors have accepted a condition like this.

[1] *Tulane Drama Review* No. 34, Winter 1966.
[2] Gielgud will return in 1974 to play Prospero.

In his book *The Exemplary Theatre* (1922) Harley Granville-Barker suggested that a National Theatre should keep between forty and fifty plays in permanent repertoire. Quite apart from recasting difficulties, the space it takes to store scenery, costumes and properties makes this impossible in a theatre like the Old Vic, while outside storage space is so expensive. Even in the new building, custom-tailored for the company, with two theatres, it is unlikely that there will ever be more than about twenty plays in the repertoire at any one time. But since 1963 the National's repertoire has been built in accordance with Barker's formulation of six categories of play: Shakespeare, the other English classics, foreign classics, contemporary English plays, contemporary foreign plays and 'recent plays of merit'. *Hobson's Choice* and *Hay Fever* come into this last category: plays which, as Tynan says, 'express their period sometimes more completely than the masterpieces which transcend their period'. Each season, he says, has had at least one play in each of these six categories.

In *The Exemplary Theatre* Granville-Barker's programme for the theatre's salvation was based on 'a plea for truth-telling ... and for the cultivation of the faculty by which the common man may hope, as a rule, to know whether he is being told the truth about things or not'. The value of theatre could be judged according to whether it can 'help to produce more fully and more freely developed human beings, and more co-operative human beings'. For Granville-Barker, in other words, the function of serious theatre was mainly educational, and this spirit survived into the founding of our present National Theatre. According to its Articles of Association, its purpose is 'to promote and assist the advancement of education' and to procure and increase 'the appreciation and understanding of the dramatic art in all its forms as a memorial to William Shakespeare'. After one financial year, 1965–66, in which the Arts Council subsidised the theatre by paying ten shillings for every pound of reckonable receipts, and the GLC made a further payment equivalent to five-seventeenths of this one, this system was dropped out of fear that it would encourage a policy of building the repertoire for the sake of its box office appeal. But the theatre still cannot afford to put on plays which are not expected to do well at the box-office.

The function of the two theatres is different, and when he was Artistic Director of RSC Peter Hall insisted that it was not in competition with the National:

> On the contrary, we each help to define the other. Their intention is to deal with the world repertoire; ours to do modern or classical plays that reflect on Shakespeare today. Their aim is to be comprehensive and catholic; and the fact that they are there removes as far as we're concerned any responsibility which we might feel that perhaps we ought to 'do' an Ibsen or a Chekhov. We can be much more specialised – which they're not being. It's our task to do *The Investigation*, and *The Deputy*, and the *Marat/Sade*, much more than it is theirs. We can be perhaps more on the frontier, and they can have a broad view.[1]

This prompted a counter-statement from Tynan:

> I don't think that Peter Hall only thinks of the timely – otherwise he wouldn't do things like Marlowe's *The Jew of Malta*. And nor do we only think of the lending library and museum aspect. We've done Frisch, and Beckett, and Brecht; and new plays too. But certainly I would not think of looking at the social and political climate and saying 'What play is going to fit in?' One would also think of things like 'What play fits the company? What play will explore some aspect of theatre that we haven't yet explored?' Every new production should break new ground but not necessarily topical ground.[2]

Apart from Frisch and Beckett, the contemporary playwrights to be represented at the National have been Peter Shaffer, Noël Coward, Arthur Miller, John Arden, John Osborne (as an adapter of Lope de Vega), Tom Stoppard, John Lennon, John Spurling, Maureen Duffy,

[1] Quoted in *Tulane Drama Review* T34, Winter 1966.
[2] Quoted in *Tulane Drama Review* T34, Winter 1966.

Natalia Ginzberg, Charles Wood, Fernando Arrabal, Carl Zuckmayer (in an adaptation by John Mortimer), Peter Nichols, James Saunders (a children's play) and Adrian Mitchell.[1] For Mitchell, who made William Blake into the helpless co-author of a kind of sub-musical, it was a piece of enormous luck to be commissioned by the National: *Tyger* would have been inordinately expensive to produce commercially for the West End.

For a writer like Peter Nichols the patronage of the National is a mixed blessing. First, because it has to plan its programmes so far ahead, there may be delays of anything up to eighteen months between the completion of a script and its first performance. Then, while the repertoire system protects a near-failure from being an obvious flop which has to be taken off quickly, it also prevents a play with box office appeal from cashing in on it fully. With *The National Health* Peter Nichols was lucky that there were actors in the company who fitted so well into nearly all the main parts, but unlucky to get only two or three performances each week, producing very much less in royalties than he could have made out of an uninterrupted run in the West End. He was particularly unfortunate in that the play had to be taken out of the repertoire because some of the actors in it were involved in the National Theatre's American tour, and by the time it was put back into the programme again there was no longer the same demand for tickets because people were no longer talking about it so much. Altogether it received 126 performances. Only playwrights who make most of their living out of the cinema can afford to give all their plays to the National or the RSC. Harold Pinter says that his plays are staged better by the RSC than they would be in the commercial theatre.

Peter Shaffer's *Royal Hunt of the Sun* received 215 performances at the National, and Stoppard's *Rosencrantz and Guildenstern Are Dead* 181, but Charles Wood's '*H*' had only 24, and the double bill consisting of *Macrune's Guevara* by John Spurling and *Rites* by Maureen Duffy had only 12. The National's most successful production to date, *A Flea in her Ear*, had 227, but *The Royal Hunt of the Sun* is the only other one to pass the 200 mark. In the five seasons from 1967–68

[1] Trevor Griffiths's play *The Party* will join the repertoire in December 1973.

to 1971–72, *The Beaux' Stratagem* (108) and *The Merchant of Venice* (138) were the only plays – besides *The National Health* – to have over 100 performances. Arrabal's *The Architect and the Emperor of Assyria* had only 22 and *Coriolanus* only 23. Stoppard's *Jumpers* had had 88 by the end of August 1972 and was scheduled for revival in 1973. O'Neill's *A Long Day's Journey into Night* had 84 by September 1972.

It is more prestigious for a contemporary writer to have his play produced at the National or the RSC than in the West End but it is almost inevitably less lucrative. Besides receiving fewer performances each week, plays are liable to be taken out of a repertoire when the demand for tickets is still quite high if the season is coming to an end or if irreplaceable actors are leaving the company. At the Aldwych in 1966 Charles Dyer's *Staircase* with Paul Scofield and Patrick Magee, and in 1970 Edward Albee's *Tiny Alice* with David Warner and Irene Worth were both taken off when they were still playing to capacity business.

While it is hard to avoid these rather invidious words 'commercial' and 'subsidised', it is a mistake to regard them as antithetical. There is a strong commercial element in all theatre which depends on the sale of tickets to a wide public, but we hear a lot of unreasoning polemic based on the assumption that there is no commercial pressure on the subsidised theatre and that commercial managements are all motivated solely by a greed for profit. To be really free from commercial pressure a theatre would have to be subsidised very highly indeed, but our government has only recently passed the two million pound a year mark in subsidising drama, compared with East Germany's twenty million and West Germany's thirty million. So even our National Theatre is under constant pressure to find ways of cutting down on costs. Originally there were sixty-three actors employed just at the Old Vic. In 1971 eighty-four actors were divided between three theatres (the Old Vic, the Young Vic[1] and the New).

The National Theatre has also to find ways of supplementing its income. In the years 1968–69 it played at the Old Vic for forty-six

[1] Though the Young Vic was far from being entirely dependent on actors from the company.

weeks during which, on average, 92 per cent of the 878 seats were full. Box office takings amounted to £234,242. And in November 1971 it was announced that the size of the company would have to be reduced – ten actors who were leaving would not be replaced.

In 1970–71 it played for 47 weeks at the Old Vic, taking £211,068 at the box office, which is 73 per cent of the capacity sale. In fact 230,410 tickets were sold, which is 83 per cent of the total number – the difference between the two percentages being explained by the popularity of the cheaper tickets. There was also a thirty-week season at the Cambridge Theatre, where £245,997 was taken at the box office, of which £196,800 came to the National, the balance going to the theatre owner. And 209,505 tickets were sold – 76 per cent of the capacity sale – while box office takings were 70 per cent of the capacity figure.

Especially when there is no income from American touring, the National needs to make as much as possible from recordings, television, films and the sale of subsidiary rights on plays. Even in 1969–70 when £87,522 was made in these ways, and when subsidies from the Arts Council and the Greater London Council amounted to £360,489, there was an overall deficit on the year of £758. In 1970–71, when only £3,528 came in from recordings, films, television and subsidiary rights, there was a deficit of £58,735, though the Arts Council subsidy was higher than ever at £375,384, and £130,000 was received from the GLC – an increase of £40,000 on the year before.

Inevitably the costs of running a company like the National are enormous. With a permanent ensemble of actors on the pay-roll, small-cast plays are not necessarily the cheapest, but productions vary hugely in what has to be budgeted for them. Leaving out the salaries of the actors, *Coriolanus* cost £16,700, of which £8,000 went on the set and £3,000 on the costumes. The remaining £5,700 was spent on the directors', designer's, composer's and choreographer's fees, the cost of re-editing a tape borrowed from the Berliner Ensemble and the hotel expenses of the two German directors. *Long Day's Journey into Night* cost only £6,200, but this did not include a fee for the director, who is on the permanent staff, and there was no composer or choreographer, only a designer and lighting designer. With only five characters, only one of whom has a change of costume, the wardrobe cost only £1,000 and the set cost only £4,100. In *The Death of Danton* the set and props cost £6,800, the wardrobe £3,500 and the fees (including director and designer) £1,900. About £1,000 ought to be added to the figures for all three plays for workshop wages, which vary according to the amount of time that has to be put in.

In 1971–72 there was again a West End season, this time at the New, and the running expenses for both theatres can be broken down in round figures like this:

Actors, musicians and stage management	£226,000
(An average of about 70 actors through the year, an average of 8 musicians paid on a performance basis and four stage management teams – two for each theatre – of four people.)	
Stage staff	199,000
(Electricians, prop men, stage-hands, storemen, drivers and so on.)	
Production fees (including contract work)	151,000
Management salaries	106,000
(Director, associate directors and all heads of departments.)	
Salaries and wages at the Old Vic	81,000
(Front-of-house staff, box office personnel, ushers and so on.)	
Production department salaries and wages	54,000
Publicity	52,700
Old Vic running costs	47,500
(Heating, lighting, water, electricity, cleaning materials, cloakroom requisites and so on.)	
General administration expenses	40,000
(Telephone, postage, stationery, travelling, office equipment and so on.)	
Authors' royalties	35,000

National Insurance and Pension Scheme   32,000
Depreciation on vehicles, machinery, lighting
   equipment and so on   29,000
Production department – general expenses   25,000
General stage expenses   19,000
   (Lighting, materials, lift maintenance and so on.)
Interest   4,500
   (On bank overdrafts and the loan from the
   Shakespeare Memorial National Theatre
   Committee.)

Both the National Theatre and the RSC have to think constantly of money, and it is not merely in the choice of plays that box office appeal is a factor. If an actor who has a large following on television expresses an interest in joining the company, his drawing power at the box office would be more of a consideration than it would if the government felt able to give the theatre not necessarily as big a margin of financial safety as the West German theatre enjoys, but at least some margin. The National Theatre executive group would never use a star actor in a part he could not be expected to play reasonably well, but no absolute distinction can be drawn between the use of stars in the commercial theatre and the use of stars at the National. Not only are plays brought into the repertoire at the initiative of an actor who wants to star in them, star actors are given a say in the choice of director, and therefore in the shape the production will take. Coral Browne was cast to play in *Mrs Warren's Profession* before Ronald Eyre was engaged to direct it, and he had to meet her before his engagement was confirmed. When it was decided to stage *Coriolanus*, the original idea was that Paul Scofield should play the part. After he decided not to, it was offered, together with several other parts, to Christopher Plummer, who accepted. A short list was then made of directors who were available and who were acceptable to the company's executive group, and it was Plummer who selected Manfred Wekwerth and Joachim Tenschert, who had directed Brecht's adaptation of the play at the Berliner Ensemble. It then turned out, after only a day or two of rehearsal, that he could not see eye to eye with them about Coriolanus's place in the play,[1] but the directors had won the support of the rest of the company and the part was taken over by Anthony Hopkins. Effectively, though, the mould of the production was determined by a star that never lent its shine to it.

It is sometimes said that the National is an actors' theatre while the RSC is a directors' theatre. Certainly Olivier himself, being more an actor than a director, saw things primarily from the actor's point of view. According to Tynan he was quick to intervene if ever the actors seemed to be at the mercy of an autocratic director. So far there has been less continuity of directorial style than was expected in 1963 when William Gaskill and John Dexter were appointed by Olivier as his Associate Directors. Of the sixteen plays produced during the first two seasons, eleven were directed or co-directed by one of them. But after Gaskill left in 1965 and Dexter in 1967, a great many plays were handed over to a series of guest directors including Jacques Charon of the Comédie Française, the Italian Franco Zeffirelli, the Swede Ingmar Bergman, Wekwerth and Tenschert of the Berliner Ensemble, and the Argentinian Victor Garcia – as if to compile an international anthology of production styles. The only startling omissions are New York and West Berlin. The appointment of Robert Stephens as an Associate Director tended, if anything, to make it more of an actors' theatre, without doing anything to increase continuity of style.

The use of designers like René Allio (Planchon's designer), Piero Gherardi (Fellini's), André Lavasseur (of the Comédie Française), Karl von Appen (Head of Design at the Berliner Ensemble from 1954) and Josef Svoboda, the Czech designer, has also helped to introduce elements of an international vocabulary. The distracting extravagances of Zeffirelli as director and Gherardi as designer were the determining factors in the two productions (*Much Ado about Nothing* and *The White Devil*) which represented the two furthest points from anything the RSC would have done in its attempts to project the real meaning of a play. The appointment of a pragmatist

[1] There had also been a misunderstanding about whether an English translation of Brecht's version was to be used.

like Frank Dunlop as Administrative Director (1968–71) seemed to make the evolution of a house style or even of a distinctive directorial policy more unlikely than ever, but by 1972 when Dunlop was mainly involved with the Young Vic, which he had created, and when Dexter was back, together with Michael Blakemore, it seemed very possible that these two (who have some stylistic affinities) could work in harness to impose a belated directorial consistency. In fact this had no time to develop. With Peter Hall at the helm, without Dexter (who will leave in 1974), and with Jonathan Miller and Harold Pinter as Associate Directors, something very different will evolve. With directors as different in style and approach as Hall, Blakemore, Pinter and Miller, we cannot expect a 'house style' to emerge, but there may at least be more continuity than before.

Probably the National will become more of a directors' theatre, though in its first ten years it was less of an actors' theatre than it ought to have been: at the Old Vic not enough priority has been given to the actors' needs. There are very few rehearsals on stage, and, with its low roof, the rehearsal room soon gets overheated. In rehearsal an actor needs all the energy he is capable of mustering – a stuffy room depresses both him and his performance. There is no green room and, apart from the canteen, nowhere to relax after rehearsals. Consequently members of the company see less of each other than they otherwise would, and actors who are not members have sometimes rehearsed with the company for several weeks before meeting all the others. The few large dressing-rooms, as usual, are allocated to the actors who spend least time in them, being on stage throughout most of the show; most of the dressing rooms, as in all old theatres, are small enough to discourage even the most gregarious small-part players from visiting each other.

It is also unfortunate that the offices are not in the same building as the theatre. In the first few years of the company's life, Olivier, Dexter and Gaskill appeared to spend most of their time with the actors, but later it seemed more and more as though the important policy-forming decisions were taken in the offices and presented to the actors some time later as *faits accomplis*. All these things will be different, of course, after the much-postponed opening of the new National Theatre building. But by 1975 the company will have been working at the Old Vic for twelve years – the formative years of its life. It was a great mistake not to spend more money and more effort on producing conditions under which the actors might have come together more as a group and worked better as individuals.

Certainly there has been much more stylistic continuity at the RSC, though not enough, possibly, to merit the phrase 'house style'. Peter Brook's four productions, *King Lear,* the *Marat/Sade, US* and *A Midsummer Night's Dream,* have stood out in complete contrast to the work of all the other directors, but most of the productions are in the hands of Trevor Nunn (who succeeded Peter Hall as Artistic Director in 1968), Terry Hands, John Barton and David Jones. Nunn, Barton and Jones are all ex-Cambridge (like Peter Hall). Terry Hands was at Birmingham University. Peter Hall still does occasional productions himself, as does Clifford Williams, who is still an Associate Artist under long-term contract to the company. But there are relatively few productions by outsiders, though Ronald Eyre, after his success with *London Assurance*, was invited to do *Much Ado*, and Robin Phillips followed *Tiny Alice* with *Two Gentlemen of Verona*, and later *Miss Julie* in the experimental season at the Place.

Continuity of production style is inseparable from continuity of design style, and whereas the National has no designers under contract, the RSC has a Head of Design – now Christopher Morley – and three other designers, who are Associate Artists. These include John Bury, the former Head of Design, who came to Peter Hall from Joan Littlewood's Theatre Workshop. A chemist by training – not a painter – Bury has always created his settings by thinking in terms of shapes, materials, textures, not pictures. He reorganised the Stratford-on-Avon workshop 'to accommodate three-dimensional design, the use of machinery and the handling of big pieces. Each set, we say, is a new machine . . . The machine does the work; you don't use it to make half the statement and then superimpose the décor on top of it.'[1]

[1] *The Times*, 5 April 1966.

Christopher Morley is similarly anti-illustrationist in his approach, and equally hostile to Craig's epic ideas and the compromise naturalism of the forties and fifties. He believes there are 'unlimited possibilities for the destruction of scenery', and that the designer should start not from the background but from the actor's face, then going on to his costume and from that to everything he sits on, handles or moves around. Or, as Trevor Nunn has put it, the chamber setting 'establishes that the most important object on the stage is the actor. His words, thoughts, fantasies and language must seem important. The actor has to be able to exist in a number of environments. So what he wears, what he sits on, the possessions directly connected with him are next in importance. The middle and far distances are not important.' Christopher Morley's intention is that nothing should ever be literally represented. His experiments in reducing the set to a single white or grey box were prompted partly by practical considerations – sometimes there is only an hour between a matinée and an evening performance of a different play – but also by a determination to find the right sort of stage chamber, stylised and gently symbolic, to give the meaning of the play its full resonance. There is a similar reaction against naturalism in Morley's costume designs, and, after going through a phase of trying to use monochrome as a means of unifying a *mise-en-scène*, he arrived at the uniform black taffeta of the RSC's *The Revenger's Tragedy*, partly through being given a very low budget. Shortage of money can lead to good results, though it would be difficult to argue that it was more of an advantage than a disadvantage to a company like the RSC.

The RSC has suffered much more than the National from poverty. The first annual grant of £40,000 from the Arts Council, plus £7,136 as a touring guarantee, went up the following year (1964–65) to £88,136 and in 1965–66 to £93,273. In these three years the National's grants from the Arts Council were £130,000, £142,000 and £188,000 and the argument was being put forward that, with two theatres to run and no contribution from the local authority either at Stratford or London, the RSC should not receive a smaller grant than the National. In 1966–67 the council was more generous to both theatres, with a commitment of £306,000 to the National (of which just under

£300,000 was actually paid). But the RSC, which had asked for £250,000, received only £153,341, and played during the 1966–67 season to over a million people – an audience twice the size of the National's. Though this grant was an improvement of £60,000 on the previous year's, it was not nearly enough to cover the high production expenses of the 1966–67 season, and the company had to economise rigorously. Some of the revivals scheduled for 1967 at Stratford were cancelled, and the London season was cut down to small-cast productions.

During the year 1967–68 when Berlin's Schiller Theater, which is about the same size as the RSC, received a subsidy of about £924,000 from public funds and took about £253,700 at the box office, the RSC's subsidy was £200,000 and its box office takings £598,395. The next year the subsidy went up to £221,308 and to £229,000 in 1969–70. The figure went up to about £295,000 in 1971–2 but this still represented a subsidy of only 30p per ticket sold, whereas the National receives about 94p for each ticket. In West Germany in 1968 the overall subsidy from public funds was 19·17 DM per ticket – well over £2. The RSC's reserves, depleted by the three years of running both theatres without any subsidy, have never recovered, and in the ten financial years from 1960–71, deficits totalling £478,817 were financed by selling investments and other invisible assets. The company cannot now afford to pay for the work which needs to be done on the heating and ventilation at Stratford-on-Avon. And the lighting-board should have been replaced in 1967.

Meanwhile the expenses of running the Aldwych are enormous. The building belongs to a privately owned company which retains control of the bars and programmes. There is little space for offices and workshops, none for rehearsals. The annual outlay for hiring rehearsal rooms comes to £9,000, while £8,000 is spent each year on storing scenery outside the theatre and paying overtime rates to stage hands for bringing it in and out.

During the year 1970–71, when £842,747 was taken at the box office and £275,220 received from the Arts Council, the total expenses came to £1,232,489. What follows is a breakdown of this figure.

Theatre operating costs   £342,663
(This includes £216,000 for salaries of front-of-
house staff and backstage staff, £42,000 for rent
and rates on the two theatres and £31,300 of
building maintenance costs.)

Production costs   327,156
(£155,000 of this went on salaries for workers in
the scenic workshop, the property shop, the
paintshop, the wardrobe and the wig department.
The balance was spent on the materials used in these
workshops, overheads, rehearsal accommodation
and facilities, maintenance costs and purchase tax.
By a grotesque and expensive anomaly, the
company had to pay over £5,000 each year as
purchase tax on the value of costumes made for
its own use in its own workshops.)

Salaries for the actors and expenses on travel and
subsistence   265,278

The World Theatre Season   86,044
(It was the RSC which paid for this and paid a salary to
Peter Daubeny, who organised it. He was always
billed as its Artistic Director, but of course he
was not an artistic director in the normal sense. The
companies that he invited were usually subsidised by
the governments of the countries they came from.
Daubeny negotiated a separate deal with each
company – usually a guarantee on account of a
percentage of the box office takings. The companies,
mostly coming for reasons of prestige, usually accepted
fairly disadvantageous terms. There was never a
profit on the season, but if there had been, it would
have gone to Daubeny, not the RSC. Originally the
season was sponsored by the *Sunday Telegraph*, which
guaranteed it against loss. From 1968 the *Financial
Times* was contributing to the cost of the
Season, and in 1970 and 1971 there were

contributions from the GLC, the Arts Council and
from an anonymous benefactor.)

Direction and Administration	66,772

(Salaries for the directors, the General Manager,
the Financial Controller, the Planning Controller,
the Production Controller, the assistants and
secretaries to these people, the accounts department,
the administrative expenses, including a subsidy to the
staff canteen at Stratford.)

Provision for repairs	50,000

(Rewiring, which has not been done at Stratford-
on-Avon since 1932, will cost £35,000, a new
switchboard will cost £30,000 and stage lighting
circuits £10,000.)

Publicity	41,639

(Including salaries of publicists, printing and
advertising.)

Share of box-office takings to visiting companies	
during the winter season at Stratford-on-Avon	25,271
Depreciation of theatre and rehearsal hall at	
Stratford-on-Avon	7,322
Professional charges –	6,097
lawyers, accountants, architects	
Expenses on gardens and land at Stratford-on-Avon	4,041
Bank charges	2,676
Library expenses (mainly librarians' salaries)	
at Stratford-on-Avon	1,660
Conferences, summer school lectures, and	
cultural liaison	1,382
Governors' expenses	515

Like the richer National, the RSC is in a financial situation which
forces it to do something lucrative each year, quite apart from
running its two theatres. There is a period each year, between the
seasons at Stratford-on-Avon, when one of the two companies is
free to go on tour. The Australian and American tours (1970 and

1971) have been financially well worth while and, unlike the National, the RSC is not debarred by the nature of its constitution from doing productions specially for film and television. (The only filming and televising the National can do are of productions which have been created for the stage.)

In 1970–71, in spite of record attendances which produced a total box office revenue of £842,747, there was still a deficit of £76,529 on live theatre performances in this country – with the Arts Council grant of £276,220 taken into account. But the income from foreign touring and work done for the other media was so high – £82,990 – that it produced an overall surplus of £6,461, the first surplus in the RSC's ten-year history. This was due mainly to the enormous success of Peter Brook's production of *A Midsummer Night's Dream*. Income from foreign touring and work for other media had never before been so high. In 1968–69 it yielded an income of £28,065 and in 1969–70 only £9,944. The best year, previously, had been 1967–68, when it produced £42,542.

The survival of both companies is assured, but the financial pressure on them is much too high. If either of them could afford to work at a more leisurely rate, not to press the actors so hard, giving them more breathing space between parts, and the directors more time for lying fallow and for pre-rehearsal preparations, higher standards could probably be achieved. In a talk to the company in January 1963, Peter Hall said it was important that 'each actor, in addition to his main work and by taking part in experiments in public, is constantly developed and re-examined by training in the Studio. We want to increase this work. And then spend more time and more care on fewer large-scale productions.' This has not been achieved.

The RSC's six-month experimental season at the Arts in 1962 was very valuable but very expensive. Side by side with revivals of plays by Middleton and Gorki, and an English première of one by Boris Vian, there were new plays by Giles Cooper, Henry Livings, David Rudkin and Fred Watson. Livings had already had a play done at the Arts in 1961, but Cooper, Rudkin, Vian and Watson were all being introduced to London audiences. At the same time, the actors in the company were presented, in public, with a challenge that could not fail to have its effect on their Shakespearean work. No private challenges inside a studio can be quite like this, and nothing has since been attempted by either the National or the RSC which could possibly have been as reinvigorating as this. The National put on a small-scale experimental season at the Jeannetta Cochrane Theatre in 1969, transferring two new one-act plays, Maureen Duffy's *Rites* and John Spurling's *Macrune's Guevara,* to the Old Vic. The RSC had its second experimental season in 1971 at The Place but though two of the three plays were new to London, none was being tried out for the first time. There was Trevor Griffiths's *Occupations*, which had been staged at the Stables Theatre, Manchester; there was Robert Montgomery's *Subject to Fits*, which had been seen in an Off-Broadway production by the same director, A. J. Antoon; and there was Strindberg's *Miss Julie*. The Place was booked again for a 1972 season, but this had to be cancelled. At Stratford-on-Avon actors have also found time to stage shows of their own for performance to the rest of the company in a summer-house they have equipped as a theatre, but instead of having fewer large-scale productions, the company does many more. In 1961 there were five in the eight-month Stratford season: in 1971 the season was only two weeks longer, but there were eight productions scheduled, all new.[1] Recent policy changes have increased the proportion of classics in the Aldwych repertoire at the cost of cutting down on plays by writers like Dürrenmatt, Peter Weiss and Rolf Hochhuth, and by contemporary English writers. Trevor Nunn is less concerned than Peter Hall to put on new plays. So far he has himself directed only one contemporary play for the company – Mrozek's *Tango*.

The problems the RSC has in running two large companies would be enormous, even if they were both based in the same town. The 91-mile gap makes everything still more difficult. The workshops

---

[1] The last, *Timon of Athens,* had to be cancelled in the penultimate week of rehearsal.

[2] A second season was arranged in 1973 to include new plays by Philip Magdalany and John Wiles, a revival of a play by Athol Fugard, a reworking of a radio play by David Rudkin and a programme of material (including a short play) by Sylvia Plath.

and most of the company's offices are at Stratford, together with most of the staff. There were 338 people on the staff in June 1971, and 269 of them were at Stratford. The directors, too, see less of each other than they would if they were all working in the same town. When Trevor Nunn took over, he appointed John Barton as Company Director at Stratford and David Jones at the Aldwych, giving each of them a fairly free hand to make decisions in his absence. During 1972, for instance, when Nunn was himself involved in directing the cycle of Roman plays at Stratford, David Jones was controlling most of what happened at the Aldwych. Since 1970 at least half the plays scheduled for production there had been suggested by him. When he took over, the theatre was averaging a capacity of 60 per cent and in order to improve on that, as he was briefed to, he had to be very cautious about putting new plays into the repertoire. The company has revived several plays which had been undeservedly neglected, like Boucicault's *London Assurance*, O'Casey's *Silver Tassie* and Gorki's *Enemies*, but the policy of having the actors spend alternate years at Stratford and London means that the Aldwych company is always about the same size as the Stratford company, varying slightly from year to year but always being determined by the largest cast of the season. While this does not altogether rule out the possibility of doing some new plays, like Pinter's or Albee's, with small casts, it makes it unlikely that the company will often take the risk of tackling small-cast plays by less established writers. Since the National, too, is including very few new plays in its repertoire, while the commercial managers, hard pressed by rising wages and rising prices, can seldom afford to take risks even when they want to, there are altogether too few openings for new playwrights.

Under Peter Hall there were meetings of the RSC directors roughly once a month; under Trevor Nunn they were at first held at two-monthly intervals and then became much less regular. Of course informal conversations can be just as useful, and the basic decisions about recruiting new members and inviting old ones to stay on are usually taken jointly by three or four or five of the directors, depending on who is available. They never take votes but go on talking until they reach agreement. They also have a method of using each other as sounding-boards for each production. At an early stage, having worked with the designer until a satisfactory model has been produced, the director will invite one of his colleagues to look at it and to listen to his basic intentions for the production. The colleague can then be very useful at a later stage, sitting in on a run-through or a dress-rehearsal or a club review and discussing what he has seen in relation to the director's original formulations.

Twenty years ago – in England at least – it would hardly have seemed possible that there could be as much collaboration between directors as there now is at the RSC. This is one of the company's biggest achievements, and though the actors no doubt gain a great deal from working together, there is little doubt that if both the Stratford and the Aldwych companies were completely recast from one year to the next, audiences would hardly notice any break in continuity. This is some index of how much the directors have gained from each other and from the situation Peter Hall created.

The reduction in the size of the company has been prompted, like the scenic simplifications, partly by a natural dialectic of reaction against the previous phase of the company's policy, but partly by financial necessity. The relative importance of these two pressures is hard to determine, but the depletion has been very marked. In 1964, the year of Shakespeare's tercentenary, there were about eighty actors at Stratford-on-Avon and between forty and fifty at the Aldwych – in 1971 there were thirty-seven at Stratford and thirty-two at the Aldwych. The advantages of having a large company are obvious: the disadvantages are that many of the actors are under-employed which, besides being wasteful, breeds disaffection. In the production of *The Wars of the Roses* there was a contingent of thirty actors employed to swell the crowd and work the scene-changes. By contract they were engaged to 'play as cast' and to understudy as required, so they had no guarantee that they would ever speak a word of Shakespeare during the whole season. Trevor Nunn feels strongly that a professional actor, with two or three years of drama school training behind him, should not be reduced to this. If Peter Hall created an RSC less hierarchical than the Stratford company had ever been before, Trevor Nunn has gone still further in the direction of democracy, introducing a system by which even the leading actors have to understudy in at least one production and have to walk on in at least one other. No actors are employed merely to understudy and to walk on. In the 1970 *Richard III* most of the actors doubled as soldiers and citizens, while Sebastian Shaw, who was playing Polonius in *Hamlet*, understudied the Priest. Alan Howard, the Oberon in *A Midsummer Night's Dream,* was the goddess Ceres in the masque in *The Tempest* and understudied Norman Rodway as Trinculo, while Rodway understudied Howard's Oberon and appeared in the *Dream* as Snout. Ian Richardson, who was playing Angelo in *Measure for Measure,* and Prospero, also played Marcellus in *Hamlet* and understudied Osric.

At the National, where there is, on the whole, less undercasting and a tendency to use older, more experienced actors, things are still more as they were under the old regime at the RSC. Derek Jacobi, after playing Laertes in the National Theatre's opening production of *Hamlet,* went on to work for six years in which he was under contract to 'play as cast'. So he never knew what his next part was going to be until he was called into an office and informed or else found out by reading the cast list on the notice board.

The general level of salaries in both companies is still low. In 1972 an actor in his late twenties with some very good work behind him joined the RSC to start rehearsing at £12 a week. This went up to £18 a week and later to his full salary – £30 a week. But in 1973 Equity negotiated a new contract with the RSC. The minimum weekly playing salary was increased from £18 to £30, and it is to go go on rising until it reaches £42 in 1977, and rehearsal salaries were increased to £25. These, too, will go on rising, and by 1977 actors will be paid full playing salaries from the beginning of their engagement. It is impossible to make any direct comparison with salaries at the National because actors there are paid a basic salary plus a fee for each performance. Equity is currently negotiating a new contract which increases minimum rehearsal and playing salaries from £18 to £25, and the minimum performance fee from 50p to £1·50. Each new RSC actor has about thirty-seven weeks at Stratford, followed probably by about fifteen weeks of a world tour, and then just over forty weeks at the Aldwych. Both companies still have some artists contracted for a period of several years but both are more flexible than they used to be in granting leave of absence for film and television work.

The more democratic orientation of the RSC may spread the big parts more evenly through the company, but inevitably, with such reduced numbers, the pressure is enormous, especially on the leading actors. For the majority of actors in both the RSC and the National, though, there would not be enough work to keep them happy if it were not for extra-curricular productions of their own staged for private performance and as a showcase in which directors can see small-part actors playing larger parts.

These private performances at the National and at Stratford are very valuable as a safety valve for energy and creativity that would otherwise be frustrated but, generally, studio work has not bulked so large in the time-table of either company as was envisaged when they began. The RSC's studio was started in 1962 as an attempt at a drama school for the company, with an annual intake of ten students. John Kane and Frances de la Tour (the original Puck and Helena in Brook's *Dream*) were among the first of them. In 1963 over 90 per cent of the company took part in studio activities, including leading members of the company, some of whom worked as tutors. There were individual tutorials on verse-speaking, voice production, movement and fencing. Concentrated work was done in rehearsing excerpts from plays, the chief object being to experiment and stretch the talent of the actors. This was particularly good for those who were playing only small parts or walking on.

Though the intake of ten students soon had to be abandoned, something of the school ideal survived. When Trevor Nunn took over in 1968, he stepped up the amount of studio activity. Apart from voice and movement classes, there are sessions in which a director sits down with a group of six or eight actors to work intensively on one of the sonnets, discussing structure, rhythm and the relationship between verse, movement and sense. According to John Barton, 'it takes five or six years for an actor to come to his full capacity in the Shakespearean idiom ... You can never quite marry up a modern acting tradition, which is on the whole psychological, with the kind of acting tradition one assumes Shakespeare wrote his plays for.' But he and other directors have certainly helped the company by holding sessions patterned on university seminars.

After five years of running the Royal Court, George Devine said, 'This place is a sort of school, after all.' Like the National Theatre, the RSC has largely continued the tradition Devine had established, and it is not an accident that Devine and Peter Hall, themselves university graduates, surrounded themselves with other graduates – Tony Richardson, Peter Brook, William Gaskill, Lindsay Anderson, Anthony Page, John Barton, Trevor Nunn, Terry Hands and David Jones. It is not merely that a university education inculcates respect for the literary values in a script, it creates an intellectual addiction to atmospheres in which one man gives mental stimulus to a group. Not that rehearsals came to be like lectures either at the Royal Court or the RSC, but actors were certainly given more mental stimulus than had generally been available in the English theatre previously, and the RSC has undeniably produced a higher standard of work throughout the whole company than could be achieved at Stratford-on-Avon or at the Old Vic during the fifties, when groups of actors neither stayed together so long nor received seminar-type coaching.

The argument is still sometimes put forward that universities are a bad training-ground for directors, that instead of familiarising themselves with methods of theatrical communication as they would in a drama school, they merely learn to fall in love with ideas. But the young English directors of the fifties and sixties, far from being narrowly academic or intellectual, did much more than the previous generation of directors to enable the theatre to communicate with a wider public. Joan Littlewood, who was working-class by birth and anti-intellectual by disposition, never achieved her ambition of building up a working-class audience.

The university graduates who created Theatregoround, the touring unit of the RSC, succeeded in taking Shakespeare's plays to a public more representative of the whole community than any audience the plays had had since the time of James I. Theatregoround has incidentally had the effect of stretching the actors involved in it, but the main intention was to take productions out to areas and sections of the community where people were not in the theatre-going habit. Working in halls, clubs, community centres and schools all over the country, the Theatregoround actors gained experience of working in different spaces and conditions, striking up lively and reciprocal relationships with audiences. Designed for mobility, the productions have smallish casts. *When Thou Art King*, a telescoping of the *Henry IV* plays and *Henry V*, was toured with only ten actors, nearly all playing several parts. Working like this they are involved more intensively. Often actors would surprise directors by showing themselves to be capable of very much more than they had revealed under normal working conditions, and the quality of ensemble work that was sometimes achieved helped to shift the RSC's policy towards scaling down the size of the company.

Theatregoround started in 1964 when it was suggested by Peter Kemp, a stage manager, that Shakespeare productions ought to be taken out to schools. Then, when an anonymous gift of £500 arrived in the company's Christmas post, Peter Hall used it to launch the new project. After being shown the plans that were formulated for it, the same anonymous donor sent a cheque for £10,000 which paid for the first three years of work. Under the leadership of Terry Hands and John Barton, Theatregoround was soon penetrating not just to schools but also to adult audiences. Performances that seemed to be aimed at bringing culture to the masses were met with immediate hostility, but by playing to schoolchildren in the afternoons, and in the evenings to parents who had heard enthusiastic accounts of the show, the company managed to make contact with a lot of people who had never seen Shakespeare in performance.

But by the end of 1968, Theatregoround had spent £17,000 more than was budgeted for it, and the governors insisted that it must pay its way. Its aims had never been defined but it had been combining abridged Shakespeare with anthology programmes, modern plays, demonstrations of how the actor works, teacher training and collaboration with teachers in schools. Forced now to cut down, Theatregoround continued with anthology programmes like John Barton's *The Hollow Crown* and Terry Hands's *Pleasure and Repentance*, a compilation he describes as 'a lighthearted look at love', with songs and texts from very mixed sources including Sir Walter Raleigh, Mickey Spillane, Tennyson, the Rolling Stones, Prévert and the Bible. Theatregoround also continued, of course, with Shakespeare, tailoring the productions to the actors and resources that were available, using the costumes left over from *The Wars of the Roses* in *When Thou Art King*. And in 1972 there were still two demonstration programmes in the repertoire – *Movement and Mime* and *The Actor at Work*. Touring is expensive, even though the company has its own bus for the actors and scenery is limited to one lorry-load. But it takes its own mobile stage and lighting equipment to every date. Financial stability was achieved in 1972, thanks to John Barton's suggestion that Theatregoround should give matinées at Stratford. Seat prices were lower than at other productions, with a top price of £1·90 instead of £2·50 but, though there were more school parties at these matineés than at other performances, the 1,400-seat theatre was not less full than usual, and about £1,000 was taken at the box office each time. These matinées did not replace the normal mid-week matinées at Stratford but were additional, so the box office takings were used to swell Theatregoround's finances, which were kept separate.[1]

On touring dates ticket prices are kept well down – usually 50p for adults, 40p for students and 30p for children. Even at school performances the children are made to pay – unless they can't afford it – so that teachers cannot make attendance compulsory. For appearances at provincial theatres like the Oxford Playhouse or the Yvonne Arnaud at Guildford, seat prices are left at their normal level. But Theatregoround is not primarily dependent on theatres. Following the single paragraph in *Flourish*, the RSC Club's quarterly newspaper, inviting inquiries, there were so many that within three months there was a five-year waiting list. Which invitations are actually accepted depends partly on the facilities of the halls, partly on how far away they are. Sometimes a whole week is clear for Theatregoround touring; sometimes the actors are needed back at Stratford the following day. But from April 1970 to March 1971, Theatregoround gave 105 performances in 61 different villages and halls, playing to a total of 55,931 people. (During the summer of 1973, Theatregoround

[1] But the extra matinées were not continued in the 1973 season.

put on a six-week season in a newly created studio theatre at Stratford, and another is planned for the summer of 1974.)

Between them, the National and the RSC have helped to enrich the theatrical scene, not only in London and Stratford and the big provincial cities that the National has visited on tour, but in a great many small towns, villages and industrial suburbs where theatre-going is almost an unknown habit. But there is also a shadow side to the picture. In a recent interview[1] Frank Dunlop pointed out that between them the National and the RSC constitute a virtual monopoly. 'Even now the openings for talent are few enough. If a young actor or director happens to be on bad terms with just two organisations, he'll be out in the cold for several years'. Dunlop would like to break the present near-monopoly by having six or twelve national theatres in London and the provinces, and while it is unlikely that any such decentralisation could ever be achieved, it is also clear that any situation which reduces free competition in the theatre is bad for it.

As Francis Place said in the evidence he gave before the Select Committee of 1832, appointed 'to enquire into the state of the Law Affecting Dramatic Literature', 'If you want to have something done as well as it can be done, you must leave it to competition.' It would be a great mistake to amalgamate the RSC and the National: the competition between them is thoroughly healthy; the weakening of the commercial theatre by withholding subsidy from it and making it unable to compete with either, is not.

[1] In *Plays and Players*, January 1970.

6 THE WEST END

'However, this is a West End show: and, to expand that sneer, this means that instant theatricality is its sole objective.' IRVING WARDLE reviewing Tony Richardson's 1972 production of *The Threepenny Opera* in The Times

The phrase 'commercial theatre' has become almost meaningless, calling up as it does a mixed image of good-looking middle-aged stars forgiving each other in luxurious drawing-rooms, leggy chorus girls in loud production numbers, whodunnits with unflappable detectives in dry macintoshes, quickfire American comedies, and the new porno with nude bodies dancing on the Lord Chamberlain's grave. 'Commercial' suggests that some plays are commodities and that producing them is a business. To apply the same name to all unsubsidised productions is to imply that actors, playwrights, directors and designers who come to one of them after working in a subsidised set-up, suddenly have compromises forced on them which curb their creativity and lower their standards.

In fact, what it usually means for the actor is a shorter rehearsal period than he would get with a subsidised company, but one in which he is free to concentrate entirely on the new play. Then he has to repeat his performance eight times a week for an unpredictable number of weeks. Then he is out of work again. For the director it means working with an *ad hoc* stage management and without the help of the large organisation (from Literary Manager to Wardrobe Mistress) which shortcuts many problems at the subsidised companies, but it is only from a percentage on a long run in the West End that the director can earn big money. The original director of *The Mousetrap* has now made over £30,000 out of it, and in a large theatre, where a success can take over £10,000 a week, 2¼ per cent of the gross can provide a useful income over a very long period. For the playwright, too, whose percentage can be up to 10 per cent, West End success is the only large jackpot to be won inside the English theatre.

Undeniably most of the money is made out of musicals, thrillers, and light comedies. *Oliver* cost £15,000 in 1960, and made over a million pounds. There have been over 8,000 performances of *The Mousetrap*. *Sleuth* and *Oh! Calcutta!* will each have made profits of over half a million pounds. In November 1972 three box office records were broken by three light comedies. William Douglas Home's *Lloyd George Knew My Father* took £11,757 in one week at the 1,123-seat Savoy; Robin Hawdon's *The Mating Game* £7,607 at the 796-seat Apollo, and Joyce Rayburn's *The Man Most Likely to . . .* £6,119 at the 850-seat Duke of York's. It is clear that most of the major successes are scored by shows that do not make any serious comment on the contemporary situation. One of the undeniable functions of the London theatre is to cater for the appetite of old and middle-aged people for reminders of the elegance and glamour they remember or think they remember from the time they were young. Most of the longest-running shows of the sixties ran because they resurrected something of the appeal of earlier decades. There were the revivals of Noël Coward's *Present Laughter* and *Private Lives*, and of Dodie Smith's *Dear Octopus*. There were nostalgia plays like William Douglas Home's *The Reluctant Peer*, Hugh and Margaret Williams's *Past Imperfect*, M. Bradley-Dyne's *The Right Honourable Gentleman* and Alan Bennett's *40 Years On*. There were nostalgia musicals like *The Sound of Music* and *Charley Girl*, and there were nostalgic revivals of musicals like *The Boy Friend*, *Desert Song* and *The Student Prince*, though these were less successful. The wave of Oscar Wilde revivals – *Lady Windermere's Fan*, *A Woman of No Importance* and *An Ideal Husband* – played on the same hunger for lost elegance, and there were many other successes like *My Fair Lady*, *Robert and Elizabeth*, *The Rehearsal* and *The Prime of Miss Jean Brodie* which owed at least part of their appeal to a rather sentimental sampling of the manners of the past.

The nostalgia industry has been equally active in the seventies, with *The Great Waltz* and *The Maid of the Mountains* at Drury Lane, a spate of revivals of plays by Coward, Rattigan and Priestley, two more William Douglas Home successes, *The Jockey-Club Stakes* and *Lloyd George Knew My Father*, an evocation of Imperial India in Barry England's *Conduct Unbecoming* and two more knowing (and more autobiographical) pleasure-trips into the past in Peter Nichols's *Forget-Me-Not-Lane* and John Mortimer's *A Voyage Round My Father*. But very few of the plays staged in London at the beginning of the seventies held a mirror up to England as it was then. In fact the vast majority of shows that go on in the West End could fairly be described as 'commercial', but while the independent producers have to make more money than they lose, they do not all go merely for the easiest money-spinners. Michael Codron might never have survived as a producer but for Terence Frisby's *There's a Girl in My Soup*, which ran at the Comedy from 1966 to 1972 and made about £300,000, but he also introduced Pinter, Joe Orton, John Mortimer, James Saunders, Simon Gray, Henry Livings, Charles Wood, David Halliwell, and David Hare to the London public.

A hundred years ago, before the word 'commercial' had come to be used as if it were synonymous with 'unsubsidised', it had very much more meaning. When the Independent Theatre was founded in 1891, its aim was 'to give special performances of plays which have a literary and artistic rather than a commercial value', and its opening production was Ibsen's *Ghosts*. Modern plays of this calibre were conspicuously absent from the normal repertoire of the London theatres in the eighteen-seventies and eighties. There were only matinées and special performances to satisfy the section of the public that wanted more serious fare. The famous Vedrenne-Barker partnership at the Court (1904–7) originated when John Vedrenne invited Granville-Barker to direct *Two Gentlemen of Verona*, and he accepted on condition that some matinées of Shaw's *Candida* could be included in the run. Irving and Tree both worked in the commercial theatre, but the profit motive was not uppermost with either of them. Tree would often withdraw productions when they were still playing to full capacity.

The need for a National Theatre was already a popular topic of conversation, and as George Rowell has put it, 'Tree took unofficial but characteristic action by making Her Majesty's serve some of the functions of a National Theatre'. His uneconomic Shakespeare summer seasons presented Londoners with several of the plays each year, well mounted, with good performances in the supporting parts. Commercialism crowded the classics out of the West End during the twenties and early thirties, but Gielgud's 1937–38 season under his own management at the Queen's revived the classical tradition within the commercial theatre, with two Shakespeare plays, one Chekhov and one Sheridan, and it was commercially profitable, as was his season at the Haymarket in 1944–45, presented by the Tennent management.

The whole of our present subsidy system rests on the almost meaningless distinction that is drawn legally between companies which distribute their profits and companies which do not. Those which do are never subsidised; those which plough their profits back into their assets can qualify for subsidy if they are constituted either as charitable trusts or in such a way that no salary is paid to anyone on the Board of Directors. Control of the company may effectively be in the hands of a paid professional, but he must be appointed by a committee of honorary amateurs, which may occasionally assert itself by overruling his decisions.

It was during the war that this legal distinction became a factor in theatre finance. Dr Thomas Jones, who had been Secretary to Lloyd George's cabinet, was now Secretary to the Pilgrim Trust, a charitable foundation which administered money for the American philanthropist E. S. Harkness. Now, at the suggestion of Lord Macmillan, the Minister of Information, it put up the money for a Council for the Encouragement of Music and the Arts, to make them more available all over wartime Britain. The Council was effectively taken over by the Government when the Treasury gave it a grant of £25,000 in 1940 and went on in 1942 to assume full financial responsibility. CEMA organised companies of actors to tour the country and subsidised independent companies like the Pilgrim Players, which staged religious plays in villages. But it would not have been considered proper for CEMA to become associated with a company which was run for profit – though there were very few which were not. CEMA supported the Old Vic, the Memorial Theatre at Stratford-on-Avon and the London Mask Theatre, which was staging modern classics at the Westminster. The Government was also subsidising these theatres indirectly by exempting them from Entertainment Tax on plays which were 'partly educational'. Entertainment Tax had been introduced in 1916 as a wartime emergency tax, and continued all through the twenties and thirties. It varied between 15 per cent of the gross box office takings and (during the 1939 war) 38 per cent, and it had to be ·paid even if the production made a loss. Exemption from it, therefore, was far more useful than a small subsidy from CEMA. The growing amateur movement had been exempt all through the inter-war period, but it was only in 1934 that the Old Vic claimed exemption and qualified for it, since it was 'not conducted or established for profit'.

In 1942 the decision was taken to exempt all non-profit-distributing companies which presented 'partly educational' plays. Naturally this caused a good deal of confusion and the injustice of the system was obvious. Many other managements were putting on plays that could be called 'partly educational', but they did not plough their profits back into their assets, so they had to pay the tax in full and could have nothing to do with CEMA, though collaboration could have been mutually advantageous.

Soon, of course, they learned how to slip under the barrier. There was nothing to stop a producer from forming a subsidiary company which would be non-profit-distributing and which would either have an independent board of directors or be constituted as a trust. H. M. Tennent, the leading West End management, formed a new company, Tennent Productions Ltd., and immediately qualified for help from CEMA in organising the first major provincial tour of the war – the 1942 Gielgud *Macbeth*, which went round the provinces for six months, ending up in the West End. By the end of the war, when CEMA was reconstituted as the Arts Council, the vagueness of the description 'partly educational' had become intolerable, and Customs and Excise was empowered to exempt all companies whose overall *policy* was 'partly educational'. This meant that Tennent Productions Ltd. could stage 'commercial' plays, provided that any profit went back into the company, to be spent, presumably, on more 'educational' ones. In 1948, when Tennent Productions had sustained some heavy losses, H. M. Tennent was able to bring it back to solvency by handing over the production of Daphne du Maurier's *September Tide*, which was profitable, though scarcely educational. Throughout the rest of the forties and well into the fifties, much of the best work in the West End was produced by this non-profit-distributing subsidiary of the most important West End management. Tennent Productions Ltd. also presented seasons at the Lyric, Hammersmith, featuring modern French plays by writers like Sartre and classical revivals with stars like Gielgud, Scofield, Eileen Herlie and Margaret Rutherford. Other managements, like Henry Sherek, followed Tennent's example, forming non-profit-distributing subsidiaries of their own, but by then the system had helped the Tennent management into a near-monopoly position. Stars were nervous of accepting offers from other producers, for fear of being dropped by Tennents. By 1947 they had effectively established a first claim on all the best touring dates and (together with Linnit and Dunfee) they had about fifteen of the best West End theatres. Monopolies are always bad because exclusiveness tends to preserve the *status quo*, but the standard of Tennent productions was extremely high and the history of our theatre in the forties and fifties ought at least to have killed off the superstition that public money must be kept away from theatrical managements that make profits.

Not only have these managements had no help from the Arts Council during the sixties and seventies, they have been seriously damaged by subsidised competition and by hostility based partly on political assumptions. The *idea* of profit is associated with the idea of capitalism, and the impresarios and their backers have been attacked as if they were gamblers interested in nothing but quick profits. The extremists would like to see commercial theatre die out altogether. 'Ideally,' writes D. A. N. Jones in the first issue of *Theatre Quarterly*, 'practically all our theatres (and concert halls, art galleries and publishing firms) would be in the public sector.' This is ambiguous, but what I think he means is that not only theatre buildings but the control of productions mounted inside them should be in the hands of either the state or the municipal authorities.

Turning points in the history of drama are seldom the result of committee action. It was a commercial manager, Donald Albery, who in 1955 produced Beckett's first play, *Waiting for Godot*, in the London theatre, after two years of trying to interest West End stars in it, and defending it against the Lord Chamberlain. It was Peter Daubeny who brought the Berliner Ensemble to London in 1956. In April 1958, when the English Stage Company at the Royal Court was already in its third year, it was another commercial producer, Michael Codron, who put on *The Birthday Party*, the first play by Pinter to be seen outside Bristol University. Very few new playwrights have been discovered by the National or the RSC; many have been discovered by the Royal Court, but probably none more important and original than Beckett and Pinter. And as Michael Codron has said, if in 1958 he had had to convince a committee that Pinter was an important new playwright, he would probably have been unable to. As D. A. N. Jones went on to admit, 'There will always, I suppose, be *avant-garde* work so original and rebellious that no establishment, however catholic and tolerant, would feel justified in offering public patronage.'

Meanwhile the combination of higher salaries, higher production costs and subsidised competition is forcing the better 'commercial' managements actually to be more commercial than they want to be. To put a show like *Pyjama Tops* into a West End theatre like the Whitehall and to advertise it as 'London's controversial sex comedy. Cast of beautiful girls and the fabulous NUDE SWIMMERS in the £10,000 SEE THRO SWIMMING POOL' is effectively to turn the theatre into one of the largest (and therefore most profitable) colonies of the expanding strip-club empire which centres on Soho. There are other producers who use the profits of long-running light comedies to finance more serious plays, and who do as much serious work as they can afford.

Relatively few serious plays now go on in the West End without having received their first production in a subsidised theatre. Managers can rarely afford to operate in the way they used to, setting up their own productions and trying them out on a six- or eight-week provincial tour, making improvements all the time before bringing the play in to London. The costs of mounting a production have risen very sharply in the last ten years. In 1963 a large-scale musical like *A Funny Thing Happened on the Way to the Forum* cost £40,000, and *Fiddler on the Roof* cost £67,000 in 1967. The cost of Harold Fielding's production of *Gone with the Wind* was estimated at about £150,000 and Bernard Delfont claimed a new record for the most expensive musical ever scheduled in England when he was planning one that would cost at least £175,000 in 1973. Comparatively simple productions like *Boeing-Boeing*, which cost £5,244 in 1962, would have cost (according to John Gale who produced it) between £12,000 and £15,000 in 1971. If *Abelard and Heloise* had been set up for the West End with a preliminary provincial tour, production costs would have been in the region of £25,000. By persuading the stars, Keith Michell and Diana Rigg, to go to Exeter to launch it at the Northcott, a subsidised repertory theatre, John Gale saved about £10,000.

A play with a very large cast, like David Storey's *The Changing Room,* could never have come to the West End if it had not started at a subsidised theatre like the Court: to set it up in the old way for a pre-London tour would have been prohibitively expensive, especially as it had no stars to draw the regional audiences. Even without star salaries it was going to be an expensive production for the English Stage Company, the management at the Court, so Michael Codron was approached, and became a partner in the production. He had already worked in partnership with the ESC over Christopher Hampton's *The Philanthropist*, another play on which they approached him. Sometimes an independent manager will take a play to them, as Michael White did with Jean-Claude van Itallie's *America Hurrah* (1967) and Michael McClure's *The Beard* (1968). There was no other theatre where he could have either play done, and he financed both productions. But the oddest collaboration of all was over David Hare's *Slag*. Although Hare had been appointed Resident Dramatist at the Court, *Slag* would never have been revived there, after its three-week run at the Hampstead Theatre Club in 1970, if Codron, who owned it, had not suggested it. The ESC paid for the production at the Court but Codron could have transferred it to the West End if he had wanted to.

Large-scale musicals like Harold Fielding's revival of *Showboat*, which cost about £125,000 in 1971, still have to be produced specially for the West End, and the box office appeal of a star like Ingrid Bergman, Deborah Kerr or Alan Bates can make it possible for a manager to set up an expensive play without a subsidised try-out. But most often one of the subsidised theatres is used as a launching pad, and on the whole this new habit is beneficial to them because of the prestige, the extra money for the production, the percentage they receive of the West End gross if the play transfers, and the possibility of casting on a higher level. The prestige factor can even lead to abuse of the new system. A reputable repertory theatre on the outskirts of London announced that its production of a new thriller was 'in association with' a West End producer. The producer had never even read the play but was allowing the repertory director to use his name because it helped to secure a better cast, actors being more likely to say yes to a part if the chances of West End transfer seem high.

The kind of play that is wanted in the West End has changed so much over the last fifteen years that the Royal Court, once the main theatre for non-West-End plays, has become one of the West End's sources of supply. Since January 1970, Donald Howarth's *Three Months Gone*, John Osborne's *West of Suez*, David Storey's *Home* and *The Changing Room*, E. A. Whitehead's two plays *The Foursome* and *Alpha Beta*, and Christopher Hampton's *The Philanthropist* (which was still running three years later) and *Savages*, have all transferred) from the Court. Both Peter Nichols's play *Forget-Me-Not-Lane* and John Mortimer's *A Voyage Round My Father* had been seen at the Greenwich Theatre, the latter in a different production. Sartre's *Kean* came to London from Oxford. Robert Bolt's *Vivat! Vivat Regina!*, Anouilh's *Dear Antoine* and Robert Sherwood's *Reunion in Vienna* came in from the Chichester Festival Theatre. Kevin Laffan's *It's a 2' 6" above the Ground World*, William Fairchild's *Poor Horace* and the musical *Trelawny* came in from Bristol, and Noël Coward's *Tonight at Eight*, Trevor Griffiths's '*Erb* and R. C. Sherriff's *Journey's End* from Manchester's 69 Theatre Company (this last via the Mermaid). Wedekind's *Lulu* in a Peter Barnes adaptation came from the Nottingham Playhouse via the Royal Court, David Mercer's *After Haggerty* and Boucicault's *London Assurance* from the RSC's Aldwych seasons, and four not-so-new plays came to London from the Yvonne Arnaud Theatre, Guildford – Coward's *Blithe Spirit*, Maugham's *Lady Frederick*, Priestley's *When We Are Married* and Henry James's *The High Bid*.

It might seem from this that little initiative is left to the West End producer, that his function has changed, that he is no longer concerned in the manufacture of the product, only in its distribution, that nearly all the goods he displays are second-hand, that all he can do is offer the playwright and the audience the benefits of an uninterrupted and unlimited run. But in fact many of the plays at subsidised theatres are put on only because an independent producer has taken the script to them. Hugh Beaumont of H. M. Tennent offered *Vivat! Vivat Regina!* to Chichester. When Oscar Lewenstein was an independent producer, he (like Codron) sometimes worked in partnership with the ESC – on Osborne's *West of Suez*, for instance. Of the many plays that have transferred successfully from the Bristol Old Vic since the early fifties, only one, *Salad Days,* was originated by the theatre's own management. Michael Codron offered Bristol Frank Marcus's two plays *The Killing of Sister George* and *Mrs Mouse Are You Within?*, and *A Severed Head* by Iris Murdoch and J. B. Priestley. Codron transferred the first two to London himself but gave up his rights to *A Severed Head*, which was brought in by Donald Albery. Albery has himself taken several plays to Bristol, including Barry England's *Conduct Unbecoming*, Iris Murdoch's *The Italian Girl* and a collage about Queen Victoria, *Portrait of a Queen.*

The system that allows this sort of co-operation between subsidised and unsubsidised managements was attacked in an article by Nick Roddick and David Illingworth in *New Theatre Magazine*.[1] They quoted some of the Arts Council's statements on its policy, to the

[1] Vol. X No. 3 (undated).

effect that it wanted 'to see a great increase in local and regional activity' and to use the provincial theatre trusts as a 'counterpart' to 'the mass media and the large-scale enterprises. They are points of defence against London tentacles.' The article suggested that the interests of the local community were not being ideally served by a theatre which was aiming at London transfers and that the subsidies from the Arts Council and from Bristol Corporation should not have been mixed with the money Albery contributed towards the production costs of *Conduct Unbecoming*. But there can be no doubt that Bristol audiences saw a better production than they would have done otherwise. Albery was able to spend far more time on the preliminaries of casting than Val May, Bristol's artistic director, could have spared, devoting three or four weeks to steady auditioning. He was also given a managerial say in the casting, the set and the shaping of the production.

Altogether the Bristol Old Vic has benefited hugely from co-operating with Albery. Val May has said that the recent improvements of the theatre might never have been made if he had not used the profits (which he was keeping in a separate bank account) to buy the adjacent plots of land as soon as they came on the market. He had not yet approached the Arts Council about a grant for reconstructing the theatre, but to delay might have been to lose the opportunity of securing the site. Committees cannot take snap decisions. Balancing losses against profits on all the plays owned by Albery that had been tried out at Bristol, the theatre has made £48,879, while Albery, his companies and investors made £53,377. Had an overall loss been made on the West End transfers, it would have been borne entirely by the private investors, not shared with the Bristol Old Vic.

The system which prevents the Arts Council from subsidising West End managers directly but allows them to collaborate with subsidised theatres in trying their plays out is no less absurd than the old system by which they formed non-profit-distributing subsidiary companies so as to qualify for the indirect subsidy of exemption from Entertainment Tax. But until subsidies are given to independent producers, they will go on becoming more and more dependent on subsidised try-outs as steep increases continue in the costs both of mounting a production and of keeping it on. Running costs in the West End are hardly ever below £2,000 a week. A straight play would normally cost between £3,000 and £4,000 a week and a musical between £8,000 and £10,000. Except when big stars are involved, relatively little of this money goes to the actors. For *The Patrick Pearse Motel* to break even at the Queen's in 1971, £3,800 had to be taken every week at the box office, but the seven actors in it were altogether receiving only £790 a week.

Forget-Me-Not-Lane had a cast of nine and, to take the exact figures for the seventh week of the run, the salary bill accounted for £738 out of £3,474. In *No Sex Please We're British* the combined salaries of the actors and stage management during the second week of the run amounted to £1,198 out of a total of £4,065. In the seventy-fifth week of *Sleuth* the actors received £848, and the week's expenses came to £3,434; and in the musical *Fiddler on the Roof* (during the 189th week of the run) the artists' salaries came to £2,342 and the total weekly expenses £9,972. In the thirty-sixth week of *Oh! Calcutta!* the artists' salaries were £1,280 and the total expenses £7,485. (This last figure is swollen by the abnormally high rental of £3,000 per week.) Michael White, who had great difficulty in finding a theatre-owner willing to house the show, ended up in the Royalty, which belongs to Paul Raymond, the striptease impresario, who took it over from being a cinema.

In the *Forget-Me-Not-Lane* figures the £2,737 that did not go to the actors is made up as follows: £897 was spent on stage expenses and staff salaries; £484 on royalties; £144 on advertising and printing; £827 on rent and fixed charges; £210 on hires and purchases of properties used in the production; £100 on the management fee; £16 on accountancy; £6 on insurance; £2 on 'sundries'. With *Sleuth*, £645 was spent on royalties; £550 on rent and fixed charges; £433 on stage expenses and staff salaries; £346 on front of house expenses; £310 on advertising and printing; £95 on hires and purchases of properties; £86 on lighting and heating; £80 on the management fee; £19 on 'sundries'; £16 on accountancy and £5 on insurance. On the weeks I have quoted, *Forget-Me-Not-Lane* took

£3,847 at the box office, making a profit of £401 for the week, and *Sleuth* took £5,337 making a profit of £1,903 for the week.

Weekly profits always tend to be smaller than they are expected to be, partly because so many of the outgoings are on a sliding scale. A show that could break even at £4,000 a week is not going to make a profit of £2,000 if it grosses £6,000: in fact the profit is more likely to be in the region of £900. As much as 40 per cent of the gross takings may be subject to percentages. The theatre owner gets 20 per cent, the star may get 10 per cent or even 12½ per cent, the author is sometimes on a sliding scale of 5, 7½ and 10 per cent, sometimes on a straight 10, the director may be getting from 1½ to 3 per cent and the designer from ½ to 1 per cent. In one recent West End production, 31 per cent was being paid out in this way: 10 per cent to one actor, 7½ per cent to another, 10 per cent to the author, 2½ per cent to the director and 1 per cent to the designer. There were also 28 other actors, 3 understudies and stage management to pay.

It was because of percentages that William Douglas Home's comedy *The Secretary Bird*, which went on running at the Savoy from 16 October 1968 to 10 June 1972, taking nearly a million pounds at the box office, made a profit only of somewhat over £250,000.

The running cost of a show dictates the size of the theatre that the manager must rent. A production may ideally call for a small, intimate theatre, but if it breaks even at £7,000 to £8,000 a week, it can be economic only in a theatre where £12,000 – 14,000 can be taken at the box office. There are plays like David Halliwell's *Little Malcolm and His Struggle Against the Eunuchs* which ran for twenty performances at the Garrick in 1966, and E. A. Whitehead's *The Foursome*, which was briefly at the Fortune in 1971, both presented by Michael Codron, which could probably have enjoyed long runs if only they could have been put on in theatres where the takings did not need to be so high. New York has more small theatres with relatively low running costs, so Off-Broadway plays can run as long as enough people are buying tickets to see them; in our most nearly equivalent theatres – the Royal Court, the Mermaid, Hampstead Theatre Club and the outer London reps like Greenwich – as soon as one production has opened, another starts rehearsing, so nothing can run for longer than the pre-arranged period – three or four or five weeks. For *The Foursome*, Codron was trying to use the 440-seat Fortune Theatre as if it were Off-Broadway. But for a play to cover its costs there, it has to take £3,000 a week, the capacity take being £4,000; whereas at the 907-seat Globe, for instance, a production could go on running without actually losing money if it were playing to only half capacity.

There is a system in New York by which some of the less fashionably situated theatres can operate either on Off-Broadway terms or Broadway terms, and a production which starts on one can change to the other. A producer with a play he wants to try out can take it to a theatre like the Long Acre or the Lyceum, paying a lower rent, lower union rates to the staff and lower salaries to the actors than he would under normal Broadway conditions, as well as charging lower prices for the tickets. Then if he manages to make the play into a success, he can switch to normal Broadway levels both in the rent and salaries he pays and in the prices he charges. Ideally of course actors and stage staff should not be made to share a risk, but in practice this happens anyway, and they are out of work if the play flops. But a system like this would be practicable in London only if we had many more theatres.

At the big theatres rent, rates, insurance and staff salaries make the overheads enormous. Even when there is no show on, Drury Lane costs £3,300 a week to run, and Her Majesty's £2,175. At Drury Lane the heating alone costs over £100 a week in the winter. Between July 1970 and September 1971 the National Association of Theatrical and Kine Employees secured wage rises averaging 28 per cent, and it is not only the full-time staff who are members. NATKE barmaids are paid £16 a week in the West End for working from just over half an hour before the curtain goes up until they finish washing up after the interval. In November 1971 at Her Majesty's, to avoid a loss on the catering, £372 had to be taken at each performance in the half hour before the show and during the interval. This is why it is so expensive to present a play without an interval. To put on *The Price*, in 1969 at the Comedy as Arthur Miller wanted it, with no interval,

Eddie Kulukundis would have had to pay an additional £125 for each performance. As a rule, theatre owners – or the catering companies who do a deal with them – keep all the profits on bars and programmes, though a participation in these could be very helpful to a producing management. On cloakrooms in the eight theatres that are run by Stoll Theatres, a subsidiary of ATV, they have been making an annual loss of £10,000. Attendants and insurance have to be paid all through the year and during the warmer weather takings are negligible. At the Apollo in 1972, the staff wages bill of the theatre-owning company was nearly £1,000 a week. With a 20 per cent share of the gross it could not agree to a break figure below £4,200 a week. This meant the show had to average not less than 60 per cent of capacity.

In any event, of course, the initial costs of a production have to be repaid out of the weekly profits, and these costs are quite high, even when the production originates at a subsidised theatre. *Forget-Me-Not-Lane* (1971), which transferred to the Apollo without any cast changes from Greenwich, cost £9,014. By the end of the seventh week only £2,199 of this had been recovered. Whereas it used to be possible to recover production costs within six weeks of opening, a manager is lucky today if he can do it within twelve. And it can even happen that a show has a very long run without ever paying for itself. *Robert and Elizabeth* was an expensive musical, and though it ran for 957 performances from 1964 to 1967, it lost money partly because the Lyric Theatre was too small for it, though a top-heavy orchestra bill was also a factor.

Arturo Ui, which was at the Saville in 1969, is another production which could have been expected to recover its costs. Both Leonard Rossiter's performance and Michael Blakemore's direction were enthusiastically reviewed and talked about, and the run was nineteen weeks. The production would have been prohibitively expensive if it had been set up for the West End, mainly because of the size of the cast, but because it was put on originally at Glasgow, then at the Edinburgh Festival, then Nottingham, it cost a mere £7,313 to bring to London. But 400 gallery seats were on sale at each performance for only five shillings each. It was good that so many students and young people came to see it, and some of them could not have

E

paid high prices anyway, but not nearly enough of the more expensive tickets were sold, and though the play took £80,929 at the box office, the running expenses came to £77,004. So when these are added to the pre-production costs, the overall balance shows a loss of £3,388.

Here is a summary of the running expenses, looking at them this time over the whole period of the run:

Actors' salaries	£21,631
Stage expenses and staff salaries	5,237
Royalties	5,656
Front expenses	474
Advertising and publicity	3,589
Lighting and heating	2,383
Rent and fixed charges	32,331
Insurance	491
Management fees	1,520
Accountancy	359
Sundries	248
Hires	2,679
Get out	128
Under-provided expenses	277

The producer is not usually risking his own money, though sometimes he does. Frith Banbury had a substantial proportion of his own backing in his production of *My Darling Daisy* which in the summer of 1970 lost nearly £34,000 during four weeks of provincial touring and four weeks in London. It can happen that a producer will go into production with a new show before he has fully financed it. Investments could be made as late as the actual day of the opening, but a producer who has gone into production without being sure that he could raise all the money from outside backers, usually ends up by risking his own money. The only one in London to do this regularly in the late sixties was Eddie Kulukundis, who was drawing on private reserves derived from a family shipping business. Most producers are very dependent on their backers, though H. M. Tennent used to be able to put up a large part of the money they needed from their own resources, but in 1965 the company had to be reorganised and refinanced. It now operates in association with an American management.

For other producers who use individual backers, a great proportion of investment money comes from Americans. The London theatre is attractive to American investors because the share is 60 per cent of the profit, instead of 50 per cent, which is what they get on Broadway. And a rich American is far more liable to be interested in investing in the theatre than a rich Englishman, because over there losses are tax-deductible and here, though the backer has to pay tax on his profits, he is allowed no relief on his losses. Hal Prince, one of the most successful Broadway producers, has said that he would be out of business if his backers were not allowed to offset their losses against taxable income. So our producers are largely dependent on Americans, whose investments in London shows are treated by their tax authorities in the same way as Broadway investments. This is an unhealthy situation because it is an insecure one. At the moment the London theatre's prestige in New York is high, and, besides being proud to be associated with it, American backers enjoy coming over here to see the shows they have helped to bring into existence. But a crisis on Wall Street or a change in American tax laws could have a disastrous effect on our West End.

One show may have as few as six backers or as many as sixty. Investments can be anything between £125 and £7,500, though they are seldom higher than £2,000. Most backers do not want to read the scripts of a new play. They trust the judgment of the producer and usually they go on investing with him if his shows are doing well on balance. But for the balance to be favourable he will need some very big successes: you lose much more on an average failure than you make on an average success. Richard Pilbrow calculates that to maintain a favourable balance, one success must be made to pay for four failures. *Beyond the Fringe* (1960) was a cheap and enormously lucrative success, but a very few subsequent failures were enough to bankrupt one of its two producers quite soon afterwards.

The producer who is looking for a theatre in London now is in a weaker position than he was ten years ago or than his Broadway counterpart is today. In New York there is about the same number of theatres, but it is hardly ever difficult to find an empty one. At the beginning of the fifties in London the Fortune was occupied by amateurs for two-thirds of the time. Today nearly all our theatres are in use all the year round, whereas the average Broadway theatre is dark for at least two or three months. It is therefore much easier for the producer to plan ahead, booking a particular theatre for a particular opening date. Here theatre owners will not commit themselves in advance. They will only say that they have a theatre which *may* become available. The producer who is also a theatre owner is obviously at an advantage. But in June 1971 Toby Rowland of Stoll Theatres, which owns eight London theatres, did not know which theatre he would be able to have for Stoll's own production of Alan Bennett's *Getting On*, scheduled to open in November. And Donald Albery has had to wait as long as a year to bring a play into one of his own theatres.

It is quite common for producers not only to put a play into rehearsal but to take it out on a provincial tour without knowing which theatre it will end up in. This means that the designer has to work without knowing the size or shape of the stage his set will have to fit, and the director and actors have to work without knowing the size or shape of the space their performances will have to fill. Normally the set is designed for a thirty-foot proscenium opening, and closed in or widened out if necessary.

It can happen that a show bound for the West End will exude so much promise of success that there is competition for it between theatre owners. The contract which booked David Storey's *The Changing Room* into the Globe in 1972 was signed before it had even opened at the Royal Court. To have delayed any longer would probably have been to lose it to a rival theatre owner. But though there were times in the fifties and sixties when theatre owners were hard pressed to find new productions, it has been decidedly a theatre owner's market since the beginning of the seventies. Whenever a show is about to come off, there are usually at least three possible replacements for it. One producer will have a play he has been touring in the provinces in the hope of bringing it in, another will want to transfer a play from Hampstead Theatre Club, another will have seen a production in one of the reps which, with a few changes, could be brought in. London audiences would be able to see a greater variety of plays if fewer theatres were tied up with long runs. In September 1972 thirteen of the thirty-two West End theatres had been occupied by the same show for over eighteen months, and in October no space could be found either for a highly praised Tennent production of Marguerite Duras's *Suzanna Andler* starring Eileen Atkins or for Robin Phillips's production of the comedy *Norman, Is That You?* starring Alfred Marks.[1] The situation is exacerbated by the package holidays which are sold to American tourists, with theatre tickets included and the air-fare substantially lower than the normal price. The tickets are almost invariably for light comedies, and many of the tourists who have bought them do not trouble to use them, but their money helps the long-runners to clog the theatrical bloodstream.

Without a fairly rapid turnover of plays the arteries harden. Long runs generally depend more on personality than on script or production. They were unheard of until the second half of the nineteenth century, when plays, becoming more naturalistic, needed the actors to assert their individuality rather than conform to type, while tickets started to be numbered and bookable in advance instead of being sold only on the night, with all seats unreserved. Nightly changes of programme gave way to long runs, and this encouraged a middle-class cult of stars, which was not new but was now exploited more than ever before by the speculators, who by the end of the century were replacing the old actor-managers. Long runs are bad for the actor, whose talent gets less exercise, bad for audiences, whose choice is effectively restricted, and bad for all the playwrights who are deprived of opportunities. Some of them are sidetracked into designing plays as vehicles for popular personalities.

Today cast changes are nearly always involved when a play runs for over six months. And here the theatre owner's interests are not necessarily identical with the producer's. The producer, thinking of his backers, his profits, his author and the actors who stay, would like to keep the production running as long as possible. The theatre-owner,

[1] *Suzanna Andler* was later seen in the same production but with a different leading man for three weeks at the Aldwych.

knowing how attendances will drop off without the star who is leaving, is reluctant to see his theatre only half full when another producer wants it for a show that would probably do capacity business at least for its first six months. So the clever producer is good at persuadings stars to stay on in a play longer than they had intended to, and good at replacing them when he has to. The run of Simon Gray's *Butley* at the Criterion might have ended when Alan Bates left the cast in January 1972, but Michael Codron managed to extend it for nine and a half months by replacing him first with Richard Briers and six months later with Alec McCowen. In London a producer also needs to be good at holding on to theatres. When one production has to come off, he will have another equally attractive one ready at exactly the right moment to go into the theatre, so that the owner is not persuaded to let it to another producer.

The deal between the producer and the theatre owner can be made in either of two ways. Under the old sharing terms, 40 per cent of the gross would usually go to the theatre owner, who would pay for the front-of-house staff and most of the stage staff, while the costs of the orchestra and of advertising and publicity would be shared. But over the last six or seven years this kind of deal has become almost extinct, giving way to the 'four walls' deal, by which the producer takes over the whole building, together with all its expenses, except only rates, ground rent, insurance and so on. He pays all the theatre staff, both front-of-house and backstage, from the manager to the cleaners. He nearly always has to pay an advance on the rental, generally between £600 and £1,300 a week on account of 20 per cent of the box office gross, and sometimes he has to pay a guarantee, when the theatre owner has to make a deposit to Equity, but of course neither the advance nor the guarantee increase the producer's overall expenses.

Normally the length of the tenure is determined by the business the play is doing. The theatre owner and the producer agree on a figure below which the box-office takings must not fall. If they do fall below it for two weeks, either can give notice to the other. Usually it is two weeks' notice but they can agree that it is to be three or four. The first week of the run is usually incomplete, with the play opening on the Tuesday, Wednesday or Thursday. So however badly the play flops, notice cannot be given until the end of the third week, and a further two weeks may have to be paid for. The theatre owner often releases the producer from this obligation but not always.

The Broadway producer can close his play the day after it opens and though contractually liable for two weeks' rent, he can be sure he will not have to pay this. In Paris, thirty performances have to be guaranteed, but after that the play can be taken off without notice. In London the producer can lose as much on taking a play off as he has on putting it on. It is also very difficult for him to calculate the right moment to take it off. He wants to keep it on as long as possible, and he may be losing between five and eight hundred a week by the time he gives notice. The final two weeks he is then forced to carry on could easily add £5,000 to his losses.

The system of fixing a level below which box-office takings must not fall is liable to be abused. A producer may have reasons for wanting to keep a show running at a loss and he cannot be stopped from buying up tickets himself to make up the takings to the required level. In April 1970 it was known that a producer whose play had opened in February at one of the West End theatres was feeding in £1,000 a week to the box-office so as to keep the production alive until he was ready with his next, which he wanted to bring into the same theatre. It can also happen that a theatre owner is guilty of sleight of hand. If he is being offered a production which seems likely to earn big profits and wants to get rid of another which is doing badly but not badly enough for him to give notice, he can instruct his box-office manager to sell less tickets. People who ring up can then be misinformed about what seats are available, and business rapidly declines.

It is more expensive to rent a theatre on a 'four walls' deal in London than it is in New York, though it looks cheaper. A New York producer with an attractive-looking show to bring in might contract with the theatre owner to pay 30 per cent of the gross up to $20,000 per week, and then 25 per cent. A musical pays a straight 25 per cent. In London 20 per cent was the usual rate, though in 1971 at the Queen's it went up to $22\frac{1}{2}$ per cent when the box-office takings passed an agreed figure, and now there is a steady push towards this level. But in New York the theatre is staffed and maintained by the owner; here the operating expenses that the producer has to pay can easily add up to £1,500 a week and are sometimes nearer £2,000. He not only has to pay for all the theatre owner's staff but also heating, lighting, window cleaning and even towels, disinfectant and lavatory paper.

In this financial climate it is not surprising that many managements go out of business and very few come into the business. In New York about 40 per cent of each season's shows are presented by new managements; in London Michael White and Eddie Kulukundis, who both emerged in the sixties, are the only producers to have become important in the West End since Michael Codron in the middle fifties. None of our independent producers is younger than about forty, which means that, however hard they try, it is difficult for them to make the right decisions on the work of playwrights who are still in their early twenties. Younger producers are badly needed, but most of the older ones are saying that if they were young today they would not want to go into theatrical management. They continue not for the money to be made but to give themselves something enjoyable to do. Almost invariably, though, they have to mix light comedies they do not particularly want to do with the more serious plays that really interest them.

In the fifties and early sixties it was less difficult to avoid escapist drama. One of the producers who came nearest to doing so was Oscar Lewenstein, who started his career as a commercial manager in 1955. He had no money of his own but found backers for his first four shows – *The World of Scholem Aleichem*, *The Punch Review*, *Moby Dick* and *The Threepenny Opera*. These all lost money so he ended up without a backer. Having no option but to get a job, he worked at the Royal Court as General Manager for George Devine. In 1958 he re-established himself in the West End with two properties, Wolf Mankowitz's musical *Expresso Bongo* and Jane Arden's play *The Party*. When Charles Laughton committed himself to playing in *The Party* it became relatively easy to raise money for it, and Lewenstein secured Paul Scofield for the lead in *Expresso Bongo*.

The Party was a moderate success, running at the New from the end of May till the middle of November, while *Expresso Bongo* ran for nine months at the Saville. It was in 1959 that Lewenstein began a very successful association with Donald Albery, who was willing to transfer three Joan Littlewood productions from the Theatre Royal, Stratford E.15, into his theatres at a time when no other theatre owner would take them. He was the active producer on Shelagh Delaney's *A Taste of Honey* and Brendan Behan's *The Hostage* with Lewenstein as his associate, and he was Lewenstein's associate on Wolf Mankowitz's musical, *Make Me an Offer*. This was less successful than the other two, but Lewenstein's other 1959 production, Willis Hall's *The Long and the Short and the Tall*, which started at the Royal Court with Peter O'Toole and Robert Shaw, was a huge success. Three of these four were made into films, and when this happens it always adds substantially to the producer's profits.

Some of the backers who put money into *Expresso Bongo* went on investing in Lewenstein's shows, and if we imagine an investor who started by putting in £500, which would have bought him a thirtieth of *Expresso Bongo*, and went on investing at the same rate over the ten years from December 1957, when the Mankowitz musical was in preparation, to November 1967, he would have emerged at the end with the modest profit of £660, although he would have participated in the profits of such productions as Ionesco's *Rhinoceros*, directed by Orson Welles with Laurence Olivier, Willis Hall's *Billy Liar*, and Osborne's *Luther* (both with Albert Finney), David Turner's *Semi-Detached* with Laurence Olivier, Brecht's *Baal* with Peter O'Toole, and the Broadway production of *Semi-Detached*.

In these ten years Lewenstein put on twenty-five shows, but he did not go on working at this pitch of intensity in the theatre. In 1962 he had become involved in the film industry, and between 1967 and 1969 he diverted most of his energy into it, working either as producer or as executive producer. When he returned to the theatre it was to work more selectively and spasmodically, with productions like the English version of Barrault's *Rabelais* in 1971 at the Round-house. Then in 1972 he accepted a full-time appointment as Artistic

Director at the Royal Court, where he had been on the board of the English Stage Company since it started in 1956 and he succeeded Neville Blond as Chairman when he died in 1970.

Just as an actor is liable to become less creative as he becomes successful, relying more on repeating what has pleased the public before and protecting his reputation by taking fewer risks, a producer, who has to consider his backers and his box-office returns as well as his own taste, may come to feel less certain of what his taste really is. At the beginning, probably, to like a play meant to believe in it, and to believe in it meant to feel capable of presenting it successfully. If he is creative – and I believe that a really good producer, like a good publisher or a good editor, has to merit the word creative – his belief in the play will almost automatically propel him into a series of initiatives which will culminate not only in a well-conceived production with the right director, the right actors, the right designer and in the right theatre, but in helping the play to find the audience it needs and the audience to find the play.

To say that if the audience does not exist it must be created would be to exaggerate. But in April 1958, when Michael Codron put on *The Birthday Party*, there was no audience for Pinter. In May 1960, when Codron put on *The Caretaker*, there was a big enough audience to keep it at the Duchess for 415 performances. How had such a large public suddenly acquired a taste for Pinter's work? There had been Harold Hobson's rave review of *The Birthday Party* in *The Sunday Times* just after Codron had acknowledged failure and cut the run short after less than a week. The BBC had commissioned some Pinter plays, first for radio, then for television. There had been a prestigious amateur revival of *The Birthday Party* by the Tavistock Rep at the Tower Theatre, and there had been a couple of West End revues, presented by Codron, with Pinter sketches in them. There had also been a few articles and a lot of conversations. But the initiatives which established Pinter's reputation were Codron's. He, more than anyone else, created an audience for him.

But just as a drama critic is wise to get out after ten or fifteen years (as Tynan did after reviewing from 1951 to 1962), and turn to something else before his palate becomes too jaded, his reactions too blunted, a producer may have only a limited lease of creative life. If he goes on too long, his ear is liable to become tuned to the jingle of coins at the box-office grille, his personal taste subtly depraved by that of the West End public. He must work on the assumption that scripts which appeal to him can be developed into shows with box-office appeal; it becomes harder and harder for him to know whether he is persuading himself that he likes a script because he believes he could make a success of it.

It is almost amusing now to remember the so-called 'dirty plays' controversy of 1964 when Codron resigned from the Society of West End Theatre Managers because Emile Littler, the theatre owner and impresario, and Peter Cadbury, Chairman of Keith Prowse, the ticket booking agency, were launching an onslaught on the Royal Shakespeare Company's choice of plays for the Aldwych and its 1962 season at the Arts. Littler said that the Aldwych season had been full of horror plays which the public did not want to see. Cadbury said that these plays and others like them reflected 'the lowest form of life' and that audiences were 'embarrassed' and 'disgusted'. Littler said that the plays were not suitable as 'family entertainment' and Cadbury complained that critics were recommending plays that appealed only to a small minority which 'claimed' to enjoy them. Codron, who was soon to put on Joe Orton's *Entertaining Mr Sloane*, was regarded as an extremist. Public taste has changed so much that what seemed outrageous then is taken for granted, and he says he is no longer confident of his own ability to keep ahead of theatrical fashion. The difficulty for a forward-looking producer is that whatever currents are uppermost, the audience's nostalgia creates a strong backward undertow.

There are also several kinds of invisible pressure on a producer to keep up a steady output. Ideally he would be able to take as much as a year or two between one production and the next, waiting first for the script that fully involved him and then for the right director and the right actors to be free. In practice the producer has to be almost as aware of his image as the actor is, and once having made a reputation he can only retain it by scoring several new successes each year. It is not enough to be actively looking for material: his activity must be publicly visible. Otherwise the agents start offering the plays he would want to someone else, and his backers may be won over by a rival with a range of tempting projects.

Of the thirty plays Lewenstein put on between 1957 and 1967 thirteen made a profit and seventeen a loss. This is an unusually high ratio of success to failure, but backers lose the whole of their investment when a play fails to recover its production costs. With *Billy Liar*, though, which cost only £6,000 and made a profit of over £80,000, £48,000 was divided between the backers.

Who are the backers? What sort of people put money into the theatre? A considerable proportion of them are people who make their living out of the theatre: of the £8,000 needed to finance John Gale's production of *The Secretary Bird*, £3,000 came from theatre people. The capital for his production of *No Sex Please, We're British* came from very mixed sources: a film company; the authors, who had a clause in their contract entitling them to a participation; two directors of a theatre-owning company; an ex-taxi-driver turned travel agent; a theatre-owner and producer; two producer–directors; two theatrical agents; a publisher of medical magazines; a writer; a stage manager; two men of independent means; four businessmen; a widow; a public relations man; a retired naval officer; a retired businessman; an accountant's wife; an employee of a consultant engineer; and a company manager. Apart from the authors, who found backers of their own and provided a fifth of the capital, a fifth came from theatre people. It was capitalised at £15,000 with a 25 per cent overcall (which means that if the producer spends more than he budgeted he can call on each backer to provide up to an extra £25 for every £100 he has invested) and this money was raised within three days.

Obviously theatre has become big business. On Broadway it grosses about $60,000,000 each season at the box office, and Off-Broadway about $1,500,000. In London there is no way of arriving at an accurate figure, for box-office takings are not published here. Takings would be lower than in New York because ticket prices are so much lower, but we have seventeen theatres with over 900 seats, which could each average half a million pounds in a good year, and if twenty smaller theatres each averaged £300,000 this would produce a total annual gross of nearly fifteen million.

It is very unfortunate that this vast complex of art, business and industry is not more efficiently organised. The film industry's methods of selling its wares to the public are highly imperfect, but the theatre's are unbelievably primitive. C. B. Cochran was one of the first London managers to use a press agent, and the practice grew after the war ended in 1945. Today each major production has a press relations officer who does what he can to get publicity for the show and its stars on television, radio and in the papers. Once the reviews have come out, the juiciest praise is carved out of its context and quoted on posters and in advertisements. If the Press is unfavourable, the producer has to decide whether the show can be nursed through the critical two or three months that have to go by before the reviews are forgotten. Reviews affect not only the number of people who come to the theatre but the frame of mind they come in. If the critics say the play is funny, the audience will be predisposed to laugh; if they give the impression that it's not, there will be noticeably less laughter than there was at the previews. But even a very good set of notices cannot keep a play alive for more than six months: beyond that it is entirely dependent on what people say about it. On the other hand a light comedy like Joyce Rayburn's *Don't Start Without Me* can survive a bad press, and so can a show with nudes of both sexes like *Oh! Calcutta!* or *The Dirtiest Show in Town*.

What else can a producer do to nurse a show? Until four or five years ago the most effective means was to arrange for a forty-minute live extract to be shown on BBC television. It was dangerous to give away the main part of the plot, but providing that the right sequence was excerpted, leaving viewers in suspense about what happened next, the bookings would come pouring in, and the canny producer would leave his box office open late on the night of the transmission to answer the telephone calls that always ensued. The boost would usually be effective for about eight weeks. But the BBC has now changed its policy about excerpts from plays, and it is only very occasionally that an exception is made. *Spring and Port Wine* would never have been the success it was if Albert Finney, whose company was producing it, had not been able to arrange for a television excerpt, compèring himself from a box in the theatre. Publicity like this can make all the difference between a very short run and a very long run. But to buy space on commercial television is extremely expensive, and, for the most part, producers are more likely to advertise plays on sides of buses and on the walls of escalators at underground stations.

Remarkably little thought has been put into the question of how to sell more theatre tickets to more people. In a sense the non-commercial RSC has shown that it is more commercially-minded than the commercial theatre in that at least it has gone out of its way to explore the possibilities of introducing theatre to sections of the public that are not in the theatre-going habit. Not that the West End managers could start a sort of commando unit like Theatregoround, but it is striking that no one has thought it worth while even to commission any large-scale market research into West End theatre audiences.

Commercial managements make arrangements for party bookings, coaches and the circularisation of schools, factories and institutions within a fifty-mile radius of London, but a great deal more could be done towards selling the theatre's wares to people who would enjoy them if only they could be persuaded to sample them. The theatre has to compete not only with cinema and television, but with pubs, restaurants, bingo halls, youth clubs, dance halls and all the other places where different sections of the community spend their leisure. Some of these are highly advertised, not just individually but collectively. We see commercials on television persuading us what a jolly evening we could be having in a pub, but the theatre is not organised in such a way that space could be bought to advertise theatre as a whole. Vast amounts are spent on advertising individual shows, but this is like preaching to the converted. Almost nothing is done towards breaking through to that huge section of the English public – about 98 per cent of it – which has no interest in theatre. What the theatre needs is some equivalent to the Milk Marketing Board.

The theatre owners are concerned with letting their theatres on good terms to a reliable management with a show that looks likely to run. The managements concentrate on the productions they have on and the ones they're trying to set up. Equity has had a long battle to get salaries – especially rehearsal salaries – up to a reasonable level. NATKE is constantly fighting to raise technicians' salaries, as the Musicians' Union is for musicians'. The Society of West End Theatre Managers, which represents a community of interest between the producers, has in the past been concerned primarily in negotiations with the unions, only recently turning its attention to marketing the product. But if, instead of fighting each other, these component elements would form a united front to fight for the cause they have in common – selling the London theatre to a wider public – each one of them would at the same time be serving its own members' interests.

It would be useful to know what percentage of London theatre tickets are sold to tourists. It has been estimated that 63 per cent of all foreign visitors to London go to the theatre. In 1968, according to the British Travel Association, 58 per cent of all organised parties of Americans went to the theatre, and there are many American travel agents who organise off-peak tours for fourteen days in London in the winter. The package the tourist buys for between $300 and $350 includes five shows, with at least one musical, one West End play and one classic. In addition to these five shows most of the tourists book seats for three to five more.[1] In October 1971, when a spot check was taken at Wyndham's Theatre, 48·1 per cent of the tickets were sold to foreign tourists.

Producers disagree about the extent to which they ought to become involved in the leisure industry. Some are anxious to co-operate with the packagers who sell theatre tickets to the tourist together with railway-tickets, hotel reservations and a trip to Hampton Court. Others insist that their function is limited to putting the plays on and that if they are put on well enough they will attract as big an audience as they need.

But even if the unsubsidised theatre were better organised, it would still need help from the Government, which has done nothing at all to help it since it abolished Entertainment Tax. A large boost could be given to private investment in theatre if only the Government would

[1] *The Theatre Today.* The Arts Council, 1970.

rule that losses made on theatrical investment should be tax deductible. The Government could also divert some of the fiscal income from television to the live theatre. But there does not seem even to have been any official discussion of these possibilities.

In 1967 the Arts Council appointed a distinguished committee to report on the state of the theatre, subsidised and unsubsidised, and 'to recommend how the position should be improved'. At the beginning of 1970 the committee decided to publish its recommendations. It found that rising costs, rising wages and rising rents were involving the theatrical manager in extra expenses he was unable to recoup by putting up the price of theatre tickets. It recommended that a Theatre Investment Fund should therefore be created on the same lines as the National Film Finance Corporation, which was set up by the Government in 1948 to invest public money in the commercial cinema. The new fund was to be used to lend reliable managements up to half the capital they needed for a worthwhile production: a corresponding proportion of the profits would flow back into the fund. According to the report, it could be established for the theatre on as little as £250,000 – about 5 per cent of the original government grant to the NFFC – and the Arts Council was to be asked to provide only £100,000 of this, which was 7 per cent of its annual grant to the Royal Opera House. The balance was to be raised by issuing shares or long-term loan stock. Lord Goodman, who was then Chairman of the Arts Council, indicated that he could secure £150,000 for the fund from private sources, and it has been said that it was in order to launch this idea of a Theatre Investment Fund that the Arts Council initiated the Theatre Enquiry. In any case, the committee appointed to carry it out recommended that the fund should be set up immediately. But it was only in 1972 that the Arts Council started advertising for a Managing Director for the Theatre Investment Fund, asking for applications to be in by 12 May, offering a salary of about £6,000, and announcing that the Fund would start operating 'in the near future'. At the end of the year it was still not operating. The delay[1] has done incalculable damage, and meanwhile the Government has withdrawn support from the NFFC – which will have an adverse

[1] It has been caused partly by legal problems.

effect not only on the British cinema but on the theatre too, since cinema earnings have enabled so many actors to accumulate reserves they have partly lived off while working in the theatre.

Meanwhile, our theatre is being gravely damaged by Value Added Tax. The perfectly justifiable evasion of Entertainment Tax by the non-profit distributing companies in the forties and fifties should have made it obvious even to politicians that the whole of our theatre cannot be dismissed as something that provides mere 'entertainment' of no cultural or educational value. But while tax concessions are being made for books and even newspapers – to tax books, the Chancellor said, would be to tax knowledge – all appeals on the theatre's behalf were rejected. During the debate in the House of Commons, he promised to increase the Arts Council's budget to enable it to offset the consequences of the tax. In a joint letter to *The Times* (29 May 1972) a Conservative and a Labour M.P. estimated that to refund even 50 per cent of the tax, the Council's resources would need to be doubled. This is very unlikely to happen, and even if it did, it would be of no help to the unsubsidised sector of the theatre, which is the one that is suffering most. Serious managements are being forced to become less serious, simply in order to survive.

Meanwhile, of course, ticket prices (which have to be agreed between the producer and the theatre owner) have been put up since the Arts Council report was published and will go on increasing. In 1971 most theatres were trying not to charge more than £2 for the best seats, though soon there were several theatres where they cost £2·25 or £2·50, especially on Friday and Saturday evenings. By the middle of 1973 the £3 barrier was broken. The top price for *Gypsy* at the Piccadilly was £3·30. But there are also 30p seats at many West End theatres, while there are very few West End cinemas where the cheapest seats cost less than 50p. Visiting Americans are incredulous at the cheapness of London theatre in comparison with Broadway, and it is remarkable how ticket prices have been so little affected by inflation. In 1874, when a theatre could be rented for £50 a week, the Bancrofts started to charge 10s. for the best stalls at the Prince of Wales. In 1952 the best stalls in most London theatres would cost about 16s. There are not many things today which cost only four times as much as they did in 1874 or two and a half times as much as in 1952.

That it has been possible to keep ticket prices so low while other prices have been rising so steeply could be used as support for the argument that the independent producers do not need subsidy. But what has been happening is that several have been forced out of the business, while the survivors, in spite of having less competition, take fewer and fewer risks. A theatre that plays safe is a dull theatre, and if they have to go on without subsidy, the few independent producers who survive will be forced down to the same level of commercialism.

7 THE ROYAL COURT

For me the theatre is really a religion or a way of life.
You must decide what you feel the world is about and
what you want to say about it, so that everything
in the theatre you work in is saying the same thing.
... The great problem is to find material to express
yourself without distorting other material. GEORGE
DEVINE. *From an unfinished book.*

Since the Royal Court Theatre was taken over by the English Stage
Company in 1956, the whole anatomy of our theatre has changed,
and the ESC has done more than any other company to change it,
setting a pattern which subsidised theatres all over England have
followed. The ESC has itself evolved into something very different
from what it used to be, but then some of the needs it was created to
meet no longer exist. The prestige of the English playwright is
generally much higher than it was in 1956; there are more outlets for
his work, and more plays are being written which reflect and criticise
contemporary life. The excitement of the ESC's first few seasons,
when new voices were reaching a new public, could not possibly have continued at the same level, especially after the creation of
two much larger subsidised companies, the RSC and the National.
But though they took away some of the kudos from the ESC, and
took away some of the plays it could otherwise have produced, they
showed no willingness to share what had become the ESC's main
concern – to find new playwrights and to encourage them to go on
writing.

There were two groups of people behind the formation of the new
company. Oscar Lewenstein and Ronald Duncan met in 1955 when
Lewenstein was arranging for Joan Littlewood's production of

Mother Courage to open at the Devon Festival, which Duncan organised in Barnstaple. Duncan was also associated with the English Opera Group and was eager to see a theatrical equivalent created. Lewenstein, who had been manager of Glasgow Unity and had been editing the magazine *New Theatre*, was concerned with the social role that theatre could play. He did not share Duncan's interest in poetic drama, but they both admired playwrights like Brecht and Arthur Miller, whose work was being ignored in the English theatre, and they decided to start a new non-commercial company. The first step was to form a committee. Lewenstein invited Alfred Esdaile, the owner of the Kingsway Theatre and the Royal Court, to join it; Duncan invited the Queen's cousin, Lord Harewood, who had directed the Edinburgh Festival, Lord Bessborough, Sir Reginald Kennedy Cox and J. B. Blacksell, who later approached Neville Blond, a Manchester textile manufacturer who had been adviser to the Board of Trade on North American imports.

Meanwhile George Devine had been trying to start a new London company, and the Shakespeare Memorial Theatre Company of Stratford-on-Avon, whose governors were already planning a London base, wanted him to run it for them. Having come into the professional theatre himself from being President of the Oxford University Dramatic Society – he played Mercutio in the 1932 *Romeo and Juliet* which Gielgud directed – Devine now had his eye on a possible associate director for the new theatre, Tony Richardson, who had directed at the OUDS and was working in television.

Lewenstein suggested to his committee that George Devine (who had written articles for *New Theatre*) would be the right man to run their new company, and so the two groups came together. Esdaile proposed that they should take a lease on the old Kingsway Theatre, which had been damaged by a bomb, and in July 1955, thanks to Blond, they were able to announce their intention of spending £50,000 on renovating it. When, instead, they finally secured a thirty-four year lease of the Court, Blond was elected Chairman of the English Stage Company and Devine was appointed Artistic Director, with Tony Richardson as his associate.

When Devine announced that the new theatre was to be a writers' theatre he was thinking of the gap between contemporary English literature and the contemporary English theatre. Drama always tends to lag behind the other arts, partly because it needs an instantaneous response from an audience. Kepler said, 'My words can wait a hundred years for a reader.' The playwright's words can't. In 1951 Devine defended John Whiting's play *Saint's Day* in a letter to *The Listener*:

> To me, it splits wide open the conventional forms of playwriting and allies itself with the other modern arts in a way that no other play has done. It helps the theatre to bridge the gap of time that exists between itself and other forms of artistic expression.

In 1955 Devine had directed *King Lear* with décor and costumes by the Japanese sculptor Isamo Noguchi, who had designed for Martha Graham's Modern Dance company. The production was artistically a failure but at least it represented an attempt to bring Shakespearean production into line with contemporary developments in the other arts. After the English Stage Company had been founded, one of Devine's aims was to attract important writers into the theatre. In post-war France the leading playwrights were the leaders of the literary profession – Gide, Mauriac, Claudel, Sartre, Genet and Camus, but in England novelists and playwrights were like two separate breeds. Nigel Dennis, for instance, had never even thought of writing for the theatre. Devine now made a great many overtures to novelists, and during the first year at the Court he staged Angus Wilson's play *The Mulberry Bush*, Nigel Dennis's adaptation of his novel *Cards of Identity* and Carson McCullers's adaptation of hers, *The Member of the Wedding*. But Devine did not achieve the results he was expecting. Nigel Dennis went on to write an original play, *The Making of Moo*, which was less successful than *Cards of Identity*. Doris Lessing's play, *Each His Own Wilderness* was awarded only a Sunday night production. Gwyn Thomas produced a very funny first play, *The Keep*, which was staged in 1961, to be followed, much less successfully, by *Jackie the Jumper* (1963). But most of the novelists Devine approached personally were unresponsive, and his advertisements for scripts yielded few of any merit.

As originally formulated by Devine, the two principal aims of the new company were 'to stage and encourage new writing in the theatre and to present the plays in true repertory'. As an actor in the Old Vic company and in Gielgud's season of 1938–39 at the Queen's, he had seen how valuable it was for the actor to ward off staleness by switching from role to role. In 1956 there was still a classical repertoire at the Old Vic, but there had been no large-scale attempt at a modern repertoire in London since the Vedrenne-Barker seasons at the Royal Court before the 1914–18 war. Devine now announced his first six plays. *The Mulberry Bush* was to open the theatre on 2 April 1956, to be joined a week later by Arthur Miller's 1953 play *The Crucible*, which had already been seen in America, in France and in Germany (even in small towns like Bochum) but not in England. The next pair of productions, to be introduced into the repertoire in May, would consist of John Osborne's *Look Back in Anger* and a double bill by Ronald Duncan, *Don Juan* and *The Death of Satan*. *Cards of Identity* followed in June and Brecht's *The Good Woman of Setzuan* in October. The first revival, Wycherley's *The Country Wife*, was added in December. So Osborne was the only unknown writer to have his work seen at the Court during its first year: 'new writing' meant the work of writers new to the theatre, not to writing.

But it was also to be a writers' theatre in the sense that more attention was to be paid to the playwrights. Devine's intention was that the style of each production should be determined by the style of the writing. He also promised that the author would never be put under pressure to make cuts and that he would always be welcome at rehearsals. This was not normal practice in the London theatre of 1945–55, where playwrights were generally denied the prominence and the influence they enjoyed in Paris. Nor has the Royal Court ever become anti-literary, even when *avant-garde* theatrical fashion was being formed around the influences of Artaud and Grotowski. At first Devine was able to pride himself on having every script that was submitted read within a week. Many of the readers were playwrights who had themselves submitted interesting scripts. Arnold Wesker and Edward Bond, for instance, were employed to read scripts, and rejected plays were often returned with comments from the play-wrights who read them.

Devine's main achievement was to build a drawbridge for intellec-tuals to ride freely into the English theatre. For over 150 years no one inside the fortress had been prepared to throw down a rope-ladder to any Henry James who wanted to climb in, and the intellectuals (like T. S. Eliot) who got in by disguising themselves still kept their dis-guises on when they were inside. Now, suddenly, intellectuals were no longer enemies. A variety of friendly fanfares had been sounded. Tynan had been using his drama column in *The Observer* to trumpet the virtues of Brecht. The three most fashionable young English directors, Peter Brook, Peter Hall and Peter Wood, were all uni-versity graduates. A play written in French by an Irish intellectual about two intellectual tramps had repeated its continental success in London. But it was Devine who succeeded in building up a collection of young writers who could catch the imagination of an audience in almost the same way as a star actor or a star director. The success of the Royal Court was due mainly to its writers.

The time was more than ripe. In 1956, except for the Arts Theatre Club, there was no platform in London for plays that could be expected to appeal only to a minority taste. But in 1957 at the Court there were five 'productions without décor', staged in the manner of societies like The Repertory Players, who occasionally put on similar try-outs – though of less experimental plays – on Sunday nights in West End theatres. Without fully dismantling the set of the current play and without paying actors more than a couple of guineas as 'expenses', Devine was able to stage well-rehearsed but visually simplified productions of plays which might never otherwise have been presented, and each production cost only £100. The first five playwrights to benefit were Charles Robinson, Michael Hastings, Kathleen Sully, John Arden and N. F. Simpson. Arden and Simpson went on to become well known as Royal Court playwrights, and subsequent writers whose plays were first tested out on a Sunday night included Donald Howarth, Ann Jellicoe, Doris Lessing, Gwyn

Thomas, Barry Reckord, Edward Bond, Heathcote Williams, David Cregan and Christopher Hampton.

Devine also formed a Royal Court Writers' Group, consisting of playwrights who had submitted scripts he liked. Two or three dozen of them were then allowed to attend rehearsals of any play at the Court and any performances that were not sold out. Devine knew how much a writer could learn from watching actors in rehearsal, and from coming again and again to the same play. Few members of the group could have afforded to keep coming back even to the plays they most liked if they had to pay for tickets each time. There were also regular Wednesday evening meetings at the house of David and Anne Piper on Hammersmith Mall. William Gaskill took charge of these sessions, treating the writers rather like a group of student actors and spending most of the time on improvisations. Many of the playwrights learned a lot about using less words and more actions and silences. John Arden, Arnold Wesker, Edward Bond, Ann Jellicoe, Maureen Duffy and Keith Johnstone all attended fairly regularly. Edward Bond has said, 'I owe a hell of a lot to the Royal Court Playwrights' Group. It taught me that drama's about relationships rather than individuals.'[1]

In 1971-2 the Arts Council subsidy to the Royal Court was £105,400, and since 1966-67 it has never been less than £80,000, but for the first six years of George Devine's regime it was never more than £8,000 and sometimes no more than £5,000. With a top price of 21s. and only 407 seats, the maximum takings at any one performance were £339 2s. 6d. which was less than half of what could be taken (even with prices as they were then) at Wyndham's with its 771 seats. There was some income from other grants and gifts (£1,067 in 1956-57; £1,917 in 1957-58) but what kept the theatre alive was the share it had of the profits made by John Osborne's plays after they transferred from the Court to the West End and to America and when they were made into films.

In the financial year 1956-57 the deficit would have been £11,327 but for grants totalling £8,067 and an income of £8,505 from transfers, tours and the sale of auxiliary rights, which produced a surplus

[1] *Plays and Players*, November 1965.

of £5,245. In 1957–58 the income from these three sources (thanks to the scale of Osborne's success) was £39,631, so, even with a larger deficit on running the theatre (£20,448) and a smaller revenue from subsidies and donations (£6,917) the profit on the year's work was £26,100. The next five years each produced an overall deficit, but the reserves that had been accumulated kept the company solvent. Then in 1962–63, with the Labour government's new deal for the arts, the subsidy went up to £20,000, coming much closer to covering the operating deficit, while the ESC's new policy of co-producing certain plays with West End managements,[1] made it possible to cut down on some of the financial risks and to step up the chances of transferring a production by spending more on it.

Productions aimed at the West End would inevitably be less individual than productions conceived and developed with the Royal Court as their only goal. But the loss of independence was partly balanced by the possibility of influencing the West End. The number of transfers from the Royal Court during the early seventies is an index not only of how much the Court has changed but also of how much the West End has. If both its plays and audiences are very different from what they were in 1955, the changes, without being wholly due to the Court's influence, derive from a complex series of social and cultural developments which were both encouraged and reflected by the Court more clearly and more forcefully than by any other theatre. Even the cinema has altered in the same direction, and writers, directors and producers who established themselves at the Court were in the vanguard of the new movement. By the beginning of the sixties Oscar Lewenstein, John Osborne and Tony Richardson had formed a company called Woodfall Films which made *Tom Jones, Saturday Night and Sunday Morning, A Taste of Honey. The Loneliness of the Long Distance Runner, The Knack* and the films of *Look Back in Anger* and *The Entertainer*.

The generation that came intellectually of age in the early fifties was encouraged to believe that all great writers were reactionaries. Lionel Trilling's influential book *The Liberal Imagination*, which was published over here in 1951, argued that the pioneers of modern

[1] See pp. 122 and 124.

European literature were either indifferent or hostile to democratic liberalism – Yeats, Eliot, Proust, Joyce, Lawrence and Gide.[1] The Marxist argument (put most cogently by Lukacs) was that no one could write great literature except from a progressive viewpoint. But in 1954 England had no novelists, poets, or playwrights of any stature who were committed to Left Wing causes. Then from 1956 onwards the new voices that made themselves heard through the Court – John Osborne, John Arden, Arnold Wesker, Edward Bond and David Storey – were all passionately and explicitly Socialist.

Devine's original aims were in no way political. But in 1956 the Suez crisis and the Hungarian uprising provoked many of the writers, directors, actors and audiences who were gravitating towards the Court into a higher degree of social and political awareness. And after *Look Back in Anger* and *The Entertainer*, which brought Laurence Olivier to the Court in 1957, it was inevitable that these plays, which were both forthright in their expression of Left Wing views, should contribute to defining not only the image but also the character of the theatre, as it was rapidly becoming financially dependent on their success. Some of the young directors whom Devine employed, like Gaskill and Lindsay Anderson, were deeply and publicly committed to Left Wing causes, and after Devine's October 1956 production of Brecht's *The Good Woman of Setzuan* (the first Brecht production in England since the Berliner Ensemble's visit in the spring) other productions at the Court tended to become more Brechtian. Brecht has remained a powerful influence on style and policy at the Court. Edward Bond's *Lear* is one play that could never have been written, directed (by William Gaskill) or designed (by John Napier) in the way it was, but for the example of Brecht and the Berliner Ensemble.

Not that Devine allowed his catholic course to be narrowed by Brechtian didacticism. Nor has the choice or treatment of plays ever been partisan in the manner of the Berliner Ensemble. During its first fifteen years the ESC mounted over 250 plays, including 140 new plays. Altogether 130 very diverse playwrights had been represented. If there is a Royal Court style of writing it can be defined

[1] *The Liberal Imagination.* Secker, p. 301.

only very vaguely. The word 'humanistic' is sometimes used, and William Gaskill talks of a hostility to 'the over-studied and the hieratic'. Lindsay Anderson claims to see a 'strongly identifiable style', and he speaks of 'a whole movement of writers working in a style characterised in ethic by a kind of non-schematic progressive conscience and in its treatment of character by a passionate concern, sometimes fierce, sometimes tender, for the individual human being'.

It may be partly because the plays have been so heterogeneous that, in spite of the existence of the English Stage Society (a club whose members can attend Sunday night productions and semi-public dress-rehearsals), the Court has never succeeded in building up a reliable retinue of supporters confident that they will be interested in seeing more or less every play that is staged, irrespective of reviews and whether or not there are star names in the cast-list. From the beginning there was extreme audience oscillation between full houses for a star like Olivier and empty houses for a play like John Arden's *Serjeant Musgrave's Dance*. Ironically, a revival today with the same cast would probably do very good business, not because of the reputations that both Arden and the play have since acquired, but because of the popularity so many of the actors have acquired – Ian Bannen, Frank Finlay, Donal Donnelly, Alan Dobie, Colin Blakely and Stratford Johns. The same pattern prevails in box office business today. In 1969 for John Osborne's *Time Present* 82·5 per cent of the seats were full, and for *The Hotel in Amsterdam* (which had Paul Scofield in it) 98·4 per cent, but only 26 per cent for David Cregan's *The Houses by the Green* – and for *Life Price* by Michael O'Neill and Jeremy Seabrook, at first only 27 per cent of the seats were full – the takings being 14·4 per cent of the maximum. But when all seats were given away free, the theatre was full every night. If they were always free it could probably be full nearly all the time, but paying theatre-goers, even at the Court, still tend to spend their money on stars.

In 1970 Scofield came back to play in *Uncle Vanya*, which filled 98·1 per cent of the seats; the Madeleine Renaud season filled 83 per cent; Donald Howarth's *Three Months Gone* (with Diana Dors and Jill Bennett) 79·5 per cent and David Storey's *In Celebration* (with Alan Bates) 75 per cent; while *The Three Musketeers Ride Again* filled 30·7 per cent and Frank Norman's *Insideout* 40·7 per cent. In 1971 the best business was done by David Storey's *Home*, with John Gielgud and Ralph Richardson, which filled 92·7 per cent of the seats, but Christopher Hampton's *The Philanthropist* filled 88·8 per cent and Peter Barnes's adaptation of Wedekind's sex tragedy *Lulu* 86 per cent, while Heathcote Williams's highly praised *AC/DC* filled only 32 per cent and Mike Weller's *Cancer* 42 per cent.

Perhaps it might have been easier to build up a steady audience if it had been possible to realise Devine's original ideal of 'true repertory'. But repertory had to be abandoned within the first year. After he retired in the summer of 1965 a second attempt at it was made by the new artistic director, William Gaskill. With Keith Johnstone and Iain Cuthbertson as his associates, he launched the new season with Ann Jellicoe's *Shelley*, N. F. Simpson's *The Cresta Run* and Edward Bond's *Saved*, but the first two were very unsuccessful and repertoire was again abandoned. Even with successful plays it could only be feasible in a small theatre like the Court if the subsidy were enormous. There are now 401 seats, and with a maximum take of £440 per performance – it was £380 until prices were raised in June 1970 – the theatre cannot but depend largely on West End transfers. Both the contributions of independent producers involved in co-productions and the share of the West End gross have to be sacrificed in order to run plays in repertoire, for the actors are needed for other productions and therefore unable to transfer.

The abandonment of one of Devine's original aims made it easier to achieve the other – to stage and encourage new writing in the theatre. The permanent companies of actors that the ESC had for the repertoires of 1956 and 1965 were both much smaller than the permanent companies at the RSC and the National, and in 1965 William Gaskill found that the selection of plays was being limited by considerations of whether they could be cast adequately from the company. This is not giving priority to the writer, and in general the playwright's intentions can be more accurately served by *ad hoc* casting. Although the top salary in 1972 was £50, the Court can attract very good actors, and a great deal of care is taken over casting. Auditions are held for each new production. Even well-known actors who had previously worked at the Court may have to go through several bouts of re-auditioning. Plays that depend on particular physical types, like David Storey's *The Changing Room* (which is about a rugby team), probably come off better at the Court, despite the smallness of the stage, than they would at the RSC or the National, where the use of the permanent company would inevitably lead to approximation in some of the casting.

Certainly the two larger subsidised companies, for which the Court set the pattern and prepared the ground, have taken over some of its functions. During the period 1956–61, the Court was the natural habitat for plays by writers like Arthur Miller, Brecht, Beckett, Giraudoux, Max Frisch, Sean O'Casey, Genet and Albee. Since the middle sixties plays by all these writers have been staged at either the National or the RSC, and relatively few foreign plays are now produced at the Court.

Although Devine's original interest was in established writers who had not yet written for the theatre, it turned out to be easier to get good plays from new writers. Productions of plays by Brecht, Sartre and Miller could make points of contemporary social relevance, but native writers have made more impact on audiences at the Court. No other explosion shook the public quite as much as *Look Back in Anger*, but there were one or two loud bangs each year. In 1957 John Arden and N. F. Simpson were introduced, in 1958 Ann Jellicoe and Barry Reckord. At first the ESC rejected Arnold Wesker's work, but later brought it to London after John Dexter had persistently championed it and the Belgrade Theatre, Coventry, had made a success with it.[1] Donald Howarth was given a Sunday night production in 1958 and his first full-scale production in 1959. Alun Owen was staged for the first time on a Sunday evening in 1959, the year in which Willis Hall's first full-length play, *The Long and the Short and the Tall*, had its first London showing. Later in the year a play by Wole Soyinka, *The Invention*, had a Sunday night showing. In 1960 the poet Christopher Logue was given a chance as a playwright when a double bill, *Trials by Logue*, was staged. In 1961 *The Keep* by the novelist Gwyn Thomas, which had been tried out the previous year

[1] See Ronald Hayman, *Arnold Wesker*. Heinemann.

on a Sunday night, received a full-scale production. In 1962 Edward Bond's first play to be staged, *The Pope's Wedding*, appeared on a Sunday night. The years 1963 and 1964 were less remarkable for debuts by writers, but in 1965 a play by David Cregan, *Miniatures*, had a Sunday-night performance, and in 1966 one by Heathcote Williams, *The Local Stigmatic,* and one by Howard Brenton, *It's My Criminal.* In 1967 David Storey's *The Restoration of Arnold Middleton*, which had been seen at the Edinburgh Traverse, had a full-scale production, and in 1968 Michael Rosen's *Backbone* had a Sunday night production, followed three months later by a full-scale one.

The last few years have been very much less impressive for launching unproduced playwrights. One reason is that there are fewer Sunday night productions and another is that though the English theatre as a whole still has the same need for new playwrights, the ESC hasn't. As Oscar Lewenstein said after taking over as Artistic Director in 1972, 'The writers we started with were foreign writers, and we hoped to find English ones. Now we have a whole body of authors who have grown up with the Court and who are very actively writing. While they continue to offer us their plays, they'll continue to form the backbone to our work.' In 1975, when the National Theatre moves into its own building, if the ESC takes over the Old Vic without giving up the Royal Court, it will be able to mount twice as many full-scale productions. But with only about nine each year, the theatre is liable to be occupied for a lot of the time with plays by John Osborne, David Storey, Edward Bond, Donald Howarth, Arnold Wesker and Christopher Hampton – to name just six of the playwrights whose work was new to London when first mounted at the Court. It would be easier to do new work if a play could be put on for two or three weeks, but it is uneconomic to run it for less than six weeks, and even with a subsidy of £2,000 a week and a continuing income from West End transfers like *The Philanthropist*, the ESC only just managed to break even in 1971–72.

Increases in Sunday overtime rates for stage management and stage staff have now made Sunday night productions very expensive, and though they have not been altogether abandoned, they have become rarer. In 1968 the Royal Court opened its Theatre Upstairs, a studio theatre created out of a room which had previously been leased to Clement Freud, who ran it as a night-club. It was announced that productions in the Theatre Upstairs would largely replace Sunday Night Productions Without Décor. It ought to be a big advantage for the playwright to be able to see more than one performance of his play, and the fact of having a second auditorium ought to have opened the door to more débuts by new writers. But the function of finding new playwrights has effectively been channelled into a backwater. In effect, though not in intention, the main responsibility for it has been delegated to the ESC's Literary Manager and to the Artistic Director of the Theatre Upstairs, who has a smaller budget, less power, less contacts and less prestige than the Artistic Director of the ESC.

Though the new theatre is too small for large-cast plays, it should sometimes be possible to try out plays in it for a full-scale production downstairs, but whereas thirteen of the Sunday night productions during the first ten years led to full-scale productions – if not the same play then at least of work by the same playwright[1] – only two of the playwrights introduced by the Theatre Upstairs during the first five years of its life have subsequently been performed downstairs. E. A. Whitehead's play *The Foursome* was produced upstairs in 1971 and his *Alpha Beta* downstairs in 1972. And Harald Müller's *Big Wolf* was played upstairs by school children in 1971 and revived downstairs by professionals in 1972. On the other hand several plays created downstairs (like Barry Reckord's *Skyvers*, Ann Jellicoe's *The Sport of My Mad Mother* and John Arden's *Live Like Pigs*) have been revived upstairs. Altogether there has been disappointingly little exploration of work by new English playwrights except when the theatre has been handed over to visiting groups like the Freehold, Portable Theatre and the Traverse Theatre Workshop Company.

[1] John Arden, Keith Johnstone, N. F. Simpson, Donald Howarth, Wole Soyinka, Christopher Logue, Gwyn Thomas, Barry Reckord, Edward Bond, David Cregan, D. H. Lawrence, Heathcote Williams and Frederick Bland.

Many of the groups invited to the Theatre Upstairs – like Ken Campbell's Road Show and Keith Johnstone's Theatre Machine – do not perform plays or need scripts. And many of the productions initiated by the ESC in the Theatre Upstairs have been of plays by established American experimentalists like Sam Shepard and Tom Eyen, or foreign playwrights like Hugo Claus and Athol Fugard. Of course it is important that their work should be seen in England, but it is unfortunate if it is being allowed to squeeze English writers out of the available slots at the Theatre Upstairs. What is more unfortunate still is that productions there do not seem to be generating as much excitement or as much discussion as the old Sunday night productions downstairs. This is partly because the fire regulations in London are so stringent that it could never be opened to the general public. It is a club theatre which seems to be offering the same kind of product as a great many Fringe theatres – especially when it gives hospitality to groups which also appear elsewhere. It is inevitably competing with those of the Fringe groups which are looking for good new writers, but when about nine hundred scripts are submitted to the ESC each year, it seems very odd that so few interesting writers are found. Of all the writers introduced upstairs in the ESC's own productions, E. A. Whitehead and Howard Barker are the only two who have gone on to make reputations for themselves. Most of the British work to be staged has been by writers who had been introduced downstairs on Sunday nights – like Howard Brenton, Peter Gill and David Cregan, David Halliwell (whose *Little Malcolm and His Struggle Against the Eunuchs* had been presented by Codron in the West End) and Stanley Eveling (whose work has been staged at the Traverse and in the West End). There have been several plays by people connected with the Court, like Keith Johnstone, Peter Gill (who had directed several productions) Jonathan Hales (the Literary Manager) and Victor Henry (who has acted in several productions). There was an interesting play by a writer from Northern Ireland – *Within Two Shadows* by Wilson John Haire—but puzzlingly few interesting débuts by English playwrights.

.   .   .   .   .

It is possible that some good plays are being missed. Script-reading is a tedious and very difficult job: arguably the ESC has put payments to readers too low on its list of priorities. Until the beginning of 1971 they were paid a reading fee of 50p per script; now it is £1. There is a pool of seven or eight readers, appointed – usually for six months at a stretch – by the Literary Manager, Jonathan Hales. Some of them are potential playwrights, some potential directors, But if too little money is spent on script-reading, at least it cannot be said that too little time is taken. Plays are never rejected until they have been read by at least two people. Normally it takes five weeks for a script to be considered. The more seriously it is being considered, the longer it takes. But it is inevitable that the script readers do their work in a different spirit from the readers in the early years when there was a genuine and exciting chance that the work of an unknown writer could be rocketed into the theatre, if only for a Sunday night. Sometimes a script is read by as many as ten different people; this can take up to five months, but there are monthly meetings to discuss scripts which are being circulated, and Jonathan Hales has a list of over thirty writers with whom he wants to keep in touch, though none of their work has yet been performed.

But if the Theatre Upstairs was intended to take over the key function of presenting the work of new playwrights, the director of the Theatre Upstairs must be a key figure, and it must be extremely important to have the right man for the job. To pay him a reasonable salary ought to be a matter of high priority. But in the year 1970–71 when £77,001 was taken at the box office, when a subsidy of £89,000 was received from the Arts Council, and when £38,029 was earned from transfers, films and royalties, the director of the Theatre Upstairs received a salary of £770 (plus a payment for six weeks when the theatre was dark). The spending on publicity and programmes was £12,515; the three artistic directors were paid £12,150, and the salaries for artists throughout the year totalled £19,140. The salaries of stage management and technical staff amounted to £17,809, those of the managerial and publicity staff to £12,022, and those of the front of house staff to £9,497. Clearly no one was overpaid, but if the actors were underpaid, the director of the Theatre Upstairs and the script readers fared worse still.

The annual cost of the permanent staff adds up to more than fifty thousand pounds, which seems high in relation to the £4,500 budget for each production: £1,500 for the set and stage properties; £600 for the actors' rehearsal salaries; £500 for cartage and staff overtime on fit-up and get-in; £400 for the director, designer and lighting designer; £515 for wardrobe materials and wages for the wardrobe staff; £275 for the stage management's and the production assistant's rehearsal salaries. In 1970–71 playing salaries for actors were budgeted at £26,000 (£500 per week), though only £19,140 was paid out. The average takings per production for the two years 1969–70 and 1970–71 were £6,530.

Even with well over a hundred thousand pounds from the Arts Council, the theatre is still arguably undersubsidised and it becomes almost impossible to explain how George Devine managed to find so many new writers and take so many risks on producing their work when his annual subsidy was only five or seven or eight thousand pounds. Had he been less of a theatrical patriarch, less authoritative or less fully committed, he could never have achieved what he did. William Gaskill had four years as sole Artistic Director from 1965 to 1969, but he then formed a triumvirate with Lindsay Anderson and Anthony Page. The artistic direction of a theatre involves a great deal of administration and planning. As Anthony Page put it, it is 'too much for one director to handle if he is to continue his own career as a director'. From October 1969 till August 1972, when Oscar Lewenstein took over as Artistic Director, the theatre was controlled either by the triumvirate or by one of the three, with the other two as his associates. And in 1970 Peter Gill was recruited as another associate.

It is unusual for a man whose experience has been in theatrical management to be appointed as an artistic director. There are some advantages in his not being a director or an actor: there is no danger that other directors or other actors will think he is offering them only the productions or the parts he does not want himself. But Lewenstein, who has been on the ESC's Council since 1956 and chaired it from 1969 to 1972, works mainly through committees and apparently his tendency on taking over the artistic helm was to be wary of making decisions without strong support from his three associate directors and his 'Artistic Committee'.

Lindsay Anderson and Anthony Page have remained on as associates, and the third, appointed by Lewenstein, is Albert Finney. Each of them is committed to directing one play each year and receives a small retainer. Otherwise no payment is made to the Artistic Committee, which consists of Jocelyn Herbert, David Storey and the three associates. They meet about once a month to advise Lewenstein on the choice of plays and on other matters of artistic policy. The Resident Dramatist (who receives a retainer and is committed to offering the ESC one full-length play each year) is also available to give advice.

It is too early to judge whether Lewenstein will be able to give the ESC the leadership it needs and to make the best possible use of the two theatres it will have if it takes over the Old Vic in 1975. Certainly this would provide a splendid opportunity to make a fresh start and to regain some of the momentum that was being lost even before George Devine retired. No one can run a new theatre for nine years without some loss of impetus, and the responsibility of running it for the next seven years was all the more unenviable because of the success he achieved at the outset. If Lewenstein is to make the most of the next period in the history of the ESC, he will have to reconsider the company's priorities. Even with two full-scale theatres and a studio theatre the number of productions would be limited, and the most important policy question of all is how to divide them between the established playwrights who were new when their plays were first staged at the Court and playwrights who are new now. In 1965 an interviewer asked William Gaskill whether his intention was to go on producing foreign authors like Ionesco and Genet at the Court. His reply was 'One doesn't have a duty to put on Ionesco as he is already established.' John Osborne, Edward Bond and David Storey are also established, but Lewenstein clearly has no intention of refusing to stage their plays for that reason. This is understandable; what is unjust is that many of the plays which are accepted would have been rejected had they been submitted under a pseudonym. It would be unreasonable to argue that the ESC should stage nothing but plays by new writers. But with two and a half theatres in hand, it would be unreasonable not to spend more energy and more money first of all on looking for new playwrights, then on launching them, then on helping them to develop.

8 THE MERMAID

The idea for the Mermaid dates back to the forties, when Bernard
Miles moved into a St John's Wood house which had once been a
school. In the back garden was an old wooden building, sixty feet by
thirty, which had been the classroom where the Christmas plays had
been staged. For some time he toyed with the idea of making it into
a miniature theatre, and, spurred on by Kirsten Flagstad's offer to sing
in it if ever he did, he made up his mind to have it ready for the 1951
Festival of Britain. A trestled Elizabethan stage was built, with a
curtained gallery, and two hundred seats were installed in the auditorium. On a Sunday night in September 1951, Flagstad sang in the
opening performance of Purcell's *Dido and Aeneas*. During the four-
week season that followed she sang in the tiny theatre twenty times,
and there were twenty performances of *The Tempest*. In 1952 there
was a six-week season during which the Lord Mayor of London
suggested that the small Elizabethan stage should be transported into
the City for the Coronation festivities of 1952. It was set up on the
Piazza of the Royal Exchange for a thirteen-week season which
included performances of *Dido and Aeneas, Macbeth, As You Like It*
and *Eastward Ho!* After seventy thousand people had bought tickets,
Miles considered he had evidence that a theatre was needed in the
City, which had not had one since the seventeenth century.

There was a bombed site in Upper Thames Street adjoining
Puddle Dock, and in October 1956 Miles was granted a lease at a
peppercorn rent. With a flair for showmanship that bordered on
genius, with persistence, energy, charm and an irresistible sense of
humour, he set about collecting the money. Within nine months
enough had been raised for the building to begin. Fund-raising

continued with a series of well-planned events that brought publicity and goodwill as well as money. For the two-week Buy a Brick Campaign, Miles had popular actors like Laurence Olivier selling bricks at half a crown each. Six thousand bricks were sold. Or people could have their names built into the foundations of the new theatre by paying half a crown to write it on a piece of paper to be dropped into a chest which would be buried. When the roof was finished a 'roof-warming party' was held and twenty Tiller Girls ran a relay from Drury Lane to the building site with a lighted torch. Meanwhile, exploiting the local patriotism of people involved in City finances, Miles was raising much larger sums of money from trusts, foundations, City Livery Companies, banks, businesses and insurance companies.

During this time, he had turned against the idea of an Elizabethan-type stage. In an article he contributed to *Encore*,[1] under the title 'Stray thoughts of an Ageing Character Actor', he wrote, 'I am sure that not enough attention had been given to the horizontal levels at which stage and auditorium meet. Sitting in the front row of the stalls with your face up against a four-foot wall is no way to see a play ... The perfect theatre is a wedge-shaped slice of a Greek amphitheatre, with twelve-inch rises and the lowest possible platform for acting, say six or nine inches.'

The Mermaid, which cost only £107,000, was designed by Elidir Davies, with a stage forty-eight feet wide and twenty-eight feet deep, raised twelve inches off the floor. The auditorium has nineteen rows of seats, with plenty of leg-room for each row, but with no one sitting more than sixty-five feet from the stage. Miles also realised the importance of making the audience comfortable outside the auditorium. The bar is in the main foyer, so the interval crowd around it is not cramped within four walls. There is another bar which serves coffee and snacks; there are two riverside restaurants, both open for lunch and dinner before, during or after the show. Not only do these contribute £12,000 a year towards the cost of running the theatre, they make people feel welcome inside the building at all times of the day. Similarly, the practice of holding art exhibitions, film shows and Sunday concerts in the theatre, as well as letting it for conferences and

[1] Vol. V No. 2, July–August 1958.

fashion shows, has brought people inside the building, many of whom would never have come there if nothing had been going on except plays.

In his article in *Encore* Bernard Miles complained of the anonymity of most London theatres. 'Who is the host at the party?' At the Mermaid he is the host, and he is an extremely good one. He has created a welcoming atmosphere and, as with the old actor–managers, you feel that you are in his hands – and sometimes in the hands of his family. He has directed sixteen plays himself, one as a co-production with his wife, Josephine Wilson, who has directed three independently. Sally Miles, his daughter, has directed seven, and Gerald Frow, his son-in-law, has written one play for the main programme, collaborated on a compilation of Noël Coward and on an adaptation of *Gulliver's Travels*, and has scripted several shows for the Molecule Club, a scheme for using theatre to help children to understand science. This use of the family, by underlining the personal nature of Bernard Miles's host relationship to his audiences, contributes to the friendliness of the ambiance, but all this time there were directors available who could have done more exciting work on the stage. Bernard Miles has all the qualities needed to bring a theatre into existence and all the qualities of a good theatrical host, but less than one might wish of the qualities of a good artistic director.

His idea about what sort of theatre he wanted had been clearly and carefully thought out; his ideas about what he wanted to do in it were considerably less definite. His own formulation of his two objectives was: (1) to give a bird's-eye view of the world's drama in ten years, and (2) to bridge the gap between highbrow and lowbrow by way of understandability. If (1) implies a serious attempt to give a sampling of all the most important chapters in the history of world drama, it has to be reported that the book has been dipped into cursorily and quite unsystematically. If 'highbrow' and 'lowbrow' refer to cultures, it is unlikely that one theatre could do much towards bridging the gap between them; if they refer to plays, they are not very useful labels. Nor has the Mermaid done much towards making plays that might be called 'highbrow' more popular or more comprehensible.

Later, writing in *The Director*[1], Bernard Miles described the

[1] January 1961.

Mermaid as 'a repertory theatre presenting for short runs plays that would never be put on by commercial managements but which nevertheless deserve to be seen, neglected English classics, foreign plays in translation, promising new plays and so on.'

When the theatre opened it was £51,000 in debt. But the first production *Lock Up Your Daughters* (a musical based on Fielding's play *Rape upon Rape*) transferred to the West End and ran for nine months. However, only seventeen of the sixty-seven productions mounted in the first seven years made a profit. Without transferring it was impossible to make more than £250 a week, even with full houses; poor box-office business could involve a loss of £1500 a week.

The Trojan Wars – two double-bills of Euripides translated by Jack Lindsay and presented in Prussian uniforms of World War I – won the description 'Pop Tragedy in battledress' from the *Daily Mail*; *Henry V* has also been staged in battledress; and plays by Dryden and Vanbrugh have been made into musicals. But like most of the Mermaid's plays these are less highbrow than middlebrow. Shaw has been the most favoured playwright, with sixteen productions of his work, including two double-bills. There have been five O'Casey productions and five original productions of Shakespeare (plus two by a touring company). Apart from four plays by Bill Naughton (*All in Good Time, Alfie, Spring and Port Wine* and *He Was Gone When They Got There*, very few new plays by new writers have been staged. The only other new writer 'discovered' by the Mermaid who was subsequently successful was Spike Milligan, whose play *The Bed Sitting Room* started its life there. Peter Dews's production of Peter Luke's *Hadrian VII* came to the Mermaid from Birmingham.

The Mermaid presented the first English productions of two Brecht plays: *Galileo* (directed by Bernard Miles who also played Galileo) and *Schweyk in the Second World War* (directed by Frank Dunlop). Arden's *Left-Handed Liberty* was directed by David William, and we have been given two Robert Lowell plays, several rarely-produced Elizabethan and Jacobean plays, two plays by Camus, the Living Theatre's *The Brig*, a production of R. C. Sherriff's *Journey's End* by the 69 Theatre Company from Manchester, two Henry

James plays, a Pirandello, a Lessing, a Molière double-bill, an adaptation by William Trevor of his novel *The Old Boys*, a revival of Pinter's *The Caretaker*, and a production by Harold Pinter of James Joyce's *Exiles*, which was subsequently taken into the RSC repertoire with some of the same cast. A few of these (like *Schweyk, Hadrian VII Left-Handed Liberty* and *Exiles*) have been worthwhile plays in worthwhile productions. Many of them (like *Galileo* and *The Old Boys*) were worthwhile plays in very bad productions, and many of them (like the two Camus (*The Possessed* and *The Price of Justice*) and the two Lowell (*Benito Cereno* and *Prometheus Bound*) were bad plays by important writers.

However quirky the choice of plays and however variable the standard of production, the Mermaid has succeeded better than any other London theatre in building up an audience of its own. People keep going back there because they like going there, whatever the play, whoever is in it, however it is produced. Judged on the basis of a ratio between the size of the Arts Council subsidy and the number of tickets sold, the Mermaid would seem to be earning its keep better than any other subsidised theatre in London. The Arts Council grants have mostly been between 25 per cent and 45 per cent of what the Royal Court has received. In 1964–65 it was £9,325 to the Court's £32,500; in 1968–69 it was £26,500 to the Court's £94,000; in 1971–72 £44,000 to the Court's £99,596. The Mermaid has 498 seats and in 1970–71 some 95,180 tickets were sold at the box office for £82,898. So each ticket sold was subsidised with 46p of Arts Council money plus 6p from the local authority. (During 1968–69, when the Mermaid's Arts Council subsidy had been only 2s. 4d. per ticket, the National's had been 18s. 9d. and the ESC's £1 0s. 9d.) On the basis of this disparity it would be possible to argue either that the Mermaid deserves a much higher subsidy or that it should not be subsidised at all, when its popularity proves that its orientation is more commercial than that of the other subsidised theatres. This raises the question of whether the Arts Council should be devoting its resources to theatres which set out to achieve a high artistic standard in the production of plays which could never appeal to more than a minority of theatre-goers, or to helping theatres which can help themselves by putting on plays with a strong box-office appeal and by working hard to exploit the building with amenities and events that will attract the public and make profits at all hours of the day. This is a question I will try to answer in the chapter on the Arts Council.

9 THE REGIONS VERSUS LONDON

In 1969, when there was a discussion at the Victoria Theatre, Stoke-on-Trent, following a programme of local documentaries, the question was raised of whether it was worth while even trying to keəp a permanent company together in a provincial theatre. Wasn't inevitable that the best actors would drift away to London, to the West End theatre, or television or films? The answer (which was given by an actor who is now working in London himself) was that for years London had been robbing the regions of talent and then corrupting it; that the Arts Council was joining in the conspiracy of preserving London's priority; that it was necessary for the regional theatres to fight back.

Even if complete decentralisation were possible, it would not be healthy for our theatre as a whole. The organism has to have a centre from which the blood flows and to which it returns. And whereas films and television programmes can be made available simultaneously all over the country, a theatrical performance cannot be multiplied. It can only be repeated by the original company or copied by touring companies. But if it is natural for talent to gravitate to the centre of the system, it is equally natural for this to be resented by people who live a long way away from it, especially now, when every taxpayer is contributing to the cost of our theatre. Why should Londoners get better value for their money than Northerners or West Countrymen?

Until the eighteenth century there were no theatres outside London. In medieval times many of the bigger towns were no worse off than London for performances of either religious or secular plays, whether presented by the church, the town guilds or strolling groups of minstrels and players. In Elizabethan England there were plenty of wandering groups, and during the summer, when the London theatres were closed, actors from them would tour the countryside, playing in inn-yards, halls and barns. Interrupted by the Civil War and the Puritan Interregnum, touring activity resumed and developed after the Restoration. It also became more organised, and the circuit system evolved as touring companies habitually revisited the towns where they had done well. Traditionally companies had been known by the names of their noble patron, but in the 1720s many of them took the name of the town in which they had established their headquarters.

Meanwhile provincial theatre-building had already begun – at Bath in 1705 – and by the end of the century there were also theatres at Bristol, York, Ipswich, Birmingham, Norwich, Manchester, Liverpool, Chester, Hull, Richmond (in Yorkshire), Brighton, Windsor and Margate. Some of these were legalised by royal patents, others by the 1788 Act which gave local Justices of the Peace the power to license provincial players for sixty days at a time. But theatrical performances were regulated by the law and the law was centred in the capital.

In most European countries, the initiative for the development of provincial theatres came from public authorities, national or regional, but in nineteenth-century England the new theatre buildings were privately owned. Some of them were used regularly by circuit companies; others were active only during the London theatres' summer recess, when troupes of actors from Covent Garden, Drury Lane and the minor theatres needed work elsewhere. The provincial theatres were also used by the profession as the natural places to obtain the training and the experience that might lead to London engagements. But the provinces were not starved at this time of star performances. Most of the important actors of the period made appearances with the circuit companies, which thrived in the late eighteenth and early nineteenth centuries. The system of hiring star actors from London started in the 1790s. To protect the interests of leading actors in the resident companies, who did not like being relegated to supporting roles, some provincial theatres tried to do without stars, but public demand for them was on the increase and so, consequently, were the salaries they could command.

In the rivalry that was to continue throughout most of the nineteenth century between touring companies and stock companies (as the resident companies came to be called) the box-office appeal of the stars – who could tour lucratively – helped to weight the balance against the stock companies. These were almost extinct by the end of the century, which meant that the provincial theatres had lost all chance of establishing independence from London. Supporting actors in the tours had no opportunity of striking roots in any local community and very little chance to develop as actors: instead of gaining experience in different roles they went on playing the same role in different towns, while the productions were modelled unambitiously on the ones that had succeeded in London. The companies were mere satellites revolving around the capital in profitable circles. Most of the theatres built in the latter half of the nineteenth century, therefore, were touring theatres. By 1900 there were over fifty of them in existence, as well as about five hundred music halls.

As the twentieth-century repertory movement developed out of the old stock system, it gave the provinces a greater measure of autonomy, though it was itself modelled on London repertory. From 1904 to 1907, John Vedrenne and Harley Granville-Barker presented a repertoire of plays at the Court including many of Shaw's, and Barker's own *The Voysey Inheritance*, together with plays by Euripides, Ibsen, Maeterlinck, Hauptmann, Schnitzler and Galsworthy. The concept of the seasons owed something to J. T. Grein, a drama critic, who founded the Independent Theatre in 1891 to produce plays of literary and artistic value, and in 1892 produced *Widowers' Houses*, the first Shaw play to be seen in London. And it was Barker's lack of commercial success at the Court which made him become the first important champion in this country of the cause of subsidised theatre.

Meanwhile Annie Horniman, the daughter of a rich tea-merchant, had been deeply impressed, while travelling on the Continent, by the subsidised repertory theatres in Germany. In 1894 she herself secretly subsidised Florence Farr's season at the Avenue Theatre on the

Embankment. The season included *Arms and the Man*, the first Shaw play to have a public performance, and *The Land of Heart's Desire* by W. B. Yeats, whose unpaid private secretary Annie Horniman subsequently became. In 1903 she spent £13,000 on buying the Mechanics' Institute Hall in Dublin and rebuilding it as the Abbey Theatre, and in 1907 she bought the Gaiety Theatre in Manchester, converted it into the first English repertory theatre and subsidised it when it opened in 1908. Of the first two hundred-odd plays that were staged, over a hundred were new. Her main interest in theatre was as a means of edifying a community, and she was responsible for the birth of a new local realism in the playwrights of the so-called Manchester School. Harold Brighouse (who wrote *Hobson's Choice*) and Stanley Houghton (who wrote *Hindle Wakes*) were the most important.

The second English repertory theatre was opened in 1911 in Liverpool, where a music hall in Williamson Square was converted. The first director was Basil Dean, who had been an actor in the company at the Gaiety for four years. The new repertory theatre at Liverpool was the first to be founded by shareholders, who wanted to make their town independent of London-based tours.

The origins of the Birmingham Repertory Theatre were very different: it grew out of amateur theatricals in the home of a young man whose family had become rich in the margarine business. After training as an architect, Barry Jackson abandoned his career to devote himself to theatre. In 1907, when he was twenty-eight, he formed a group called the Pilgrim Players which put on twenty-eight productions in local halls, and turned professional in 1913, when he built the theatre in Station Street, the first theatre in England to be designed specifically for repertory. He had only 450 seats to fill in a city with over a million inhabitants but, though he had high standards both in his selection of plays and in the productions he gave them, he lost £100,000 of his own money. In 1934 a public appeal was launched for £20,000. Birmingham is a very rich city, but only £3,000 was raised. In 1935, when he handed the theatre over to a local trust, it became the first civic repertory in England.

The early growth of our repertory movement was interrupted by the 1914–18 war and continued only desultorily after it. Good companies were started during the twenties at Oxford, Hull and Cambridge, though none of these survived for long. But more were founded in the thirties, and by 1939 there were about fifty repertory theatres in England, though very few had high standards. Most companies had weekly changes of programme and many had twice-nightly performances. Hardly any had suitable buildings: the majority were housed in touring theatres with no space backstage for making or storing scenery. These would usually be too large and insufficiently intimate, mostly with orchestra pits and stages large enough for a musical. The auditorium would often seat between 1,800 and 2,500 people, whereas 500 to 850 seats would have been enough for a rep. Nor did the existence of these reps diminish the hegemony of London, since most of them tried to fill the empty seats by producing West End comedies and thrillers as soon as the London managements released them.

Regional audiences usually have a long wait, because the managements which have bought the exclusive right to produce a new play naturally want to exploit their property to the full. Since visitors from the provinces constitute a substantial percentage of West End audiences, it would be throwing business away to let a play be staged by repertory companies while it is still running in the West End. And for a management that is sending out a post-London tour, a repertory production could be direct competition. At the same time it has to be acknowledged that there are towns like Salisbury and Exeter which have reps but no touring theatres, so a management would lose nothing by releasing a play to selected reps immediately it finishes its West End run. It would obviously be more complicated to give some towns preference over others, but it could be done. Current practice is generally based on principles that were evolved when there was much more touring than there is now, and certain revisions could well be made.

Pre-London tours today are much rarer than they used to be. Managements can no longer afford to use audiences as guinea-pigs for eight or ten weeks in the touring theatres of Bradford, Hull, Nottingham and other cities, while making adjustments to script, production and performances. They have now come to depend more on reduced-price previews in London for 'running the play in', and when there is a pre-London tour it is often only for two weeks – usually at Brighton and one other date. Post-London tours are longer but much rarer. Altogether touring has dwindled almost to vanishing point, but then it has been declining steadily ever since films began to bulk large in our leisure life. From about 1910 onwards, Victorian and Edwardian touring theatres all over the country were being converted into cinemas. Between the two world wars over a hundred and fifty theatres were either closed or made into cinemas or music halls. Before the 1939 war began, there were about a hundred and thirty touring theatres; now there are about thirty. Some have been made into reps. The Cheltenham Opera House, a 750-seat Victorian theatre, which was latterly in spasmodic use for rep seasons, closed in 1959 and reopened a few months later as the Everyman, controlled now by a non-profit-distributing company which could apply for rate reductions and subsidies and did not have to pay income tax (or Selective Employment Tax, when this was later introduced). Approximately half of the surviving thirty touring theatres belong to local councils and half to private companies. Not all of them are in use all the time as theatres: some are used for Bingo; some are left dark except during the pantomime season. Howard and Wyndham, the company which owned most of the biggest and best, has sold some of them to municipalities and would willingly sell more, but it is not always easy to agree on the extent to which the current unprofit-ability of the theatres affects their value. A town council has the power to prevent the property from being developed in any other way, but is under no obligation to compensate the owners for the loss of potential commercial value or even to take this into account when negotiating to buy.

Different town councils have solved the problem in different ways. Some have bought the theatre, some taken a lease on it. Some have set up a non-profit-distributing trust to control the theatre. Some, like Norwich Corporation, control it directly. Other municipalities, like Hull and Sunderland, have guaranteed their theatres against loss. As soon as a theatre is taken over by the municipal authority it acquires charitable status as a non-profit-distributing body. So it no longer has to pay income tax, and its rates are halved. As it comes to belong, theoretically, to the local community, it is more likely to become a focus of local life.

The whole history of regional theatre could be seen in terms of a tug-of-war between resident companies (whether stock or repertory) and the touring system. In Bristol today the touring theatre, the Hippodrome, is still the rival of the Old Vic; in Oxford the Playhouse, the home of the rep, is the rival of the New. There may be some people who go to one theatre one week and the other the next, according to what is playing, but most theatregoers develop a basic preference for one sort of show or the other. The attraction of a tour is that it often has a starrier cast and a more lavish production than would be viable if the show were scheduled for a life-span of only two or three or four weeks. On the other hand a repertory production can be purpose-built for the local community, and the actors can develop a relationship with the local audience, which gets to know them by seeing them in a succession of different roles. Companies in the new civic centres have tended to foster this relationship by giving members of the audience opportunities to meet the actors personally and discuss the plays. One problem involved here is that of time. The schedule is always a tight one and the more social events there are, the less time there is for rehearsing and learning lines.

At some periods of regional theatre history, touring has been in the ascendant; at others stock or repertory companies. Currently rep is in by far the stronger position, mainly because of the help that the Arts Council has given it. Not that it was the Arts Council's aim to damage any part of the regional theatre, but, just as in London it has been prevented by its constitution from assisting companies which can make profits that would be distributed to backers or shareholders, it held back – until recently – from subsidising tours sent out by these managements. Meanwhile many unsubsidised reps which would formerly have been classified as 'commercial' were able to reconstitute themselves on a 'non-commercial' basis when subsidy became available.

Thanks largely to Arts Council's new policy of contributing to building costs, nearly half the forty-odd reps have new buildings. The touring system has meanwhile had to sustain the crippling combination of subsidised competition, continued dependence on antiquated and deteriorating buildings, rising costs and the growing reluctance of successful actors to spend time away from London. An index of the change is that theatrical digs have practically disappeared.

So very few tours are being sent out today that the municipal authorities which have taken over responsibility for large local theatres are finding it extremely hard to book attractions for them. The situation is anomalous because the Arts Council, which cannot subsidise the managements that could send out tours, can be called upon to assist the theatres which have been transformed into charitable and non-profit-distributing bodies and which are suffering from the scarcity of tours. It would obviously be a mistake not to keep the old theatres alive. Many of them are ugly, shabby and difficult to heat, but the new repertory theatres are mostly too small for operas, ballets, musicals and the spectacular shows which are so popular with regional visitors to the West End and which ought to go on being available outside the West End. In its report *The Theatre Today* (1970) the committee appointed by the Arts Council recommended local authorities to spend money on renovating theatres they take over and even on making structural alterations.

It is no use expecting a public which has forsaken a tatty and dingy old building to resume its patronage unless the theatre is refurbished and provided with such amenities as a spacious foyer, comfortable seats, easily accessible cloak-rooms and bars and food-counters, a good sized booking-space instead of a little box in the wall, plenty of well-kept loos. On top of this, few of these old theatres have had a coat of paint, inside or out, for years, and their heating and ventilation are usually obsolete. It is equally important that back-stage facilities should also be radically reconditioned if the co-operation of actors is to be won back in the rehabilitation of touring.

But the more money municipalities spend in this way, the more likely they are to turn to the Arts Council for help, and the more necessary it becomes to justify the infusion of taxpayers' and rate-payers' money by stimulating touring activity so that the theatres can be filled.

The National Theatre, the RSC, the Royal Opera and Sadler's Wells Opera are all doing less touring than formerly. There are other sub-sidised ballet and opera companies whose primary object is to tour—the Festival Ballet, the Ballet Rambert, the D'Oyly Carte, the Scottish Opera, the Welsh National Opera Company and the English Opera Group. In the large regional cities these have often done as well at the box office as the bigger, London-based companies. There are also three subsidised theatre companies which tour. Neither has a theatre of its own.[1] Prospect Theatre Company was started in 1963 by Toby Robertson, Iain Mackintosh and Richard Cottrell. Since 1968 the Arts Council has provided most of its subsidy, and in 1973 the British Council began to champion it, sending it on a Mediterranean tour of summer festivals with three productions, including *Pericles*, made almost into a musical. Ian McKellen, who starred in Prospect's *Richard II* (1968) and *Edward II* (1969), formed the Actors' Company. In 1972 and again in 1973 its appearances at the Edinburgh Festival were followed by three months of touring. Richard Cottrell left Prospect to form the Cambridge Theatre Company, which has also done some touring since 1970. There is also a department of the Arts Council known as DALTA (Dramatic and Lyric Theatres Association) which exists to co-ordinate touring by the available companies, but there are not nearly enough of them to supply the theatres that depend on tours, even though DALTA, against all the Arts Council's principles, is now beginning to work in conjunction with commerical managements over touring productions.

Equity has proposed a scheme by which six new companies would be formed and based in existing theatres from which they would tour

[1] The Meadow Players, the company at the Oxford Playhouse, used to tour, but by refusing to continue its subsidy on an adequate level, the Arts Council has now forced it to close. The final season of the Meadow Players was given at Oxford in the summer of 1973.

three or four of the other 'No. 1' theatres in their area. A circuit of twenty-five to thirty theatres could be kept alive in this way, but the Arts Council, which would have to finance the scheme, has argued that it cannot afford to maintain so many theatres. Its own Theatre Enquiry committee put forward a more modest proposal in *The Theatre Today*, listing a dozen theatres in Britain, nine of which were already municipally owned, as being of 'paramount' importance and suggesting that they could provide an adequate circuit for visits by touring companies. 'In terms of the product likely to be available, however, we find it difficult to believe that it could supply enough productions of quality for more than a dozen No. 1 theatres.' The dozen selected for the 'Paramount List' were the Alexandra, Birmingham; the Theatre Royal, Brighton; the Bristol Hippodrome; the New Theatre, Cardiff; the King's, Edinburgh and the King's, Glasgow; the Grand, Leeds; the Royal Court or the Empire in Liverpool; the Opera House or the Palace in Manchester; the Theatre Royal, Newcastle; the Theatre Royal, Norwich; and the Oxford New. Only nine of these are in England and the selection also ignores the existence of resident repertory companies which would compete with six of the nine touring theatres, while large areas, especially in the south-west, would still be left completely theatreless. In any case the question of how even these theatres could be kept supplied with 'product' remains unanswered. The Equity suggestion is more sensible, and it would be feasible if neighbouring local councils would co-operate to set up trusts to finance the new companies. Of course it would be difficult to bring as many as six into existence, and even six would not be enough to fill twenty-five to thirty theatres all through the year. Nor could casting by the new companies be as starry as that of London-based tours. The majority of the regional audience would probably prefer a mixed diet of home-grown products and starry London shows alternating in the same theatres. Ideally (if only the Arts Council could revise its principles) it should also subsidise the London managements to send out enough tours to keep each of these twenty-five to thirty theatres busy when the new regional companies were playing elsewhere.

Unquestionably new companies are needed. It is sometimes proposed that the larger reps should send out tours, but they could not serve the immediate locality so well if they had to diffuse their resources over a wider area. The rep at Lincoln used to have two companies, which alternated between playing at the Theatre Royal and touring to Scunthorpe, Rotherham and Loughborough, but when Philip Hedley was director there in the late sixties, he abandoned the touring in order to concentrate on the relationship with the local community. Other reps have experimented with tours to outlying districts, but many have given up, trying instead to encourage organised coach parties to come in from the surrounding towns, offering substantial reductions in ticket-prices and (with the Arts Council's help) subsidising the cost of transport. There was one year in which the rep at Northampton used £400 of Arts Council money to bring 8,500 people to the theatre, increasing takings by £1,600.

But a feeling of dependence on money that comes from London is almost as dangerous as dependence on productions that come from London. It will be much better if more local money can be raised for theatre from both public and private sources. As the Regional Arts Associations take over more responsibility, perhaps local authorities will contribute more generously. This question of where the money comes from is inseparable from the question of what kind of show it pays for, and while there can be no immediate prospect of cutting out all dependence on London, a process has already been started by which a better balance may be achieved.

10 REPERTORY

*A theatre must create its own work otherwise it
cannot discover its own identity – it has no identity
if it has made no truly important decisions of its
own.* PETER CHEESEMAN

In theory all the forty-five subsidised reps in England are uncommercial. In practice some are much more commercial than others in their orientation – in the way they are run, in the priority given to box-office appeal and to considerations of transfer possibilities: not only new plays but also revivals may be selected and cast and produced with one eye cocked calculatingly on the West End. The old battle of the regions versus London is by no means over. But there is now a good deal of regional theatre for regional theatre's sake.

Some theatres start their lives with a definite policy. After the money for the Bolton Octagon had been raised, mostly locally, and the theatre opened in 1967, the brochure contained a statement: 'We are intending to appoint a playwright and a musical director so that we can create our own plays in much the same way as Joan Littlewood was doing at Stratford East during the nineteen fifties.' She also served as a model for Philip Hedley when he was director of the rep at Lincoln in the late sixties. He had trained at the East Fifteen Acting School and he picked many of his actors from its graduates. Like Joan Littlewood he spent a large proportion of his rehearsal time doing improvisations into which mime, song and dance were introduced, and he never blocked moves in advance. In Colchester, when the Mercury Theatre opened in 1972, it was said that the hexagonal shape of both the stage and the auditorium would help to create new audiences and new tastes, but that it was unlikely to become an *avant-garde* theatre because it served a country town and the surrounding rural area.

At the Yvonne Arnaud, Guildford, which opened in 1964, the aim is to provide a local alternative to an evening in the West End, which is only half an hour away by train. There is no permanent company, casting is as starry as possible, and revivals of Maugham, Coward and Priestley are characteristic of the programme planning. The policy at Stoke-on-Trent could hardly be more different, depending as it does on a permanent company and on staging just about as many new plays as old ones. Most of the new plays are created specially for the theatre.

Some reps (like Harrogate) are still accommodated in Victorian touring theatres or (like Salisbury) in converted church halls or (like Hornchurch) in converted cinemas, while many have brand new buildings. They vary in size from 167 seats (the Castle Theatre, Farnham, shortly to be replaced by a new building) to over a thousand (like the new theatre at Sheffield), and in shape from proscenium to in-the-round. All are controlled, nominally, by boards of directors, but some boards do very little beyond making the key appointments – director, general manager and so on. Here too there is no common pattern. Usually the Director of Productions or Artistic Director is in a superior position to the General Manager or Administrator; sometimes, as at the Thorndike, Leatherhead, the theatre and its artistic policy are controlled by an Administrator, who engages a series of directors. Sometimes the policy is conservative, commercial and designed to attract a middle-aged to elderly middle-class audience; sometimes it is experimental and likely to appeal to a younger or more mixed audience. Most reps now change their programmes fortnightly, but a few do it at three- or four-weekly intervals or run in repertoire. Some have permanent companies; some cast each play separately from London.

The usual assumption behind programme planning is that the town determines the theatre's policy. Generalisations are made like 'You can't do Orton in Bournemouth', or 'Northampton people don't like Pinter', and cases are quoted of an unsuccessful production which may have been unsuccessful because the previous productions in the season or in previous seasons had built up a particular kind of audience and a particular kind of audience expectation. Of course locality is a factor: Peter Cheeseman's concentration on local sources, effective at Stoke-on-Trent, would not work for audiences of holiday makers at Folkestone, and the commercial policy which is so successful in Guildford would not be in a university-dominated city like Cambridge. But it has been estimated that given a town with a population of half a million, 1·6 per cent will come to the theatre, and which 1·6 per cent you get will depend mainly on the policy, publicity and position in the town. One cannot discount altogether the existence of theatre-going habits in the town, but habits can be changed, particularly when there is a young population. In 1963 most people would have said that no audience could be found in Liverpool for a rep that was going to base its programme on Shakespeare, Beckett, Genet, Arrabal, Osborne, and other playwrights of comparable intellectual calibre. But the Everyman opened there in 1964 and survived. In fact, once, when the board of directors forced a pot-boiler into the programme, it did the worst business of the season.

It is not enough to say that the reps vary in their policy: the truth is that they vary in the extent to which they have a policy. Nor is it merely a matter, for the director, of compromising between what he would like to do and what he feels is required of him. The pressures on him may push him in different directions. He has to consider the Arts Council, the board of directors, the local town council (which may be subsidising the theatre and may have representatives on the board), the box office, the supporters' club, and the actors, who cannot work well unless they are kept reasonably happy; and if they are a permanent company, one of the director's most important jobs is to develop it as an ensemble.

It is not easy to keep a season on a straight course of continuity. If a play by Henry Livings or Luigi Pirandello does bad business at the box office, the temptation is to push an Agatha Christie or a farce into the programme as quickly as possible to improve the box-office average and to conciliate the patrons who stayed away and may go on staying away. But this sort of 'tacking' is very bad for the company's acting style and it scares away the audience which perhaps could slowly be built up if there were a consistency and a continuity in the programme-planning. A great deal of lip-service is paid to the ideal of 'catering for all tastes' and putting 'something for everyone' into the programme. In practice this means aiming almost everything at people with almost no taste. But admittedly it is easier to evolve a well-defined policy in a small theatre than in a large one.

When Barry Jackson was running the Birmingham Rep he claimed that nearly all the plays he did would be equally well worth staging in twenty years' time, and his claim was more or less justified. But the million pound replacement for his theatre which opened in October 1971 with 900 seats, a proscenium arch and an orchestra pit, was launched with an American adaptation of *Pride and Prejudice* as a musical; *Roll Me Over*, a new comedy by Bill Canaway; *Good-Time Johnny*, a musical based on *The Merry Wives of Windsor*; and *Noggin the Nog* – 'the popular children's TV series for the first time on stage'. The size of the theatre forces the artistic director to bid for popularity. Obviously the old theatre in Station Street, built in 1913 for £17,000, was out of date. It was also cramped and unattractive. But its 453 seats were latterly hardly ever full except for *Hamlet* and a revival of *1066 and All That*. With £640,000 of City Council money and £150,000 of Arts Council money available, no one was going to campaign for making the new theatre as small as the old one. But it remains to be seen whether it will in any sense by a continuation of the Barry Jackson tradition. The fact that Peter Dews, the director, left within nine months of the opening was not a good omen, and by March 1972, £110,000 had been lost. The Arts Council agreed to pay £88,000 towards the estimated loss of £142,000 for 1972–73, and Birmingham City Council agreed to contribute £44,000.

On the whole, the infusion of so much money into the repertory system by the Arts Council and by local councils has done much more good than harm. In 1957 most reps were still changing their programmes weekly and actors were mostly paid salaries quite close to the minimum, which was £6 10s. 0d. a week. Students and probationary members of Equity could be paid less. Birmingham was the only monthly rep, the Bristol Old Vic and the Manchester Library Theatre were three-weekly, and there were two three-weekly touring companies: the Midland Theatre Company, based on Coventry, and the West of England Theatre Company, whose base was Exeter. There were six fortnightly reps – the Bristol Little, the Birmingham Alexandra, Hornchurch, Ipswich, Nottingham, and Sheffield. And, apart from summer seasons, there were seventy-four weekly rep companies in England, eight of which were performing twice-nightly – Bradford, Great Yarmouth, Leeds, Leicester, Nottingham Royal, Sheffield Lyceum and Stockton. For giving twelve performances each week (as well as rehearsing next week's play and learning lines) actors were paid the twice-nightly minimum of £7 10s. 0d. Some good productions were done in the better reps and even, occasionally, in the weekly ones, but there was too little time and too little money for high standards to be maintained. The plays were mostly well-tried London successes, and some directors depended heavily on French's Acting Editions, which often contained detailed stage directions copied from the West End prompt book. What the provincial audiences were seeing were reproductions of stage business that had been effective in London. But none of the reps had enough money. In the financial year 1958–59 twenty-two theatre companies outside London were helped by the Arts Council and about £44,500 was paid out to them; in 1971–72 help was given to nearly seventy rep companies, theatres, groups and arts labs outside London, and their subsidies amounted to nearly £1,500,000.

In 1958, when the Belgrade Theatre opened at Coventry, it was the only new theatre to have been built in Britain since the war and the first ever to be built here at the cost of the municipality, but in the same year Harold Macmillan, who was then Chancellor of the Exchequer, invited the Arts Council to undertake a survey 'of the cultural building needs of London and the whole country' and to make recommendations about what should be done. A Committee of Enquiry was appointed and the second part of its report, dealing with 'The Needs of the English Provinces' was not published until 1961. By then a couple of new civic theatres had been opened at Scunthorpe and Rotherham,[1] but still no more repertory theatres. Nor was the Arts Council able to help: it could assist a theatre with its runnng

[1] At Scunthorpe in a new building, at Rotherham in a converted chapel.

costs but it had no funds and no authority to make grants towards building costs. Nottingham Playhouse, which was started in 1961 and opened in December 1963, cost £370,000 and it was financed with money which had remained in the possession of the city council because it had been transferred from one account to another just before the gas industry was nationalised. The only other new repertory theatre to open in the early sixties was the Phoenix, Leicester (October 1963), which had taken only six months to build and cost only £29,180.

It was in 1965 that the Arts Council was given funds to contribute towards the costs of new buildings, and by March 1971 £1,575,500 had been paid out for new theatres and for restoring or improving old ones. The Yvonne Arnaud Theatre, Guildford, was the first to benefit from the new 'Housing the Arts' scheme. A local trust had been formed in 1961 and an appeal launched to raise £200,000, but delays, design alterations, increased building costs and interest on loans raised the final cost of the theatre to about £362,000. The Arts Council contributed £31,000 and later another £27,000; the Corporation provided a valuable site very cheaply and a capital grant of £20,000, but most of the money came from local commercial and industrial companies and private individuals. Building was started in 1962 and the theatre opened in 1965; if the money could have been found quickly enough to obviate delays, at least £50,000 would have been saved.

The Arts Council has hardly ever contributed more than 25 per cent of the cost of a new theatre, but its example has encouraged civic authorities to be more generous, and since 1965 there has been a rush of theatre-building. The Manchester University Theatre, which also opened in 1965, was financed by the University. In 1967 the Octagon was opened at Bolton, and in 1968 Billingham Forum, the Gateway at Chester and the Northcott at Exeter, another university-sponsored theatre. (Neither Billingham nor Exeter benefited from the Arts Council's Housing the Arts grants, though both have their running costs subsidised by it.) The Arts Council did, however, contribute to the building costs of the Gardner Centre, a theatre belonging to Sussex University, which opened in 1969. The other important new theatres to open in 1969 were the Greenwich Theatre –

a new stage and auditorium built inside the structure of an old Victorian music hall – and the Thorndike at Leatherhead, which cost £440,000. It contains only 530 seats as against Nottingham's 750, but building costs had risen steeply during the sixties. The Leatherhead Property Trust, which owns the site, contributed £90,000 and the Urban District Council £10,000. The Arts Council made an original commitment of £50,000, but has actually contributed £100,000. As at Guildford, a large proportion of the money was raised by a public appeal.

In 1970 the Playhouse was opened in Leeds, which used to be the largest city in Western Europe with no rep. Its population (494,971) is nearly double that of the Swedish town of Gothenburg, which has five well-patronised theatres. The year 1971 saw the opening of the new theatre at Birmingham, the Duke's Playhouse at Lancaster, the Crucible at Sheffield and the Wyvern at Swindon. In 1972 the reconstruction of the Bristol Old Vic was completed and the Mercury opened at Colchester. New theatres are also being built at Bromley, Derby, Essex University, Farnham, Hornchurch and Leicester, there will be one at Ipswich. So amends are finally being made for the thirteen post-war years of complete inactivity and the subsequent slowness in following Coventry's lead.

A new theatre building has a great proselytising value for attracting new audiences. At Leatherhead seat prices were increased by 40 per cent when the new theatre opened, but the box-office takings were doubled. The old playhouse at Nottingham had only 467 seats and the city's population is nearly 300,000 but some productions there did very poor business. On the other hand averages were levered up by putting on more commercial plays, which could fill over 90 per cent of the seats. When the new theatre was built, with its 750 seats, it was essential to enlarge the audience. Ostensibly the local council is subsidising the theatre at the annual rate of £22,000, but the theatre has to pay the council nearly £27,000 each year in rent and instalments and interest on the 'loan' of the money that the building cost. The Arts Council subsidy for 1970–71 was £68,151, but the reason John Neville gives for resigning from his very successful directorship of the theatre in 1968 was that his Arts Council grant was pegged for three successive years. During his regime capacity was usually above 85 per cent and he never had recourse to Agatha Christie. His programme included *All's Well that Ends Well*, and a double bill of *Oedipus Rex* and *The Tricks of Scapin*, which had not been seen in Nottingham for ninety years.

The restaurants that have opened in Nottingham since the new theatre was built have changed the pattern of evening life in the city. They have also changed the pattern of theatre-going habits. If you know you are going on to a restaurant when the play ends, you do not sit in the theatre in quite the same way as you do if you are going straight home. The presence inside a theatre building of a restaurant, a coffee bar and bars that are open during all the normal licensing hours makes a big difference. People get into the habit of using the building before and after the show, staying in it for hours, feeling welcome inside it. The Belgrade, Coventry, with its large foyer, its bookstalls, its restaurant, coffee bars and its space for exhibitions had set the new pattern a year before Bernard Miles's Mermaid opened in London, designed with the same notion of attracting people into the theatre building at all hours of the day.

While we are far better off now than we would be without so many new buildings, we ought not to be complacent about them. There have been grotesque mistakes in design, as at Guildford, where the fly-tower is too low and the stage too wide. Many of the new theatres lack backstage storage space and sight-lines are often bad. At Coventry the facilities for flying scenery are inadequate and the workshops are not attached to the theatre. Though no theatres were built here in the forties or fifties, it was not inevitable that the English architects who started designing them in the sixties should have made so many mistakes: there could have been much more reference to old English and new European buildings, and more consultation with theatre technicians and designers. Local architects are often employed –as local feeling often demands that they should be – but at Colchester, where this happened, Christopher Morley, the RSC's Head of Design, was retained as consultant. Though consultants have been used all too rarely, three organisations have been created: the Association of British Theatre Technicians, which was formed in 1961, the

Society of Theatre Consultants, founded in 1964, and the Theatres Advisory Council, which started operating in 1963. Though they all came into existence too late to obviate the early mistakes, they are currently helping to disseminate technical knowledge.

Whatever is done to make technical expertise available, the motives for building theatres are not always likely to produce good ones. Local government, for the most part, is in the hands of men who are not interested in architecture or the arts. If municipal authorities have spent so much more of their ratepayers' money on new theatres in the sixties than they did in the fifties it was not because the new decade had miraculously transformed Philistines into lovers of the arts. It was largely for reasons of local prestige. A chain reaction had been started. If other towns are building new theatres, our town must have one too. When a theatre is intended to be a civic monument, it will be designed as a civic monument, constructed in the most expensive, impressive, durable materials and sited in the most central space available. Later on the theatre company may be charged high rents, and much later on, when the building is out of date, councillors will argue that they cannot afford to replace it because so much was spent on it. In an article in *The Stage* called 'Keep Theatre Cheap, or Do We Have to Build the Taj Mahal?' Peter Cheeseman quoted a remark Stephen Joseph had made at a discussion about the new National Theatre building: 'The most important thing . . . is to make it inflammable, so that by the time they realise they've made a mess of the building it will have burned down and they can start again.'

Even within the decade there were cases of plans which were out of date before the theatre had been built. In October 1964 Ipswich Town Council decided that its new Civic Centre should include a theatre, which it would itself build, and then lease to the local repertory company. Though the company was used to a stage nineteen feet by twenty-one, and an auditorium with 345 seats, plans were drawn up for a theatre large enough to accommodate full-scale touring opera and ballet. Delays ensued, and by 1969 the building would have cost about £500,000, and the trustees of the local rep were then invited to suggest ideas for a cheaper theatre. A smaller building was designed on the lines of the Octagon at Bolton, with movable seats to allow possibilities of end-stage, thrust, or in-the-round arrangements, and this will probably not cost more than about £400,000.

Even in big towns big theatres are dangerous. Costs are no doubt going to go on rising and even if actors' salaries do not rise as they should during the next few years, most reps are going to need substantial increases in subsidies. In 1968-9, every 38 pence that the public spent at the rep box offices was matched by 31 pence of subsidy – 23½ pence from the Arts Council, 7½ pence from local authorities. Even if ticket prices go up, as they will no doubt have to, and even if subsidies go up proportionately, the trend in the direction of big theatres is likely to create a downward trend in artistic standards. Big theatres make better civic monuments, and town councils, anyway, tend to prefer them to be large enough to accommodate touring musicals, operas and ballets. But the larger the theatre, the harder it is to be adventurous or creative. Fewer new plays can be tried out. Casting, production and set design must be calculated to please a large audience – not only to make the necessary money but because no company can be good when playing to a vista of empty seats.

Perhaps it is unrealistic to expect civic authorities to be concerned about artistic standards, but it is reasonable to suggest (as the Arts Council's own Theatre Enquiry committee suggested) that if less of the government's money were being spent on theatre buildings – it is not the Arts Council which earmarks it for this purpose – more of it could go towards raising wage levels and production standards. And if only local authorities would accept the committee's view that it should be their responsibility to provide and maintain a theatre without making the company pay, the whole situation could be vastly improved. While a degree of Arts Council patronage stimulates municipal spending on the theatre, there may be an optimum beyond which Arts Council munificence has a shrinking effect on local generosity. Why should the ratepayer's money be spent on something that can be paid for out of the taxpayer's money? It is unfortunate that there are no principles and no consensus on where the frontier should be set between the responsibilities of local councils and those of the Arts Council. Both have contributed to building funds, both have contributed to running costs. How much each contributes to either is largely a matter of chance.

The source of the trouble lies in the relationship between government and local government, between Parliament and the municipal authorities. The Local Government Act of 1948 provides that:

(1) A local authority may do, or arrange for the doing of, or contribute towards the expenses of the doing of, anything necessary or expedient for any of the following purposes, that is to say –
(a) the provision of an entertainment of any nature or of facilities for dancing;
(b) the provision of a theatre, concert hall, dance hall or other premises suitable for the giving of entertainment or the holding of dances;
(c) the maintenance of a band or orchestra;
(d) any purpose incidental to the matters aforesaid, including the provision, in connection with the giving of any entertainment or the holding of any dance, of refreshments or programmes and the advertising of any such entertainment or dance.

The third subsection of the same section states:

(3) The expenditure of a local authority under this section (excluding capital expenditure, but including loan charges) shall not in any year exceed the product of a rate of sixpence in the pound, plus the net amount of any receipts of the authority from any such charges or payments as are referred to in the last preceding subsection.

The setting of a maximum rate of six (old) pence ($2\frac{1}{2}$p) in the pound could have been interpreted as meaning that some such spending is recommended, but no minimum was suggested and in practice it was left to local councils to decide for themselves how much they wanted to spend, how it was to be divided between buildings and running costs, and how much of it was to be spent on dances and bands, how much on theatres and art exhibitions. At the

Municipal Entertainments Conference of 1970 many speakers urged that the sixpenny rate should become mandatory. This was the view that Lord Goodman took when he was Chairman of the Arts Council, and a pamphlet issued in May 1972 by the Local Government Information Office predicted that legislation for the reorganisation of local government would remove set limits on entertainment expenditure. But during the twenty-four years it has been in force, the restriction has never had any restricting effect on the vast majority of local councils. The actual spending on the arts and entertainment has been only a small fraction of the spending authorised. A survey of local authorities' expenditure in England and Wales during the year 1964–65 revealed that the average outlay on the performing arts was equivalent to just under one-third of an old penny of the rates – about 5 per cent of what was authorised. Since then the situation has improved, but not nearly enough. According to the Arts Council's report for 1970–71, thirty local authorities had provided reps with up to 0·25p, and five had provided 1p, but for the majority the spending was about 0·01p. At Leatherhead, when the new theatre opened in 1969, the Urban District Council raised its annual grant of £500 to £1,500. This, which represented one eighth of a penny rate, was denounced as 'a millstone round the necks of the ratepayers'.

The Greater Manchester Authority's contribution to the area's theatre programme in 1971–72 was equivalent to a quarter of a penny rate. This amounted to more than any other local authority was spending on professional theatre, but the comparative generosity was necessary because the two theatres of the Library Theatre Company are both under direct control of the local authority and therefore not eligible for Arts Council support, whereas if they were controlled by independent trusts they would be.

Here the problem of responsibility for local theatres is particularly complicated. There are more people living in a ten mile radius of Manchester's Piccadilly than there are within the same radius of London's. There are five theatres in the Manchester–Bolton–Oldham area, which between them received £97,780 in 1971–72 from local authorities and £60,822 from the Arts Council. A committee formed by the North West Arts Association, the regional equivalent of the

Arts Council, has proposed that all government subsidy for theatre in the area should be channelled through the Association, and that the Greater Manchester Council, rather than the district authorities, should be responsible for local subsidy. It is possible that this combination of local centralisation with national decentralisation would help to remove some of the anomalies of the present situation. Considered in relation to the size of the local population, Arts Council subsidy is currently 2·14p per head, whereas Oxford receives 64p per head and Nottingham nearly 25p.

Speaking in the House of Lords in 1972 Lord Eccles said, 'We ought to employ new techniques and try much harder than hitherto to offer to all parts of Britain equally attractive opportunities to participate in the arts.' This is impossible, but he made a valid point when he went on to argue, 'If we want the arts to flourish in any region, whether near or far from the centre of London, a larger proportion than at present of the activities in that area must be locally based, promoted and financed.' The question is how to bring this about.

An initiative which may turn out to be very fruitful has been taken by the Joint Repertory Committee, a new body composed of representatives of the Council of Regional Theatres, the Theatrical Management Association and Equity. Alarmed by reports that Lord Eccles had said Arts Council subsidies would be 'stabilised' over the next three years, the Committee informed the Arts Council of its intention to launch a campaign to raise both Arts Council and civic subsidies. This led in 1972 to the idea of a Festival of Regional Theatres which would 'illustrate the quality and range of work presented' by them and might help to inculcate a better atmosphere in which local authorities would become more generous in their help. The scheme now has the support of the English Tourist Board, the Theatrical Management Association and of regional arts associations.

Initiatives like this might gradually help to kill the idea that as a social and educational amenity a theatre cannot be compared with a public library because it is a place of entertainment. In 1970 £45,000,000 of money collected from rates was spent on British libraries, while less than £1,000,000 was spent on the theatre. At

Leatherhead the Urban District Council had been voting the library at least £40,000 a year.

There will be no easy solution to this problem, especially when local councillors can use the argument that spending on theatre is unpopular. In reality, of course, while all ratepayers think that rates are too high, only an infinitesimal minority take the trouble to find out how much of their money is being spent on entertainment, how much on libraries and how much on the men who slowly sweep leaves into little carts. Theatre will always appeal only to a minority, but so, unfortunately, do books. There is also the danger that the more a council contributed to a theatre, the more it would interfere in the running of it, and that interference, like the policy of building larger theatres, could force artistic standards downwards. In July 1972, after a year in which business at the box office had deteriorated at the Theatre Royal, York Corporation made a £20,000 guarantee, but on condition that it was given more control over running costs. Eleven of the sixteen governors resigned; the remainder had all been appointed by the Council.

On the other hand a great deal of good work is currently being done by companies like the one at the Northcott, Exeter, in developing closer relations with different parts of the local community. By starting a youth club in the theatre itself, by sending out groups of actors to perform in schools and hold discussions with the children, by allowing the theatre to be used for conferences and by offering help to amateur groups, a theatre can demonstrate its value as a social amenity, engaging more local sympathy, which must eventually filter through to the minds that make decisions about using the money levied from the ratepayers.

Generally the tendency of the last fifteen years has been in the direction of breaking down the barrier that used to be fortified by footlights. Following the example of the RSC's Theatregoround – and of Roger Planchon's company at Lyon on which it was partly modelled – companies have been going outside the theatre to meet members of the public in a variety of different environments. Basic attitudes have changed. Instead of making acting into a mystique, actors are now eager to explain it, demonstrate it in the classroom. Actors used to be careful to avoid meeting members of the public on the way into or out of the theatre; now situations are contrived especially for meetings. Make-up is used less and the little that is used can be seen in broad daylight. If we have not quite reverted to sixteenth-century techniques of advertising the performance by parading through the streets in costume, we have certainly broken down many of the formalities that accompanied the rigid actor–audience separation of the proscenium theatre.

Where plays are created specially for the local audience, there is a possibility of a deeper commitment to the area, particularly when a feeling can be developed among the company and a climate of working that makes the actors want to return year after year. One of the two main reasons this climate exists at Stoke-on-Trent is that the theatre is not in the centre of the town. It is in Hartshill, halfway between Hanley and Stoke, and almost as close to Newcastle-under-Lyme as to either of them. The community is a small one and the atmosphere more like that of an industrialised village than a big city. The people who live there still behave as though the five Pottery towns (Tunstall, Burslem, Hanley, Loughton and Stoke-on-Trent) had never been amalgamated into the City of Stoke-on-Trent.

The other reason is that it is continuing a tradition started in 1966 by Stephen Joseph, a man who deserves to be commemorated alongside George Devine as having pioneered the way towards the present situation in our theatre. The son of Hermione Gingold, he had a drama school training before taking a degree at Cambridge, later taking another one (in Drama) at Iowa. In 1955 he formed a company called Studio Theatre to perform new plays while exploring the possibilities of theatre-in-the-round. After starting with Sunday night productions in the Mahatma Gandhi Hall in Fitzroy Square, he moved from London to Scarborough, where he ran a summer season in the municipal library and toured to theatreless towns in the area. In the winter he earned money as a lorry-driver and lecturer. He discovered and collected playwrights: James Saunders, David Campton and Alan Ayckbourn went on writing for him season after season.

Newcastle-under-Lyme's town council eventually offered him a subsidy and even held out the prospect of building a theatre-in-the-round for him, and he found Peter Cheeseman by advertising for a manager to help him establish his first permanent base. When Newcastle abandoned the idea, they went ahead on their own, though they could spend only £5,000 on converting the cinema they found in Hartshill. When they opened in 1962 with Peter Cheeseman as Artistic Director – Joseph accepted a Fellowship in Drama at Manchester University – David Campton was company manager and Alan Ayckbourn was stage manager. Both also acted in the company as well as writing for it. Peter Cheeseman continued Joseph's policy of collecting writers. After writing regularly for the company since 1964 Peter Terson was resident dramatist for 1966 and 1967. Tony Perrin was resident dramatist for 1968 and 1969, while Ken Campbell was both writing and acting for the company. Peter Cheeseman has described[1] how

a temporary shortage of writers when Alan Ayckbourn left us in 1964 to do *Mr Whatnot* forced me to consider a way of taking on the function of writer ourselves, as a working group, and it provided the opportunity to use local subject matter. We could create our own show in our own way. The documentaries are not written, but constructed from primary source material gathered during a preliminary research period, and then rehearsed collectively by researchers, consisting of the resident dramatist, myself and the company in committee. They are then created on the floor at rehearsal.

The Knotty, for example, was based on the history of the North Staffordshire railway. *The Whitby Lifeboat Disaster* was an imaginative reconstruction of an event of 1861. Adaptations of Arnold Bennett novels centred on the Five Towns have been particularly successful, and in 1970 *Anna of the Five Towns* played to better business than either *Coriolanus* or *The Death of a Salesman*. Fourteen per cent of the population of Stoke-on-Trent have been to the theatre at least once – a much higher percentage than in most towns – but it is not merely

[1] In *Theatre Quarterly* Vol. I No. 1, January–March 1971.

the people of the immediate locality who attend: 45 per cent of the audience come by coach. It takes a long time to build up a following of this sort. In 1962 the average business was 28 per cent of the capacity, in 1971, 65 per cent.

Following Stoke-on-Trent's example, other reps became more local in their orientation during the later sixties. In the West Country, smugglers who figured in local lore became heroic figures in productions of the Orchard Theatre Company; in mining areas of Nottingham and the North-east Alan Plater's *Close the Coalhouse Door* (created at the Newcastle Playhouse) enjoyed more success than it could have had in the South; and the Sheffield Playhouse production of a play about a local trade union leader, *The Stirrings in Sheffield on Saturday Night* by Alan Cullen, who had acted with the company for two seasons, brought many people to the theatre who had never been there before. Generally regional plays today are much less likely to be long-range missiles aimed at the West End or arriving from it, and, like Stoke, many other reps are creating documentary and semi-documentary plays based on local history.

But relationships with a community depend on permanence in the company. The residents need to become familiar with the actors, the director needs to become familiar with the area and the people. And a director who takes over an existing rep is likely to find this relationship harder to establish than a director who starts when the theatre is opened. It can be very difficult for the director who is appointed to take charge of a large rep which has already changed hands several times in a town he does not know, where the inhabitants lack the unity that the word *community* implies. As Warren Jenkins found when he took over at Coventry in 1966, natives of the city seemed to be in a minority. The motor industry had attracted a mixture of Indians, Poles, Irish and Guianians to settle there. With post-war buildings in the centre of the city, which had been gutted by German bombs, and new bungalows outcropping on the fringe, old people were saying that they could hardly recognise their birthplace. Clearly local history and local traditions could not be tapped in the same way that they might be in a smaller town with a smaller theatre and a permanent company. London is only seventy-five minutes away and

Stratford-on-Avon only nineteen miles away. In any case Warren Jenkins felt that higher standards were achieved in regional theatres which cast each production separately with actors from London. This meant abandoning all hope of creating an ensemble.

Of course, if reps were subsidised on a level which made it possible for them to pay top salaries of £100 a week, it might be possible to keep higher-calibre actors for longer. But there are very few companies which can go to this level even for guest stars, and permanent companies are made up of actors willing to live on very much less. Even in the larger reps the majority of the actors are not earning more than £40 a week. In most of the smaller reps, the actors are earning between £20 and £30 a week, and there are many where none earn more than £20. Not that directors or administrators are well paid either. They seldom earn more than £40 or £50 a week, while businessmen in positions of comparable responsibility would be earning over twice as much.

Most reps cannot afford assistant directors or guest directors except very occasionally. And, besides directing most of the productions himself, the artistic director has to do a great deal of administrative work. When Caroline Smith took over as Artistic Director from Anthony Tuckey at Farnham, she had an assistant director who did alternate productions, but she still found that only 25 per cent of her time could actually be spent on preparing her own productions and working with the actors. The rest of it went on budgeting and finance, on casting, programme-planning and on the indispensable chatting that is necessary to preserve good relations with the actors and with officials of local organisations like Women's Institutes. She decided she had no time for reading new plays. 'I know that I can wade through fifty new scripts and not find one possibility: so I have tended to take the easier way out and do either new translations such as *The Crib* by Eduardo de Filippo or neglected classics such as *The Artful Widow* by Goldoni.'[1] The only new plays created during her first two years at the theatre were the children's plays, written by the stage director, and the texts used on the schools tours, which were

[1] *Plays and Players*, June 1969.

written by the youth liaison officer. But, at York, Richard Digby Day, who was appointed Artistic Director in 1971, has been reading an average of ten scripts a week.

The pressure on the artistic director's time obviously limits what he can do in striking up relationships with the local community, and the actors too, when there is a permanent company, are liable to be kept so busy, with a rehearsal, a performance and lines to learn every day of the week, that they can neither do what they otherwise might as ambassadors of the theatre in local society nor put down roots by cultivating a life outside the theatre and becoming members of the community. But more time can be bought only by more money.

The necessary involvement of actors and director in their prime function of getting the plays on gives extra importance to the role of the Administrator or General Manager, who, as well as co-ordinating the various departments of the theatre, controlling the finances, publicity and the front-of-house, and standing in the foyer to talk to the patrons, must take the main responsibility for liaison not only with the community at large but with the board of directors which effectively represents it, being composed mainly of local worthies. There are not many boards which consist entirely of the local authority's nominees; most boards are self-appointing. The board is the governing body of the theatre but in many cases it is like the British electorate in having real power only once in five years – or whenever it is that a decision has to be taken about renewing an artistic director's contract or appointing a successor. But board meetings are more frequent than this and members naturally want to feel that they are contributing to the formation of the theatre's policy. They also want a say in the play selection, though they don't generally want to read scripts and wouldn't know, even if they did, how a script might emerge in performance.

The report of the Arts Council's Theatre Enquiry tried to formulate a demarcation between the responsibility of the board and the responsibilities of the artistic director. The board, it suggested, should have jurisdiction over the budget, the buildings, general policy, seat prices, negotiations with the Arts Council and local authorities, and over theatre amenities, while the artistic director's duties are to choose the plays and the actors, and plan the productions. 'There are many Boards known to us,' the report goes on, 'which have never vetoed a play even though they have had doubts about some of the choices.' But there have been many clashes between boards and directors, sometimes resulting in the departure of the director and an interruption in the continuity of artistic policy. John Neville might have stayed on at Nottingham if he had had a better relationship with the board, and at Leeds in November 1971 it was only because the company united against the board that Bill Hays was able to stay on after it had announced its decision not to renew his contract; he left in the summer of 1972. He had been appointed in September 1970 but of the seventeen directors of the trust that employed him, only seven were still in office in November 1971 and three of these, including the Deputy Chairman, resigned over his dismissal. One of the others said there had been caucus meetings before the board took the decision against renewing his contract. The main crux, according to Bill Hays himself, was their attempt to manoeuvre him into a position where they could dictate the choice of plays.

As Hazel Vincent Wallace, the Managing Director of the Thorndike at Leatherhead, has put it, 'The temperament needed in a really imaginative and creative director is almost certainly not the temperament which can deal patiently and tactfully with a board of well-meaning local residents who have a love for the theatre but no professional knowledge.' In her view the administrator is the key man who should be able to interpret an artistic director's hopes and dreams to a seemingly uncomprehending board and 'to weld all elements of the theatre into a harmonious and creative whole'. A good administrator can certainly do invaluable work as Aaron to the director's Moses, but at Leatherhead there is no artistic director and less continuity of artistic policy than there might be.

The Yvonne Arnaud at Guildford is run by Laurier Lister, a very able administrator whose previous experience was mainly managerial. His original appointment was as Director, Administrator and Licensee, and though he now has the title Artistic Director and does sometimes direct himself, he employs a succession of guest directors and is not concerned to develop any continuity of style in the productions.

Ideally a rep might be run like the RSC, with an artistic director who is only one of several like-minded directors who share the productions. But the theatre would need subsidising on a German level for this to be financially feasible.

One of the unsatisfactory features of the present repertory system is the lack of openings for new plays. The Arts Council has tried to foster them by offering special guarantees in addition to the normal subsidy, and though this has made a difference, playwrights are still complaining that their scripts remain unread for months after they have been submitted, and artistic directors are still complaining that they are too busy to spend time on script-reading. It is also hard, in most towns, to get an audience interested in a new play without having money to spend on star actors or intensive publicity. Provincial moral prejudices can also be a factor. When Robert Chetwyn was directing at Coventry (1965–6), Michael Codron offered him a pre-London showing of Joe Orton's *Loot*. He was eager to put it on but board members thought that local audiences would have been too shocked by it, so the opportunity was turned down. Later, during Warren Jenkins's regime, after the play had been seen in London, it was included in the Coventry programme.

Nor is it merely a matter of morality. In 1962 Arnold Wesker, who has fought hard against the tradition of taking it for granted that the regional theatre will follow in London's wake, offered his play *Chips with Everything* to six reps for production simultaneous with the Royal Court première. Only one rep – Sheffield – accepted, but since then the play has had a number of rep productions. It is easier to sell a play to a regional audience once it has been a success in London.

Another dispiriting fact about audience habits is that the appearance of a not very talented actor who has been starring in a popular television series is a much bigger draw than a new play by a very talented writer. It is to be confronted with a face, not a mind, that most people come to the theatre, and many of the reps nearer to London have been cashing in on the possibility of using television stars in unadventurous revivals. With things as they are at the moment, this is inevitable, but the important question is whether it needs to go on being inevitable. Not that the box office appeal of stars is ever likely to end, but thanks partly to the theatre-in-education movement and partly to the fact that young people today have more time, more money and more opportunity to become interested in drama than their parents or grandparents did, there is the possibility of developing a more discriminating audience at the same time as developing a more reciprocal relationship between the stage and the auditorium.

We cannot afford to leave this to happen of its own accord. The theatre has to sell itself, and in the provinces, as in London, too little is being done to reach the people who have never given themselves an opportunity of finding out whether plays are something they could enjoy. The structure of audience-formation has changed: it no longer depends as it used to on the family unit. Television has taken over as a family entertainment, and generally people go less often to the theatre in family groups. Consequently theatre publicists are having to approach potential theatregoers through their membership of clubs and work-groups. At Coventry an interesting and successful experiment in public relations was made in 1970, when the Belgrade Theatre appointed publicity agents to go out and promote its interests in factories, youth clubs, schools and colleges. A sales team of three people was employed, and each of them was given a different area of local society to cover: industry and local commerce, including trade unions; local government including the police, the fire brigade, nurses, teachers and so on; social groups and youth clubs. The objective was not just to sell theatre tickets by offering price concessions for block bookings, but to encourage people to make more use of the theatre building, with its restaurant and bars. Later the Belgrade also started a 'Rent-a-Play' scheme to tour small-scale productions around pubs, colleges and schools in the Midlands.

Substantial results can be achieved by campaigns such as this, and one disadvantage of subsidy is that it is not necessarily helping a company to help itself. The report of the Arts Council's Theatre Enquiry claimed that subsidised companies 'on the average, recover 75 per cent of their expenditure at the box-office and manage to make ends meet with only 25 per cent of subsidy from local funds.'

Most of the subsidy is not local, but the figures published in the same report for the year 1968–69 showed that at twenty-two of the forty provincial theatres listed for England, the total box-office receipts for the year were less than the total subsidies, and in several cases very considerably less. At Birmingham the box-office revenue was £29,031 and the subsidy £54,000; at Lincoln box office £13,250 and subsidy £37,917; at Billingham box office was £19,573 and subsidies (mainly from the local authority) came to £72,000; at Exeter box office £20,330 and subsidy £47,840; at Stoke-on-Trent box office £13,031 and subsidy £29,515. Of these theatres Birmingham was playing to an average of 56 per cent capacity; Lincoln to 44 per cent; Billingham to 49 per cent; Exeter to 71 per cent; Stoke-on-Trent to 46 per cent.

Of the thirty-two theatres for which 1971–72 figures were available in July 1972, eighteen were taking less at the box office than they were receiving in subsidies from the Arts Council and from local authorities:

	Box Office	Subsidy
Bolton	22,600	22,800
Bristol	71,699	75,000[1]
Canterbury	24,357	26,250
Cheltenham	22,231	29,011
Chester	24,015	39,959
Colchester	19,460	38,930
Coventry	78,570 (estimate)	82,050
Crewe	6,900	20,300[1]
Derby	21,877	29,250
Harrogate	16,812	19,450
Hornchurch	27,484	35,750[1]
Ipswich	17,574	29,600
Liverpool	60,438	64,600[1]
Manchester 69 Theatre Co. (including tours)	18,845	31,500
Oxford (including tours)	61,434	75,505[1]

[1] Figures for the local subsidy were not yet available. The amounts included here (ranging between £2,000 and £20,000) are taken from the budget estimates.

	Box Office	Subsidy
Sheffield	55,879	82,000
Stoke	21,059	41,280
Watford	25,524	34,200

At some theatres the box-office takings are three or four times the size of the subsidy. At Guildford £99,873 was taken at the box office and £25,000 received from the Arts Council, plus about £2,375 (according to the budget estimate) from the local authority. At Oldham £32,814 was earned at the box office and the only subsidy was £11,000 from the Arts Council.

In 1970 (taking the calendar year as opposed to the financial year) Oldham took £28,593 at the box office, which produced a profit of £1,089. The 1971 takings were £30,919 but there was a deficit on the (calendar) year of £3,000. The policy is to mix worthwhile plays (like Arthur Miller's *The Crucible* and Joe Orton's *Entertaining Mr Sloane*) with light comedies like *Butterflies Are Free*, *Barefoot in the Park* and *Birds on the Wing*, and commercial farces like *Big Bad Mouse* and *Chase Me Comrade*. But this, surprisingly, made a loss, while Ronald Gow's adaptation of *Tess of the D'Urbervilles* made a very good profit. Joyce Rayburn's *The Man Most Likely to …* was seen by 3,573 people and made a profit. Mart Crowley's *The Boys in the Band* made a profit and *The Crucible* made a loss. No pattern emerges from these results, and at Oldham, as at most other theatres where the policy is not to have a policy, it is impossible to know whether an audience could be built up for a consistent programme of good plays.

It is nearly always taken as axiomatic that in time of financial stress a theatre can survive only by lowering its standards. But with the aid of the right publicity to involve new sections of the community, it is quite possible that many of our theatres could do better business by raising their standards. This is a risk that could only be taken with backing from the Arts Council, but it is high time it started devoting less of its resources to building and more to raising standards. At the moment it is spending a vast amount of the taxpayers' money on subsidising the same thrillers, farces and lightweight comedies which are staged in the West End without subsidy and which, in the regions, cannot even be counted on to attract a big audience.

In the sixties several of the larger provincial reps opened separate 'studio' theatres for productions expected to appeal only to a small audience. There are many advantages in this system. Where the company is a large one it helps to engage the energies of under-employed actors and challenges them with more taxing roles. And, particularly in university towns, it helps to involve a younger and more intellectual element in the population which otherwise might stay away from the theatre altogether. But there are also disadvant-ages. One is that it divides the audience and puts plays which may intrinsically be better than those on the main bill into a lower cate-gory, to be staged more cheaply and simply, with less expensive and less experienced actors. Another is that it tends to siphon off experi-mental elements away from the main auditorium, which becomes a place in which less risks than ever are taken. The studio becomes a safety valve of the wrong sort. In some ways it is better to have a theatre with two auditoriums than to have two rival reps, splitting the audience completely, as at Liverpool, but in other ways it is worse. At least competition is a stimulus which may spur a company into putting all its resources into a good, new, unsafe play.

Yet another disadvantage is that the studio can be damaging to Fringe activity. At Birmingham, for instance, there was already an Arts Lab in the town. Now that the mammoth new Repertory Theatre has opened its studio, it is not only audiences that may be diverted away from the Arts Lab but local subsidy. The corporation, already committed to subsidising the rep which it helped to build, may feel it has to cut back on its assistance to the Arts Lab, though it grew directly out of a local need and has already helped to create a local audience for the studio theatre. This is characteristic of a situation in which the Fringe is effectively extending the theatre's audience but (just like the commercial theatre) suffering from having to compete with a highly subsidised rival.

11 THE FRINGE

One of the reasons our theatre has acquired such a large Fringe is that so many people have discovered there are pleasanter, more fulfilling ways of spending their lives than by doing repetitive jobs in a factory, shop or office. Twenty-five years ago it was a social axiom that, except for the privileged few, self-expression had nothing to do with work. Office-girls could spend their evenings doing amateur dramatics and coal-miners might paint during the week-end, but hardly anyone dropped out of the work continuum to devote the bulk of his time to practising an art. Today there must be ten or twenty times as many people who can be described, loosely, as artists. Their standards may not be high and they may work only sporadically at their art, subsisting partly on national assistance and partly on casual labour, but they have opted for a non-routine life, sacrificed all prospects of a pension. Art has become particularly hard to define where design is involved, but nearly all the arts have grown fringes. The theatre, mainly because it enables artists or would-be artists to work collectively, has the longest.

Fringe theatre companies are even more heterogeneous than repertory companies. Some have premises of their own, some have only a brief lease (six months or a year) on the space they are working in. Many never stay for more than two or three weeks in one place, and some seldom for more than two nights. Nearly all are short of money. Some pay salaries to their actors, usually less than the Equity minimum; others are constituted on a co-operative basis, sharing box-office takings or performance fees, but in many the actors receive no payment at all. Many of the actors come from the working-class, most of the directors and organisers from the middle-class. Some groups are highly professional; some untidily amateurish. Some are politically or ideologically oriented, some exist to fulfil a definable social function or to serve a particular community. Some work from ideological premises which are explicitly or implicitly critical of established values, others exist outside the established theatre only because the people involved cannot get jobs inside. Some are dominated by writers, some by directors, some by actors. Many have no right to describe themselves as experimental.

What our theatre has today is not so much a fringe as a series of fringes which are all growing on the same head of hair, but not without some grafting from New York. The deepest of the native roots is probably in the Independent Theatre, founded in 1891. But in the nineties, when London critics were practically unanimous in savaging a play like Ibsen's *Ghosts*, it was easy to differentiate categorically between commercial plays and the new 'plays of ideas'. Virtually none of the plays then performed in the West End Theatre seem, eighty years later, to have any artistic or literary value.

Fifty years ago the commercial theatre was still uniformly commercial, and even the classics would have been ignored but for the existence of societies like the Stage Society, the Phoenix Society and the Fellowship of Players, which presented experimental productions in West End theatres on Sunday evenings and Monday afternoons. The actors were paid only a token fee and the profession was still a relatively small one but, because there was no television and little filming, actors in a long-running West End play would have no work to do during the daytime and be glad to spend two or three weeks rehearsing a classic or a non-commercial modern play which was going to receive only two performances. Some of these 'non-commercial' plays turned out to be very commercial, like R. C. Sherriff's *Journey's End*, which might never have been given a chance in the West End if it had not been tried out first by the Stage Society in December 1928.

The twenties also saw the birth of small theatre clubs like the Gate, which opened on the top floor of a Covent Garden warehouse in 1925, transferring in 1927 to Villiers Street, off the Strand. It was taken over in 1934 by Norman Marshall, who reopened it with a play by Ernst Toller, and it survived till it was hit by a bomb in 1941. The Q Theatre, which opened at Kew Bridge in 1924, had a slightly longer life-span and there were other small theatres, like the Boltons, the Embassy, the Torch, the New Lindsay and the Watergate, which survived into the early fifties. But from about 1952 until 1957, when the Royal Court's Sunday night productions started, there was hardly any opportunity for non-commercial plays to be tried out cheaply. There have never been as many uncommercial outlets for playwrights in England as there are today, but it is easy to forget how new this situation is.

Off-Broadway is very much older than its English counterpart. The Provincetown Players was an experimental group which started in 1916 and in 1924 began operating in conjunction with the Greenwich Village Theatre. It lasted till 1929. The Living Theatre was started in 1947, and acquired its own theatre in 1951. This was closed in 1963 by the Internal Revenue Service, but the group survived, touring mostly in Europe and America. It has been the model and inspiration for many subsequent groups all over the world.

It was also in 1951 that the Circle-in-the-Square was opened for arena productions. It started with a revival of *Dark of the Moon* and its second production was another revival, Tennessee Williams's *Summer and Smoke*, with Geraldine Page. In his book *The Season*, William Goldman has called Off-Broadway 'primarily a theatre for old plays and new actors'. The Broadway minimum salary was already $150, so unknown young actors who could not break into employment on this salary level naturally gravitated downtown, effectively providing the energy which was to make Off-Broadway theatre into the colossus it has become. By the beginning of the seventies there were about seventy companies in existence with an aggregate box-office gross of approximately $1,500,000.

Off-Broadway has come more and more to depend on backers; production costs and ticket prices have risen; and Hollywood money has entered into the bloodstream. The film rights of *Your Own Thing*, an Off-Broadway musical, were sold for $500,000. What came to be known as 'Off-Off-Broadway' has almost the same relationship to Off-Broadway that Off-Broadway had to Broadway in the fifties. Off-Broadway had become comfortable, well-heeled and traditional, lodged in conventional theatre buildings; Off-Off-Broadway was more urgent and radical, sometimes austere, based mostly in cafés, clubs, churches. Joseph Chaikin, director of Open Theatre, which brought Jean-Claude van Itallie's *America Hurrah* to the Royal Court in 1967, has said, 'Off-Off-Broadway is really an attack on the fourth wall.' It depended less on revivals, more on new plays, improvisational techniques, scripts evolved out of a relationship between the playwright and the company. The most influential Off-Off-Broadway theatre has been Ellen Stewart's Café la Mama. Her policy has been described as one of encouraging just about anybody who thinks he's written a play. 'If a play is talking to me personally, if a play beeps to me when I'm reading it, we do it,' she says. 'I'm interested in the New Theatre, subliminal theatre that explores or seeks to manipulate man's inner emotion.'

Of the many attempts to launch similar theatre companies over here in the fifties, the only one which took root was made by an American, Charles Marowitz. In 1957 he started a group called In-Stage which operated in a tiny angular theatre in the British Drama League building in Fitzroy Square. The first work of Murray Schisgal ever to be staged was staged here – *The Tiger* and *The Typists* in a double bill – and James Broom Lynne's *The Trigon* was premièred. Camden Borough Council helped the enterprise with a subsidy and, with some interruptions, Marowitz was able to carry on working, in different places, with different playwrights and different actors, until he got a cellar of his own in 1968 and called it the Open Space.

The other American refugee who did a great deal towards creating the situation we have now was Jim Haynes. He ran the Traverse Theatre which opened in January 1963 with sixty seats in an Edinburgh tenement and rapidly built up a large young audience for small-scale productions of a mixture of plays, many of which were by new or *avant-garde* writers. Seventy-five premières were chalked up within four years: forty of plays by British writers, thirty-five of plays by Americans or Europeans. The Traverse served as the model for the small theatres which sprang up in England and Scotland during the next few years. The Close Theatre, a studio adjunct of the Glasgow Citizens' Theatre, was the first, and this, in turn, served as the model for the studio theatres developed by the larger English reps, and by the Royal Court. It was Jim Haynes who arranged for the Café La Mama company's visit to Britain in 1967.

It brought Paul Foster's *Tom Paine* and Rochelle Owens's play *Futz*, about a man's relationship with a pig, and Sam Shepard's *Chicago* and *Melodrama Play*, all directed by Tom O'Horgan with a loose Dionysiac physicality that contrasted sharply with the tightly disciplined professionalism of Joseph Chaikin's Open Theatre, which was also seen in England for the first time in the same year. But it was O'Horgan's style that impressed itself on the minds of several directors (like Max Stafford-Clark) who were going to be important in the British Fringe, and the name La Mama began to figure in the names of English groups. There was a group called London La Mama which ran workshops in what it described as La Mama techniques. The Wherehouse/La Mama company was started by Beth Porter and her husband, who had both acted in Ellen Stewart's theatre in New York. The same year, a group of eight actors splintered off to form itself into a separate company called The Freehold. Directed by Nancy Meckler, another American, it became an ensemble in which genuinely experimental work was done to explore the range of the actor's physical and vocal expressiveness. It remained one of our best Fringe groups until 1973, when it disbanded. Groups that stay together too long are liable to lose their collective creativity, especially when it all has to be channelled through the work of a single director. The People Show, which has survived since 1965 with no loss of creative energy, is a small group (four or five) with no director. Two of the present five members have been in the group since the beginning, but new talent can be assimilated in the same way that a new jazz musician can become integral to an existing group. There are no rehearsals, and performances are rather like jazz concerts of surreal images, with one player dominating, then another, the rest giving support as needed.

·   ·   ·   ·   ·   ·

Though Jim Haynes, indirectly, has greatly influenced the London Fringe, his own efforts to operate in London were abortive. In 1966 he joined forces with Charles Marowitz and Michael Geliot to create a London Traverse at the Jeannetta Cochrane Theatre. Then in 1968 he started an Arts Lab in Drury Lane. This could have been kept alive if the Arts Council had not decided against rescuing it with an emergency subsidy. But even in its short life-span it exerted a considerable influence and brought into existence several groups which have survived. The People Show had already been started in 1966 by Jeff Nuttall, who wrote scripts for it to perform in the basement of a bookshop in Charing Cross Road – Better Books. When performances in the bookshop were stopped, the People Show became the resident group at the Arts Lab. Pip Simmons formed a company to put on a series of 50-minute plays there. David Hare and Tony Bicat, who were later to form Portable Theatre, collaborated to compile a show out of Kafka's Diaries.

When the Arts Lab was closed down, Pip Simmons had to find other venues, and David Hare and Tony Bicat wanted to take their productions to a variety of non-theatrical contexts. So, in the same way that sixteenth-century groups of touring players built up a circuit of towns they could successfully revisit, a new network of regional bases was created, mostly in university towns, some on campus, some outside it. With over forty universities, most of them new, England now had a very large student population, spread all over the country, and it formed the basis of the new audience. Many of the Fringe groups took to touring, and non-Fringe groups like the RSC's Theatregoround and Prospect Theatre Company started to visit the same dates.

It was in 1969 that the intervention of the Arts Council had a big effect on Fringe theatres. In 1968–69 subsidies were given to Charles Marowitz's company Camden Playhouse Productions (£2,355) and to Inter-Action Trust, an organisation set up in 1968 by another American emigré, Ed Berman, to take art to the community. It was given a subsidy of £2,300, and Portable Theatre was given £89. In theory all the new groups could benefit from the New Drama Guarantee Scheme, by which £250 could be provided for the production of a new play, but in practice relatively little money was handed out, because the groups that worked improvisationally could not submit scripts to be considered under the scheme. After six months in which members of the Arts Council's Drama Panel tried to consider work in performance, the Panel asked the Council to make a 'general grant' to groups which did not work from scripts. A great deal more money was given out in 1969–70, much of it going to groups that did not use scripts. Marowitz's subsidy was slightly reduced, while Inter-Action's was more than trebled and Portable's rocketed to £2,922. Nancy Meckler's group, the Freehold, was given £1,852; the Wherehouse Company £500; and the Soho Theatre £280. All these companies benefited again in 1970–71 and (except for Inter-Action's) all the grants were increased, while other groups were added to the list – the Brighton Combination, the People Show, the Pip Simmons Theatre Group, Keith Johnstone's Theatre Machine, Quipu Basement Theatre, the Actors Circus, the London Theatre Group, the Black Box, and Ken Campbell's Road Show. In all, £21,675 was doled out, plus £3,965 under the New Drama Scheme. Portable Theatre received £6,125, the Actors' Circus £87. In 1971–72 the total subsidy to Fringe theatres was nearly quadrupled – about £91,000 was divided between forty-five companies, but only seven of them received over £5,000 and nearly 50 per cent of them were given less than £2,000 each. In all less than 4 per cent of the total drama subsidy went to the Fringe.

Naturally the possibility of receiving official subsidy encouraged the formation of groups. New ones proliferated but, as with the reps, the Arts Council's policy was to increase the subsidy to companies it had already supported rather than take on new ones, and this tends towards perpetuating the *status quo* and reducing the possibility of rapid change, which is essential to what ought to be happening on the Fringe. Most of the newcomers had to prove themselves by surviving without subsidy. Many failed. Of the thirty-two groups listed in the first issue of *Theatre Quarterly* (January–March 1971) only sixteen were still in existence by the summer of 1972. Groups now began to proliferate less in London, where living expenses are high, but more in the regions. Many of the new groups operate only outside London –

John Bull Puncture Repair Kit, Bath Natural Theatre, Landscapes and Living Spaces, Ritual Theatre, Yorkshire Gnomes, Last Knockings, and Phantom Captain. Meanwhile the London groups which became successful and subsidised also became different. The Freehold, for instance, was unable to pay salaries to its actors when it started; everyone was given an equal share of the takings. In 1972–73 the company was receiving £6,000 from the Arts Council which covered 60 per cent of the salary bill for ten actors at £20 a week each. There were also a number of highly paid foreign bookings. At Zurich, for instance, the group received £500 for each performance. The actors were given a bonus for these dates.

The disadvantage of big money for a Fringe group is that commitments become more binding, freedom of movement curtailed. Ideally a small experimental group should have the same privileges as a highly subsidised company like the Berliner Ensemble, which can simply postpone the opening of a production if it is not ready. Subsidy and success force a group to be reliable, where sometimes standards can be maintained only by reneging on a booking. Groups also have to frame their policy to accord with the forms that have to be filled in. While the Arts Council sometimes insists that a group which has given a show three months of rehearsal should give it an equivalent period of performances, even if it turns out to be no good.

Since the Arts Council's Experimental Drama Committee was formed, reliance on balance sheets and estimates of audience sizes has been even greater than before. Nor does it always pay to make one's returns straightforwardly. Directors of Fringe companies often sense that Arts Council officials want them to misrepresent the facts especially when figures would reveal a deficit. One company was recently invited to make a deficit of £1,000 disappear by pushing it forward into the accounts for the following year.

One of the problems of the London Fringe is that it has no building equivalent to the Cité Université in Paris (which has a number of auditoriums for events and experimental shows) or to Joseph Papp's New York Public Theatre (which houses shows that could not have been staged elsewhere). The Institute of Contemporary Arts has done disappointingly little for Fringe Theatre, and the Roundhouse is too large and too expensive for most Fringe groups, though it could have become an ideal base if some of the Arts Council's Housing the Arts funds had been devoted to developing it by building a complex of small auditoriums into the space which is now going to be used for a new office block containing only one small auditorium. A new café theatre may also open in the vaults under the Roundhouse.

Nor do we even have a regular Fringe Festival in London, though we are the only large European capital without one. Rents are so high that it could only be organised if the Arts Council or an enlightened borough council (like Camden) made a suitable space available. David Aukin (who is Nancy Meckler's husband and has done valuable work as an impresario for a lot of Fringe groups) organised a festival in 1971 at the small Cockpit Theatre and succeeded in covering his costs by charging 90p a ticket. There is no knowing how large the audience might have been if prices had been lower. For a large part of the potential public it is a choice between an evening's free televiewing and a visit to the theatre. Certainly the Fringe audience is quite different from the theatregoers who can spend over five pounds on two tickets, interval drinks and a meal afterwards. When William Gaskill organised *Come Together*, a mini-festival of Fringe groups at the Royal Court in 1970, with all the seats taken out of the stalls, the crowds that bought tickets consisted mainly of people who never came back when the seats were put in again. But when a thousand pounds was spent on taking over four theatres in Lambeth and getting twenty-seven groups to take part in a Free Theatre Festival, about 3,500 people came. Some of them were children of thirteen or fourteen who could not have come if they had had to pay. Normally their parents decide whether or not they are to go to the theatre, but this is the age at which habits are formed.

The Festival was organised by Peter Oliver, who has been the director of Oval House youth club since 1960 and has been extremely helpful to the groups, giving them free rehearsal space and the use of the club's theatre. Many of the groups like the People Show, the Pip Simmons group and the Freehold, which were homeless when the Arts Lab was closed, found they were so welcome at the Oval that it virtually became their London base. The other important base for the groups was the Mickery Theatre in Holland. It was in Loenersloot, but now it is in Amsterdam. Ritsaart ten Cate, who runs it, has had a big influence on the English fringe.

There are many groups based outside London and many of the London groups spend a great part of their time on the road doing one- and two-night stands. There is still no central agency to deal with bookings but in 1971 DALTA, the Arts Council's Touring department, published *Groupvine*, a booklet containing details about some of the small touring groups – dance groups, music groups, puppet groups, theatre groups, and 'Touring Art and Mixed Media'. Thirty-nine theatre groups were listed in the first issue, fourteen of which were based outside London, though three of these were resident rep companies. DALTA has now, rather belatedly, become involved in the Fringe touring circuit with a scheme called Stopovers, and the Regional Arts Associations are also beginning to commit themselves.

The group which in 1970–71[1] was receiving by far the largest subsidy (£9,055 compared with Charles Marowitz's £4,190) was Inter-Action, which was started in 1968 by another American emigré, Ed Berman, an ex-Rhodes Scholar and radical empire-builder who claims not to be interested in the theatre, only in drama. After writing and directing some early Fringe plays at the Mercury Theatre in Notting Hill, he set up Inter-Action as a trust 'with the central aim of making the arts, especially drama, more relevant to urban community life and working to break down the cultural barriers that exist in group situations'. By the end of 1968 Inter-Action had several subsidiary companies. Doggs Troupe is a street theatre group which gives partly improvised performances for children. The members of it live communally, like the Living Theatre, and are paid £7 a week each. There are workshops at which they learn and practise games and techniques they will subsequently use and teach, applying them equally to acting and to therapy in the sessions they hold at youth clubs, mental hospitals and remand homes. At the same time, Berman was successfully launching a season of lunch-hour productions in the basement of the Ambiance Restaurant in Queensway, and he retained

[1] In 1971–72, Inter-Action received £19,450 and Marowitz £8,820; in 1972–73, Inter-Action £21,000 and Marowitz £14,000.

this name Ambiance for lunch-hour productions elsewhere. Berman's success helped to encourage the proliferation of lunch-hour theatres we have now, but the idea had already been tried out by a smaller group called QUIPU, organised by playwright David Halliwell and actor David Calderisi, who were putting on lunch-time performances at the Arts in 1966, while several other groups were trying out the London audience's interest in lunch-hour theatre. There were also midday performances at the Little Theatre Club in Garrick Yard and at the Jeannetta Cochrane, then in the hands of the London Traverse. In 1968 Quipu, now without David Calderisi, but with two other actors, Walter Hall and Carl Forgione, resumed at the Arts, and it was after this that Berman began his operations at the Ambiance.

He also joined forces with the young Israeli director Naftali Yavin, who died prematurely in 1972, to form TOC (The Other Company) a group which did very intensive studio work and kept the same actors for much longer than most Fringe groups manage to. In December 1970 they gave London audiences the first chance to see a Peter Handke play, *Offending the Audience,* and two of the same four actors (Judy Monahan and Robert Walker) appeared in Yavin's excellent 1972 production of Handke's *Self Accusation* when Inter-Action had opened a theatre of its own, the Almost Free Theatre, a converted bingo hall in Rupert Street. Like Jim Haynes's Traverse Theatre, Inter-Action has deeply influenced the way our Fringe has developed, by inviting foreign groups which have served as models. The Bread and Puppet Theatre from New York was seen at the Oval in Kennington, and the Grand Théatre Panique, which Jérome Savary had formed in Paris with the help of Arrabal, came to the Mercury Theatre. This company evolved into the Grand Magic Circus, which was seen at the Roundhouse in 1972. The seventies will no doubt see much more exchanging of influences between the un-orthodox theatre groups of different countries, and already at least a start has been made towards the creation of an international circuit.

Berman excels at involving groups of people, young and old, in games which create a feeling of contact, and, more consciously than most people in the English theatre, he is experimenting with the wide overlap between playing games and acting. Writing plays himself under the pseudonym Ed B, he made great use of verbal games. He was interested in the way that puns, jokes, songs and games, both physical and verbal, could produce pointers to the common multiples of human experience and could release emotion that produces a sense of togetherness. The techniques that he teaches to his followers are equally useful when they are acting, and when they are working with groups of children or mentally handicapped adults. Tom Stoppard, who more than any of our other playwrights makes punning into a constructional principle, wrote a play, *Dogg's Our Pet*, which was staged when the Almost Free Theatre opened in 1971.

The Off-Broadway technique of 'Environmental theatre' has been used by Marowitz, Berman and other directors on the English Fringe. Once the rigid separation between actors and audience has been broken down, not only can the playing area be extended into the auditorium, but the audience can be contained, in some sense, within the set. In a Victorian proscenium theatre this is impossible, but in the Open Space, the Almost Free Theatre and in many of the miscellaneous spaces our Fringe Theatre is using, the seating can be rearranged and the work of the designer extended till it is no longer a picture the audience is looking at but an environment it is sitting in. Nor is it only the auditorium that can be remodelled to create the atmosphere a production demands. A spectator's receptivity is inevitably conditioned by what happens to him between the moment of stepping inside the theatre building and settling into his seat. The familiar experience of moving from the traffic-noises, the illuminated shop-windows and the crowded pavements of Shaftesbury Avenue into a foyer which looks rather like a party where everyone has an overcoat on and no one has a drink, of being directed to one of several entrances according to what kind of ticket we have, of giving the ticket up to be torn by a man in uniform, of buying a glossy programme and following an elderly usherette into an auditorium where people in other seats are talking in low expectant voices – all this is doing more than we realise to programme our expectations. The people who arrived at the Open Space in July 1968 to see its first production, *Fortune and Men's Eyes* by John Herbert, had to clamber down an iron fire escape under surveillance of a prison guard with a

machine gun. After having their finger prints taken and waiting outside a cell door, listening to an impersonal official voice over a loud-
speaker, they were led through the set, which consisted of four prison
bunks on their way to their seats. The impact of this experience
helped to make the play into such a success that it was transferred to
the West End, but in the Comedy Theatre, with a different foyer, a
different stage-auditorium relationship and different audience expectations, it lasted only six weeks. For the December 1971 production of
Picasso's play *The Four Little Girls* the whole interior of the Open
Space was elaborately restructured by Marowtiz, Carolee Schnee-
man, Penny Slinger and Robin Don. On the way in you had to
duck your head to pass through the small toyland doorway, and
the whole interior was transformed into a childhood fairyland. You
sat down on uneven spangled banks and the spangles stuck to your
clothes.

Berman has also been experimenting with environmental theatre,
both inside and outside theatre buildings. The Doggs Troupe takes
a kind of theatrical experience to children in their own environment
of street, playground, amusement park, and Inter-Action takes
experimental shows to areas like Notting Hill, where social problems
are particularly apparent, and involves audiences in group improvisations. Berman also believes in drama written for non-theatrical
environments, and has himself conceived a play for performance in a
swimming pool, with part of the audience in the water. Another of
his plays *The Nudist Campers Grow and Grow*, which was performed
at the Ambiance, effectively impaled each spectator on the alternative
of stripping off too or feeling like a voyeur.

Of the English groups which are not directed by Americans, some,
like the People Show, owe virtually nothing to American influences;
others, like the Pip Simmons group, owe a very great deal. Pip
Simmons attributes the vitality of the American scene to 'the crudity
of their media, the crudity of their history'. He started from experiments with word-games but came to depend more on pop music
and violent physicality. He says of Norman Mailer that he 'communi-
cates physically – and English writers almost never work that way'.
He derived one of his shows from Chaucer (*The Pardoner's Tale*)

and one from Lewis Carroll (*Alice in Wonderland*) but *Superman* was deliberately constructed out of clichés and used the story-line of a comic Simmons had read. It was also about rock-and-roll. The next show *Do It!* was based on the book by the Yippie leader Jerry Rubin about the storming of the Pentagon and the attempt to break up the Democratic Convention of 1968 in Chicago. 'How would an audience react if they were provoked in the way the kids threw shit at the pigs (= police)? So our actors ran through the audience in a very obscene way. We were asking "If you'd been a guard at the Pentagon, what would you have done?"' In the final production before the group disbanded in 1973, *The George Jackson Black and White Minstrel Show*, the audience had to dodge bits of half-chewed banana which were spat out, and to make bids during the auction of nigger slaves.

The urgent buttonholing, the strident assault on an audience's ambivalences and the crudity of some of the means employed to make an impact are characteristic of many Fringe groups. The cult of physicality is of course partly a reaction against the main tradition of English acting, which relies more on the voice and the head than on the rest of the body, and it is inevitable that the abolition of the Lord Chamberlain's censorship (1968) should be celebrated by an over-exploitation of the theatrical possibilities of nudity and simulated sex. Though there are some Fringe groups which are not afraid to be subtle, there are many whose premise seems to be that audiences cannot be gripped or held except by a series of shock effects. This method produces diminishing returns. One of the reasons it was cultivated was that during the four formative years 1968–71, none of the groups (except for Charles Marowitz's) had a permanent home of its own. They were all moving about from place to place, in and out-side London, with no hope of building up a regular audience or the kind of style that can only be evolved in a relationship with one. As David Hare has said of his experience with Portable Theatre, 'Literary values don't survive on the road . . . You must have plays with a strong physical force. You have to find the lowest common denominator for a show.' In their first production, the Kafka adaptation, he says, 'We bashed and bashed our audiences with a long steady stream of neurosis.' Their production of Howard Brenton's play *Christie in Love* was effective, but even an intelligent cultivation of stridency is liable to defeat its own objects, and Portable Theatre went through a phase in which the directors tended to produce deafening effects for their own sake, or, at worst, deceive themselves about their own motives for wanting to shock. *Lay-by*, the co-operative work of seven playwrights, could neither focus nor conceal its relish for the pornography it was trying to satirise. It featured a photographer taking a shot of a girl sucking off his own cock. Later on, confronted with a man wearing an enormous pink dildo, she bit the end off it. In the final scene naked male and female corpses were daubed with paint by two hospital attendants who then stewed them in a large vat and started to eat them.

One of the reasons for the amorphousness of a Fringe Theatre is that it represents a mixture of reaction against the existing theatre and overflow from it, a convergence of those who would like to revolutionise it and those who would prefer to be working inside it. John McGrath is a playwright who made quite a mark while he was still an undergraduate at Oxford. He went on to have a good deal of success in the theatre, in television and in films – he adapted Len Deighton's novel *Billion Dollar Brain* for the Ken Russell film and scripted *The Bofors Gun* from his own play. But he came to feel that his writing was being distorted by the system that used it and to dislike the Welfare State atmosphere that struck him as pervading the repertory system and the RSC equally. He decided to form a company of his own, which he called the 7:84 Theatre Company, as a reminder that 84 per cent of Britain's wealth is in the hands of 7 per cent of the population. Some of the champions of the Fringe deny that the pub theatres are part of the Fringe scene but – though only a small proportion of the 7:84 Company's work is done in pubs – McGrath sees them as a way of reaching the 98 per cent of the population that does not patronise the theatre and the 93 per cent that owns only 16 per cent of the national wealth. Once they're in a pub, if there is a show on upstairs, people willingly go up to have a look at it. He wants to do plays for 'the ordinary people of London who wouldn't dream of going to a West End show'. He has also put on lunch-time shows. 'People don't feel it's a special occasion.'

The 7:84 Company is a Socialist group and many of those involved in it are Marxists. They want to remind working-class people that they are being exploited and to persuade them that their values are better than those of the middle or upper classes. But most of the lunch-hour companies and the pub companies tend to be less ideologically oriented. Frederick Proud and his wife Verity started their Soho lunch-time theatre instead of trying to get jobs in the existing theatre. After nearly four years of putting on lunch-hour productions, they moved into a basement provided rent-free by the Regent Street Polytechnic. The Arts Council gave them £1,706 in 1970–71 and £3,200 in 1971–72, but they can pay the actors only about £5 per production, with no rehearsal salary, a main incentive being the opportunity to be seen working by agents and directors. The productions usually cost about £100 to mount and there are productions of new plays, which enrich the writer by £50.

Fringe groups are always splitting like amoebas, and Walter Hall and Carl Forgione left David Halliwell's Quipu to form their own Basement Theatre, which has functioned in several different Soho basements, and above ground elsewhere. They had a grant of £2,344 for 1970–71,[1] and Walter Hall had to work as dresser at the Royal Court to earn extra money. Even successes like the 1972 production of William Trevor's *Going Home* are only moderately lucrative, and casting is very difficult since actors are being asked to work for nothing. For a part in one production the director ended up with the sixty-fourth actor he approached.

At the King's Head in Islington an American couple, Dan and Joan Crawford, provide the audiences with a cheap but good meal followed by a play which they can watch from tables while they go on drinking. Productions cost between £600 and £1,100. Sometimes actors are paid, sometimes not. Sometimes other companies' productions are brought in, like the Basement Theatre's *Going Home*. Inspired by the success of the King's Head, Ind-Coope announced their intention of having ten theatre-pubs and the first opened in April 1972 in the spacious new 100-seat theatre which

[1] £3,024 in 1971–72.

had been installed at The Bush in Shepherd's Bush. It was run by the Alternative Theatre Company, which at first had John Neville as one of its directors. Another director was Brian McDermott, who had been directing at the theatre in the King's Head for the Crawfords, and the first production of the new company was a revival of one which had been seen there – David Parker's adaptation of John Fowles's *The Collector*, directed by John Neville.

From every point of view it is good to have outlets for one-act plays. Ten years ago very few were ever staged; double bills and treble bills tend to be less popular in ordinary theatres than full-length plays, but a playing time of an hour is ideal for a pub theatre, and in the less formal drinking atmosphere there are also different audiences with different expectations. It may be true that the brewers are mainly interested in pub theatre as a means of selling more beer, but they are also making more live theatre available.

It is inevitable that some groups, in launching an offensive against the methods of establishment theatre, succeed so well in doing so, attracting so much of a following that they become an establishment themselves. Aiming to infiltrate the existing theatre, they become absorbed into it, refreshing its bloodstream, but losing their own identity in the process. But, at the same time, new groups are emerging almost daily. However exclusive the profession makes itself, nothing can stop the small groups from proliferating through amoeba-splits in which each half rapidly grows to the size of the original whole and through the formation of new groups which emerge out of someone's desire to find self-fulfilment in self-expression shared with other people.

John Ford, who was editor of the theatre section of *Time Out* until October 1971, and again from March 1972 until June 1973, has done a great deal to encourage, co-ordinate and publicise the activities of small theatre groups, and the premise behind his influential columns was that there was nothing rare or special about theatrical talent. His policy has been 'to encourage people to make theatre since it is one of the cheapest, most effective and accessible forms of expression'. He also introduced a free classified advertisement service. 'Use it for any-thing you want in theatre'. Some advertisements for actors specify that they must be Equity members; others carried some such phrase as 'training not essential if right type', or 'professional ability but willing to live off bookings'. And there were theatres like The Kindred ex-tending an 'anyone can do it' invitation to writers. Every one-act play submitted was staged in a rehearsed reading. 'In L. A.,' prompted *Time Out*, 'there are truck-drivers who have found out they can write plays. How about you?'

Other acting groups are coming into existence out of a desire to make political statements. 'Why do it?' asks an article headed 'How to Use Street Theatre', in the pamphlet *Culture and Agitation* pub-lished by Action Books. 'The group should come together in response to a political need, not out of an arty desire to try street theatre. Existing groups have grown from the need to find a more direct form of political communication than leaflets or posters ... Decide the political area where you feel a street play could be most useful (tenants, squatters, strikers, school or university students, women's liberation, colonial exploitation). In fact, your group will probably come together because of involvement in a particular local issue or situation, so this question settles itself.'

Given marks for political commitment and for professionalism, some Fringe groups would rate zero on one and highly on the other, some would rate fairly high on both, some very low on both, but one advantage they all have in common is their smallness. The sheer size of theatres like the RSC and the National makes it inevitable that actors, directors, administrators, technicians and secretaries do not get to know each other as well as they could if there were fewer of them. It is not merely that there is a better feeling running through a produc-tion when the relationships behind it are more personal, but new ways of working can be explored in which writer, director and actors can give each other more and take more from each other. Normal theatrical practice is that neither the director nor the actors see the script until it is complete, and though there may be a few pre-rehearsal weeks in which the director can work with the writer, suggesting cuts and revisions, the only contributions the actors can make to the script are the minor ones introduced during rehearsals, when everyone is under pressure.

Some of the best Off-Off-Broadway work (like *America Hurrah*) seems to have been developed out of situations in which the conventional separations of function between writer, director and actors have been broken down. Over here a start has been made in the same direction and it may well be that the most valuable achievement of the Fringe during the seventies will be the discovery of new means of collaboration in the preparation of a production. By the end of the sixties, Max Stafford-Clark, who had been director of the Traverse at Edinburgh, had already withdrawn to form a subsidiary company and to devote himself to working with it. Finding that the three-weekly changeover system allowed too little time for preparatory work on the text, he formed the Traverse Theatre Workshop company. Before it was disbanded it involved writers like Stanley Eveling, John Spurling and Howard Brenton in collaborative work with the actors. While Brenton's play *Hitler Dances* was being prepared – 'written' is no longer quite the right word – author, director, actors and musicians worked very closely together in an old theatre outside Amsterdam. After four weeks of improvisations and experiments with the company Brenton went off to work on his own. 'I had a much wider vocabulary than a writer usually has because I knew the work of the actors. I could draw on all the explorations and relationships of the last month – a physical vocabulary – as well as what was in my head.' His new script was then reworked with the company. Other writers (like John McGrath and David Halliwell) who have formed groups of their own are also having the opportunity to work closely and co-operatively with actors. Halliwell said that he started Quipu so as to be in charge of his own destiny. He felt he was being treated like a child when he merely handed a script over to a management and waited to see what would be done with it.

It is also possible for a group like Traverse Theatre Workshop or Portable Theatre to go on working on a production after it has had a public run. With no problems of keeping an expensive cast together or storing bulky scenery or keeping a theatre open, the company can withdraw into a workshop situation, using the experience that was gained in public as a basis for more work done in private between writer, director and actors. Like *Hitler Dances*, the Portable production of Christopher Wilkinson's *Plays for Rubber Go-go Girls* benefited from this process of going through more than one edition. The area where writing techniques overlap with production techniques can be explored particularly well in this way. Experiments can be made in connecting areas of experience which are not usually connected, and in switching from one style to another. Themes can be developed simultaneously on different levels, or time sequences can be mixed and the actors can exchanges roles in mid-action. More than one actor can be used to play a single part. The narrative line can be dropped and picked up again; music or poetry can be used to carry it forward. There are very few reps in which the production becomes inseparable from the play but there is a growing number of Fringe groups where this happens. Never before has there been so much opportunity for making discoveries of new ways in which writer, director, actors and musicians can help each other.

12 CULTURE AND THE ARTS COUNCIL

In any form of society towards which we are likely to move, it now seems clear that there must be, not a simple equality (in the sense of identity) of culture; but rather a very complex system of specialised developments – the whole of which will form the whole culture, but which will not be available, or conscious, as a whole, to any individual or group living within it ... One can imagine a society in which the practice and enjoyment of the arts would be very much more widely diffused. But there are dangers, both to the arts and to the whole culture, if the diffusion of this abstracted part of the culture is planned and considered as a separate operation.
RAYMOND WILLIAMS *writing on* T. S. ELIOT *in* 'Culture and Society 1780–1950'.

In 1945, the year that the Council for the Encouragement of Music and the Arts was reconstituted as the Arts Council, John Maynard Keynes, who stayed on as Chairman, made a speech on the radio: 'The purpose of the Arts Council of Great Britain,' he said, 'is to create an environment, to breed a spirit, to cultivate an opinion, to offer a stimulus to such purpose that the artist and the public can each sustain and live on the other in that union which has occasionally existed in the past at the great ages of a communal civilised life.' The only period of English theatrical history which can be called great in this sense is (as I suggested in Chapter 2) the Shakespearean period, when the culture and the language were totally different from what they are today, though Lord Keynes, in his book *A Treatise on Money*

(1930), had suggested that the greatness might be explained in economic terms:

> We were just in a financial position to afford Shakespeare at the moment when he presented himself. . . . I offer it as a thesis for those who like rash generalisations, that by far the larger proportion of the world's great writers and artists have flourished in the atmosphere of buoyancy, exhilaration and the freedom from economic cares felt by the governing class, which is engendered by profit inflations.

The Elizabethan theatre could not have developed as it did without patronage from both those who benefited directly from the nation's prosperity and from the poor. The fact that productions which depended more on the spoken word than on spectacle could appeal so strongly and so immediately to such a mixed audience can be explained only as a result of the unity of the culture. In Raymond Williams's terms, the whole of it was available to any individual or group living within it. Or as W. B. Yeats put it in the essay 'What is Popular Poetry?': 'The art of the people was as closely mingled with the art of the coteries as was the speech of the people that delighted in rhythmical animation, in idiom, in images . . . with the unchanging speech of the poets.'

I owe this quotation to Professor L. C. Knights, who wrote a book review in Vol. II No. 4 of *Scrutiny* and an essay in Vol. V No. 1, which add up to a cogent refutation of the Keynesian view. The force and vividness of Elizabethan English is as evident in the prose as in the verse drama, and Knights provides the best explanation I know of what he calls the 'muscular content' of the language that 'enabled physical states to be portrayed with such immediacy':

> O so I was tickled in the spleene with that word, my hart hopt and danst, my elbowes icht, my fingers friskt, I wist not what should become of my feete, nor knew what I did for joy.

Compared with the polite prose of the Restoration, Elizabethan prose is, as Knights says, 'closer to folk speech, to the English of ploughing, carting, selling and small town gossip. . . . Not only was the relation of word and thing, of word and action, far more intimate than in a society that obtains most of its more permanent impressions from books and newspapers, a large number of Elizabethan words and phrases are the direct equivalent of action – gestures of sociability, contempt or offence (the Elizabethans had a particularly rich vocabulary of abuse).' Both the written and the spoken language were dynamic. Words not only demanded continuous mental activity from the reader or listener: they all but involved his body. The appeal was simultaneously to the imagination and the physical senses.

Knights was writing in the early thirties. Forty years later it would have to be said that English society obtains most of its more permanent impressions from television. According to Anthony Sampson's *New Anatomy of Britain* (1971) 94 per cent of British homes have television sets, and families watch them for an average of eighteen hours a week – 'far more than any other European country and twice as much as Belgium, Italy or Sweden'. This is now the dominant factor in our culture, and the image now has a different relationship to both the spoken and the written word. Whereas the radio play is in the tradition of verbal theatre – as in Elizabethan drama, the words and the sound effects create pictures in the listener's mind – the television play is in the tradition of the film, leaving equally little to the imagination. A television play or a film may be a work of art, but it costs the viewer no effort to respond to Tuesday Weld's face or Raquel Welch's bosom, and the eye is continually diverted. So we are conditioned to expect instant gratification. It takes less effort to watch *War and Peace* on the screen than to read Tolstoy's prose, though quite a large proportion of the people who enjoy the dramatisation would enjoy the original if they had not got too far out of the reading habit to make the effort. Some actually do go on to read the book, but then the images created by Tolstoy's words have to compete with the more vivid images that a visual medium has implanted in the memory.

Less mental effort is involved in sitting in an audience at a poetry reading than in reading a book of poetry. Very little mental effort is involved in responding to pop poetry, pop music or pop art, but whether these are alternative arts, inferior arts or anti-arts remains to be seen. At the same time there is an audience for Britten and Francis Bacon, whose work forms part of the same culture, but a part of no interest to the majority of the public. Meanwhile the language itself has been weakened, divorced from physical action, diluted by the repetitious superlatives of the advertising men. The sermons and the moral dicta that were detonated so often on Elizabethan eardrums derived from the well-written stories of the Bible; the commercials and the catch phrases which force themselves on to our consciousness are full of the phoney effervescence of copy-writers and the platitudinous promises of politicians. Instead of being involved physically by the spoken and written word, we have defensively to cultivate non-responsiveness.

What can be done to improve the situation? There are those (like Dr F. R. Leavis) who say that in any period it is only a small minority that is capable of a genuine personal response to first-rate works of art and literature. The alternative view is that, given the right education and the right opportunities, a large public could become capable of responding to the best plays, the best music, the best poetry. The question of how much our culture would be changed and how much it has already been changed in the process of being extended is not usually faced either by the state, which has finally taken over responsibility for making the arts available to a wider section of the English public, or by the Arts Council, which has to administer the funds that are made available. The assumption is that culture can be popularised – within limits – without debasing it. Very little thinking goes on about what the limits are.

When the Council for the Encouragement of Music and the Arts was founded in December 1939 to boost public morale during the war, the founder members held very similar views about what could be done. Dr Thomas Jones was a firm believer in the civilising properties of adult education. Lord Macmillan was the Minister of Information. Sir Walford Davies was a proponent of popular education in music. Kenneth Clark was later to become famous by lecturing about Civilisation on television. William Emrys Williams had been

Secretary of the British Institute of Adult Education and had originated the 'Art for the People' scheme for circulating paintings, most of which were privately owned, in small towns and rural areas. These five were later joined by Thelma Cazalet, who was nominated by the Board of Education, and L. du Garde Peach, an energetic champion of amateur drama. When Dr Jones retired in 1942, John Maynard Keynes became Chairman. He had been concerned for years with the problem of patronage for the arts, and in 1930 he had formed the London Artists Association to support painters of merit who were not earning as much as they needed. He believed that the pleasures of the arts could be made available to a far wider public, and when CEMA evolved into the Arts Council, he arranged for the Treasury to take over financial responsibility for it from the Ministry of Education, which would probably have allowed it less independence. In his 1945 broadcast he said:.

> I do not believe it is yet realised what an important thing has happened. State patronage of the arts has crept in. It has happened in a very English, informal, unostentatious way – half-baked if you like. A semi-independent body is provided with modest funds to stimulate, comfort and support any societies or bodies, brought together on private or local initiative, which are striving with serious purpose and a reasonable prospect of success to present for public enjoyment the arts of drama, music and painting. . . . But we do not intend to socialise this side of social endeavour. . . . The artist . . . cannot be told his direction. . . . The task of an official body is not to teach or to censor, but to give courage, confidence and opportunity.

In August 1946 the Arts Council of Great Britain, which had been announced in the House of Commons in June 1945, was formally constituted as a Body Corporate under Royal Charter with the object of 'developing a greater knowledge, understanding and practice of the fine arts exclusively, and in particular, to increase the accessibility of the fine arts to the public throughout Our Realm, to improve the standard of execution of fine arts and to advise and co-operate with Our Government Departments, local authorities and other bodies on any matters concerned directly or indirectly with these objects.' This is a fairly vague formulation, and priorities are left undefined, but in 1967 a new charter was issued which redefined the objects and arranged them in order:

(a) to develop and improve the knowledge, understanding and practice of the arts;

(b) to increase the accessibility of the arts to the public throughout Great Britain; and

(c) to advise and co-operate with Departments of Our Government, local authorities and other bodies on any matters concerned whether directly or indirectly with the foregoing objects.

This is still vague. It is presumably in the general public that the knowledge and understanding of the arts are to be developed, so (a) overlaps with (b) and there is still no answer to the question of whether priority should be given to raising the standard of artistic activity or widening the public for it. Lord Goodman, however, the Chairman from 1963-71, provided a clear definition in a speech he gave to the House of Lords in April 1967:

Our major emphasis is on cultivating new audiences for the arts. The question of improving the standard and quality of those institutions which are still there is of great importance, but it is not our paramount consideration.

Both the policy-forming and the administration involve a complex collaboration between professional artists, professional administrators and distinguished amateurs. In many ways our system is preferable to having the whole apparatus in the hands of politicians and civil servants who have no involvement in the arts, but government by committee is always government by compromise, and the people who would be most valuable on the committees are often the people who have least time to spare for voluntary work.

Of all the committees that are exercising control over our theatre, the Arts Council and its Drama Panel are the most influential. Subsidy is now the life-blood of nearly all our theatres, and in deciding how to apportion the three million pounds that the government spends on drama each year, these two committees are effectively determining not only which companies will survive, but how much freedom they will have to do what they want to do. Like the reps' boards of management, the committees consist of men and women who for varying – but not invariably altruistic – motives, undertake a great deal of work without payment.

It is the Minister responsible for the Arts who appoints the Chairman of the Arts Council and up to nineteen other members. The Chairman can ask for anyone he wants to be appointed, and the Secretary-General and other members of the Council can put suggestions to him. The appointments are for a five-year term. (Lord Goodman was asked to continue in office for two extra years which overlapped into the regime of the Conservative government, although he had been appointed and re-appointed by the Labour government.)

The Council depends on several advisory panels and committees including the Art Panel, the Drama Panel, the Literature Panel, the Music Panel, the Art Film Committee and the Experimental Projects Committee. Panel members are normally appointed for three years, and nominations for new members can be made by anyone on the Council or the existing panel or the permanent paid staff. (The Drama Department consists of a Drama Director, six drama officers plus secretaries, while DALTA, which deals also with opera and ballet touring, has a separate staff, which is being increased, now that it also has a regional office.) Nominations for the Drama Panel are considered by the Drama Director and the Panel Chairman, who passes them on to the Council, which makes the final decisions. The Council also appoints from among its own members the Chairman and Deputy Chairman of each panel. The Chairman is usually appointed for only one year, but he can be re-appointed any number of times, and, unlike the other panel members, he does not have to retire at the end of three years.

While most of the personalities involved, then, are selected by the Minister or the Chairman or by people who have themselves been selected by one of these, it would be unfair to suggest that all the thinking done by the Council and its panels is orthodox Establishment thinking. In 1972 seven of the twenty-eight members of the Drama

Panel were under thirty, and several were involved in Fringe theatre. There are usually two or three playwrights, one or two designers, a few actors, actresses and directors, a critic, a theatre administrator, a few members of repertory theatre boards and a few people connected with local government. But no one is there as a representative of any organisation.

In a letter to the *Guardian* in November 1971 the playwright James Saunders suggested that the structure of the Arts Council made it inevitable that the thinking of the panels should reflect the thinking of the Council itself, which in turn reflected that of the Establishment that put it there. The same argument is sometimes put forward about educational systems. In *Man and Society* Karl Mannheim wrote, 'Education does not mould men in the abstract but in and for a given society.' State control over both education and the popularisation of culture is more apparent and very much more one-sided in Communist countries, but is it possible, in any society, that the state should give ten million pounds each year to a committee which is itself completely autonomous and which allows complete autonomy to the orchestras, art galleries, opera and ballet companies and theatres it supports? My impression is that the theatres being subsidised have never had complete autonomy in practice, but that the idea of autonomy has prevented the Council from being as useful or as positive as it could have been.

The doctrine of autonomy is partly an evasion of responsibility. If the Council is committed by its Charter to the object of developing and improving the practice of the arts, is it right that it should hand over large sums of money to theatres all over England without making sure that the money is used towards raising artistic standards? The only major rep in England which does not receive help from the Arts Council is Windsor. The others, having accepted money, are theoretically free to spend it exactly as they please, but in practice they are limited by their own ideas of what the Arts Council expects of them, and in fact their freedom would probably be greater if only the Council would issue a clear directive. Surmise is usually more restricting than certainty. Town councils which support a local theatre financially usually have at least one representative on the board of management to act as a spokeman for the civic viewpoint. Members of the Drama Panel, obviously, do not have time to keep in close touch with the activities of nearly a hundred theatre companies. Members of the permanent staff do travel round the country to see performances and to attend meetings of the theatre boards, where they join in discussions but do not vote. In 1971–72 they attended 227 meeting and saw 599 shows. Usually they reckon to visit each subsidised company at least once a quarter. But with only seven officers and a great deal of work to do in London, it is inevitable that more attention is paid to facts and figures as they appear on paper than to the actualities of theatrical performances. The Drama Officers receive minutes of all meetings, as well as notices, accounts and box-office returns. Any major change of policy (like a return from three-weekly rep to fortnightly) would be reported at once to the Council itself, and the next quarterly payment could be withheld, but extreme measures like this are hardly ever taken.

The Drama Panel is only an advisory body with no executive authority: all it can do is make recommendations to the Arts Council itself. In practice, though, its power is restricted not so much by the Council as by the pressure of the past. Principles are evolved which are never formulated, but which persist in spite of all the changes of personnel and personalities. It is not only the Drama Panel which includes practical men of the theatre. Nicholas Barter, who had worked with the RSC's Theatregoround and had been Director of Productions at both Lincoln and Ipswich, was appointed to the full-time staff in 1970; almost all the other Drama Officers have had experience in the theatre as actors or technicians or administrators. But the initiatives that individuals can take are limited. Certain changes are made and sometimes a subsidy shoots up by several thousand pounds (as the Pip Simmons group's did from £1,110 in 1970–71 to £7,311 in 1971–72) but for the most part policy is conditioned by a consensus which seems to reside more in silence than in the spoken word. This is one of the main dangers, especially when there is no basis of agreement about priorities. Is raising the standard of performances more important than spreading the availability of performances?

Having once started operating without a definite policy, it is very hard to evolve one when the pressure of urgent practical problems is unremitting, and when there is no possibility of demanding more time from the unpaid Council and Panel members. It is partly the time factor that makes it so hard for the Council to discuss the premises from which it works, to appraise its own policy in general terms or even to take new initiatives. The tendency is always to preserve the *status quo*, to base each year's activity on the previous year's. The natural pose of Panel members is defensive – partly because they are under constant critical fire: from those who are being subsidised, but only on a small scale; from those who are subsidised heavily, but still cannot afford to run their theatres as they would like to; and from outsiders who see the anomalies in the situation without seeing what has produced them. The Arts Council is redistributing money that the Government has taken away from the taxpayers, and if it gives some of it to Fringe groups which are openly working towards the subversion of society and the state, this can – according to your viewpoint – look like super-subtle Establishment strategy or self-destructiveness worthy of the central character in Max Frisch's play *The Fire Raisers*, a middle-class muddler who goes on being polite and helpful to two arsonists with designs on his house. But if the Council boycotted the radical groups it would be attacked as reactionary.

It is still the Government that determines the total budget for the arts, but nothing is earmarked except capital funds like Housing the Arts. It is the Council that takes the decision (which in most continental countries is taken by a government minister) about how the bulk of the money is to be split between the various arts. In theory it is the advisory panels that make detailed recommendations for the budget of each separate art, but in practice a question like this cannot be settled by a committee of busy people who all have other jobs and who meet once a month for a few hours. Budgeting on this scale is a job for professionals, and it is the full-time staff who prepare a draft budget to submit to the Drama Finance and Policy Committee, which is a sub-committee both of the Council itself and of the

Drama Panel. All its minutes are circulated to all members of both committees and it is possible for any member of the Drama Panel to attend any meeting of the Finance and Policy Committee. Adjustments can be made to the draft budget, but with limited discussion time it is impossible to do more than go briefly into each item, and inevitable that the recommendations of the full-time officers will be largely accepted, the theory being that these must already reflect the feelings of the panel, since all the officers have attended all the major meetings through the year.

The Drama Officers usually draw up a budget based on the minimum that they think each company will need. This is then reviewed by the Finance Director and the Secretary-General, who submit it to the Minister, who then negotiates with the Treasury. Alternatively these negotiations may take place without a draft budget. In that case the Minister will tell the Arts Council what its grant for the year is to be and the Finance Director will then make tentative allocations for the various arts.

Usually the proposed drama budget is discussed at two or three meetings of the Finance and Policy Committee, each lasting three or four hours, and then at a meeting of the whole Drama Panel. The budget is normally based on the previous year's, with increases to cover rising costs and allocate the additional money the Treasury has made available. If the officers have made any departures from previous practice, they explain their reasons, and discussions can lead to readjustments, but it is seldom that any radical change is made or that there is much disagreement either from the Finance and Policy Committee or from the Drama Panel. Discussion usually goes on until general agreement has been reached. In his first three and a half years as Chairman, J. W. Lambert asked for a show of hands only about four or five times.

Another example of the power of the Drama Officers is provided by the case of the Old Vic. In theory there were four possibilities of what could be done with the building when the National Theatre company gives up using it in 1975. It could be let to a commercial producer, to a subsidised company, run as a touring house, or the Old Vic Company could be revived. This is what the Governors of the

Old Vic would most have liked but, when approached, the Drama Officers expressed the opinion that the Council was spending so much on the National, the RSC and the ESC that it was very unlikely to subsidise another London company devoting itself to a mainly classical repertoire. The question was never actually discussed by the Drama Panel or the Council itself, but this reaction from the Officers was enough to move the Governors towards accepting the idea of leasing the theatre to the ESC. Whether the ESC will have its subsidy increased sufficiently to run two theatres all through the year has not yet been decided; other companies may also be invited to the Vic.

In 1971–72, when £1,640,000 was spent on the Royal Opera House and £1,118,153 on Sadler's Wells Opera, £415,72 was spent on the National Theatre and £295,030 on the RSC. About £1,422,000 went to the reps and about £91,000 to the Fringe. Over £500,000 was spent on touring (mostly through DALTA), and only £26,219 on drama bursaries, £30,610 on training schemes and £57,264 on promoting 'new drama and neglected plays'. If it is obvious that new blood needs constantly to be pumped into the theatrical system, it is equally obvious that the Fringe contains the best available supply of blood donors, but the Art Council's spending indicates that new writers and experimental companies remain very low on the list of priorities. The total spending on forty-five Fringe companies was only twice as much as the Mermaid's subsidy for the year, while over £25,000 of public money went to the Yvonne Arnaud, Guildford, whose policy was not evolved to make the maximum contribution towards developing and improving the knowledge, understanding and practice of the arts.

If the Arts Council increased its allocation to the Fringe by dint of reducing grants to the reps, the economies they would have to make in order to survive – unless local authorities were persuaded (or compelled) to help – might have the effect of lowering standards. But there is a great deal the Arts Council and its Drama Panel could do to raise standards in the reps and to help new playwrights, if only they would abandon the idea of giving autonomy to all their client theatres. The Council's 1967 report said 'There is no *prima facie* case for subsidising work which the public is ready to support to such an extent as to give a reasonable return to the artists and promoters concerned.' It would seem to follow that subsidised theatres should not be allowed to spend public money on Agatha Christie thrillers, mindless musicals and commercial farces like Philip King's *See How They Run* (which was at Nottingham in June 1972). But they could only be stopped by a more direct involvement in programme planning. Standards of acting and production are directly affected, because a company which hurtles about between Shakespeare, Philip King, Strindberg, Rattigan, Brecht, Coward and Christie is not seriously working towards the development of ensemble style.

One of the considerations that may have militated against intervention in the affairs of repertory theatres is that any assumption of responsibility by a central authority is liable to discourage local spending. But the vast sums of money which have been paid out through the Housing the Arts fund towards the cost of new regional theatres have helped to produce a situation in which artistic standards are more likely to be lowered than raised by the prospect of easy money from the state. Town councillors sometimes clamour for the largest possible theatre buildings, though it is far easier to maintain high standards in small ones. And the larger the theatre, the greater its obvious claim to Arts Council subsidy, even when its programme of plays is rather lower than middlebrow. There is now very little commercial theatre outside London, but is it not for the Arts Council to put pressure on the new subsidised managements to stage better plays than their commercial predecessors? Of the numerous theatres whose subsidy is as high or nearly as high as their box-office revenue, only some should be left entirely to their own devices, because only some are doing well enough artistically. The rep at Oxford, which, until it closed in the summer of 1973, was consistently putting on programmes of far better plays than most reps offer, could have been kept alive if the Arts Council had increased its subsidy sufficiently.

There are also ways in which the new playwright could be helped. Cash awards could be given to promising playwrights as they are to novelists and poets. There was a system of direct 'bursaries' for playwrights but this is only being continued where applications could not be considered under any of the other schemes. The English Stage

Company could be given a special grant for Sunday night productions. Reps could be offered a special subsidy to pay star actors to appear in worthwhile plays by new writers. There is already a scheme to encourage new drama by offering up to £750 – but usually £250 – for the first performance (and possibly another grant for the next production) of a new play that the Council approves, plus £150 for the writer, but these grants can be used up by very small theatres (like Billingham and Farnham) and then the Council seldom goes on offering subsidies to give larger theatres an incentive to do the play. If the Artistic Director of a company wants to commission a play, to employ a resident playwright, or to have a writer seconded to the theatre over a short period, the Arts Council will consider the possibility of sharing the theatre's expenses, but not nearly enough is done to encourage theatres to take any of these initiatives.

Having failed in the past with some of the initiatives it has taken, the Arts Council tends to think it can act only in response to 'local demand'. But 'local demand' is a myth. The theatre at Stoke-on-Trent, for instance, was not brought into existence because of local demand but because of exceptional individuals like Stephen Joseph and Peter Cheeseman who happened to find a base in Stoke-on-Trent. But the Arts Council does little to encourage or help individuals. In Lord Goodman's introductory note to the Council's 1967 report he spoke of the 'function to improve the working conditions of artists'. In his Introduction to the report on the last year of his Chairmanship, 1970–71, he sounded a self-critical note which is all too rare in Arts Council pronouncements: 'We have, perhaps, been most remiss in our failure to improve the living conditions of the creative and performing artist.' A Stephen Joseph of the seventies would still have to find some job like lorry-driving to stay solvent, and might still end up accepting an academic post instead of persevering in the practical theatre.

During 1970–71 there were sixty-two grants (some of which were for double bills) under the First Professional Productions scheme and eleven for Second Professional Productions. Where it is not a full-length play, the grant to the theatre is £80 and to the writer £50.[1] On

[1] These amounts have now been increased to £100 and £80.

New Drama Bursaries and expenses the Council paid out £3,740. So rather less than £10,000 would seem to have gone directly to playwrights during a year in which the total spending on drama (including touring subsidies, drama school subsidies and capital grants to theatres under the Housing the Arts scheme) was £3,419,413.

Obviously the richer our theatre is as a whole, the better it is for our playwrights, but even the few regional artistic directors who would be seriously interested in employing resident playwrights or commissioning new plays cannot always persuade their boards to let them. In 1972 Stoke and Nottingham were the only two regional theatres to employ a resident dramatist. The prospect of an additional £250 sometimes helps them to convince the board that it is a worthwhile risk to include a new play in the programme, but without a star actor it is difficult in most towns to attract an audience to a new play. (One way the Arts Council could help would be to start a special fund to subsidise guest appearances of star actors in new plays.) Eventually, no doubt, the Council's Drama Panel will become aware of how much it is effectively damaging our young playwrights by its neglect of them. By then many of them will have given up the unequal fight, and those that have not will be able to reply, as Dr Johnson replied to Lord Chesterfield, 'The notice you have been pleased to take of my labours, had it been early had been kind, but it has been delayed till I am indifferent and cannot enjoy it, till I am solitary and cannot impart it, till I am known and do not want it.' A reserve fund could be kept for the promising new Fringe companies which still occasionally emerge with little prospect of surviving without subsidy. Inquiries could be made about how much script-reading artistic directors are doing. The company at Stoke and Fringe groups like the Traverse Workshop Company have demonstrated how much can be achieved when playwrights, directors, actors and musicians have time to collaborate, but the Traverse Workshop Company is already defunct and the Arts Council has done almost nothing to encourage this sort of collaboration.

It would also be helpful if the Drama Panel would make a statement of principle about what standards it expects of subsidised theatres and how the size of a subsidy is determined. At the moment it could not do this because it has no clear principles, and subsidies are determined mainly by the pressure of the past. At the more commercial of the subsidised theatres, artistic directors do take the Arts Council's feelings into consideration when they are planning their programmes. They know they cannot get away with a non-stop flow of light comedies, whodunnits and farces, so they throw in the occasional modern classic as a sop. It would be helpful to both sides if the Drama Panel first of all made up its mind about what sort of standard it expected in programme planning, and then issued a clear directive.

A certain amount is being done to maintain standards at subsidised theatres, but very little is done to raise them. Ups and downs are inevitable in any company, but a decline sometimes sets in which neither the artistic director nor the board seems able to check, and it has happened that pressure has been applied by representatives of the Arts Council. Once alerted to reports of slipping standards, the Drama Director can ask his staff to keep an eye on the theatre, and can send someone to cover every production. He could also ask members of the Drama Panel to watch performances and he could commission a private report. He could then meet the Chairman of the theatre's board and suggest what ought to be done. He could even recommend that a new artistic director be appointed. If the Chairman and the Board were impervious to advice, the Council could stop the subsidy, but this has never yet happened because of artistic standards. Only two theatres, Barrow-in-Furness and Bournemouth, have been struck off the subsidised list, and the reason was lack of local support from either audiences or civic authorities, or both.

It may be that the Council is slowly moving away from its policy of *laissez-faire*. Although it came to nothing, a move was made in 1972 which could have led to a departure from the policy of non-intervention. This involved an educational theatre club. Some members of the Drama Panel felt strongly that its standards were not high enough to justify its subsidy. This verdict was passed on to the Arts Council, which asked the Panel to reconsider it. The idea was then mooted of offering a subsidy on condition that the club took on a specialist on educational drama – and the Panel suggested two names – as consultant. The Council accepted this idea, and so did the club, and though it was never put into effect, it is to be hoped that a principle was evolved that might eventually lead to the practice of making or continuing a subsidy only on certain conditions. Of course, this would increase the Arts Council's power and, of course, there would be violent opposition in which words like 'totalitarianism' and 'censorship' would be bandied about. But in practice, since subsidised theatres cannot but have some kind of relationship with the power behind the purse-strings, it is possibly better that it should be more direct and more focused on qualitative artistic considerations, rather than on budgets, statistics and minutes of meetings.

Meanwhile the amount of help that the Council can give to its 'client' theatres will soon be increased very appreciably by the introduction of what it calls 'the rolling triennium'. When the Arts Council was started, there was talk of a quinquennial grant from the Treasury, so that subsidies could be planned over a long term, but, until 1972, grants were annual and the Arts Council was usually unable to make any announcement until February or March about what each theatre's grant would be for the financial year that was about to start in April. Nearly all theatres operate on very tight financial margins and almost every attempt to plan ahead artistically – to secure or commission plays or to engage actors for a permanent company – involves financial commitments that spread over a period of several months. Financial worries are not conducive to concentration on the work in hand and, while all client theatres could be fairly sure that their subsidy would not be reduced, it was usually unpredictable whether it would be increased enough to cover rises in costs, and often theatres have received large subsidy increases which would have been very much more useful if only they could have known about them six months earlier. But thanks partly to pressure that has been put on the Treasury by the Department of Education and Science, it will soon be making its commitments to the Arts Council on a three-year basis, and the Council can in turn guarantee minimum subsidies to each client theatre for the next three years.

Criticism of our system of state subsidy is often based on the erroneous assumption that there is always unanimity between the Treasury, the Minister with responsibility for the Arts, the Chairman of the Arts Council, the Secretary-General, the members of the Council, the Chairman of the Drama Panel, the members of the Panel and its various sub-committees and the Drama Director and his officers. While it is true that all these individuals are appointed from above and that it is unusual for anyone to appoint people whose outlook is totally different from his own, there is a limit to the degree of like-mindedness that can be expected in any collection of personalities associated with the arts. It is interesting that none of the important disagreements seem to have had anything to do with the differences between Labour and Conservative attitudes. Lord Eccles and Patrick Gibson are a tandem with perhaps less sympathy for Left Wing causes than Jennie Lee and Lord Goodman, but the tendency for the Council to continue along the track that has already been laid down is always very strong, and it is clear that there will be no brutal sacrifice of the ideal of fair shares for the regions in favour of an *élitist* cultivation of excellence at the centre.

There is a dialectic of internal disagreement but it has very little to do with political parties. Sometimes it produces a step forward, as in the departure from the tradition of non-intervention in the case of the educational theatre club. Sometimes a disagreement between the Drama Panel and the Council leads to a reactionary conclusion, as with the decision in 1968 not to give Jim Haynes's Arts Lab the £7,000 without which it could not survive. From the viewpoint of several members of the Council, some of the activities going on in the Lab were immoral; from almost any point of view the Lab could have been run better than it was. Towards the end hippy communes were in residence and usually in evidence. Actors had to rehearse in rooms littered with inert bodies. If the principle of non-intervention had been shrugged off a few years earlier, the money could have been offered subject to conditions which could have been formulated in a way that would have both raised the Lab's artistic standards and given a sop to the critics of its moral standards.

But as the Government involves itself more and more in the nation's cultural affairs, the need is becoming increasingly obvious for a more co-ordinated cultural policy and a greater alignment between it and the policy controlling Higher Education. We can no longer afford a system in which the semi-independence of bodies like the Arts Council and the BBC is regarded as justifying a situation in which one pulls in the opposite direction to the other. Obviously the BBC has a very strong influence on the cultural situation. The abandonment of the intention that its second television channel should be pitched on a higher cultural level than the first and the jettisoning of the Third Programme were both severe blows to the cause for which the Arts Council is meant to be fighting. The way in which arts programmes and discussions are currently being crowded out of both television and radio is another triumph for the Philistines. It is not enough for the Government to pay conscience money to the Arts Council; the brain must inform itself of what both the left hand and the right hand are doing.

The question of morality is an invidious one. Throughout the history of Western civilisation artists have laid themselves open to charges of immorality with both their behaviour and their works of art. Conventional morality changes but never quite catches up. The reactionary position taken up by Emile Littler and Peter Cadbury during the 'Dirty Plays' controversy of 1964 would be completely untenable today, but Lord Eccles has expressed concern at the use of public money to pay for plays 'which affront the religious beliefs or outrage the sense of decency of a large body of taxpayers'. One advantage of having an Arts Council which is not a government department is that the Government itself is absolved from direct responsibility for the choice of art and plays subsidised, and it is easy to see why the Council itself has held on for so long to its principle of neutrality. But as more and more theatres are needing and receiving more and more public money, the Council is coming to be regarded almost as if it were a vast uncommercial management, an employer, a rich investor involved in sleeping partnerships with about seventy theatres.

Governmental machinery always gets adapted very slowly to changing situations, and already the large increases in budgets have in some respects overloaded a system which was worked out to deal with smaller amounts. In 1971–2 the total government grant-in-aid to the Arts Council was £11,900,000 – 27·8 per cent higher than it had been the year before. In January 1973 Lord Eccles announced that for 1973–4 it was to be £17,300,000, which represented a 27 per cent increase on 1972–3.

In spite of the well-meaning efforts of Arts Council members and officials to cope with their enormous responsibility, too little is done to adjust to the rapidly changing situation. The broadside that Charles Marowitz launched in 1971 in the *Guardian* ought to have provoked some fundamental reappraisals, but, instead, the affronted official response was to paper over the cracks. Although letters were written by the Secretary-General and several other people in defence of the Drama Panel and its methods, none of them faced up squarely to the gravest of the charges Marowitz was making: that the members of the panel which advises on the distribution of the official largesse are mostly connected with one or other of the companies which are benefiting. The Panel then included the Administrative Director of the National Theatre, the Associate Director of the Young Vic, the Chairman of the English Stage Company (Royal Court), the Artistic Directors of the Birmingham Repertory Theatre, the Library Theatre, Scarborough, the Midland Arts Centre and Theatre Centre (a children's theatre company), the Managing Director of Birmingham's Alexandra Theatre, and members or ex-members of the boards of management of the theatres at Leicester and Coventry. Marowitz said that panel members sometimes went out of the room during discussion of applications for grants from companies that employ them; sometimes they do, more often they do not. The Secretary-General wrote to the *Guardian* saying it was totally untrue 'that people giving this public service abuse their positions in any way'. Two days later, Mr Hugh Jenkins, MP, wrote that he had known only one case of a panel member 'persistently and openly arguing his own case'. But obviously if some of the panel members discussing budget proposals think that the officers of the Drama Department have been over-generous to a theatre where standards are slipping or where the programme planning is too commercial, it is more difficult for them to say so when the Artistic Director is sitting on the other side of the table.

The present system must also put an intolerable strain on any panel member who works for a theatre which is being allocated more money than he thinks it deserves. How can he say so? The House of Commons Select Committee* on Estimates, which investigated the Council's working methods, suggested that the panel should include more working artists, and the question has been asked how this can be achieved without appointing employees of theatres that receive grants. The answer is simple. In London there are plenty of actors, directors, designers, producers and administrators who are not on the permanent payroll of any of the subsidised theatres. Outside London there are admittedly fewer, but there are directors, artistic directors and even administrators who have had considerable and recent experience of working in the regions but are not currently on the permanent staff of a subsidised theatre.

It is now quite hard to remember the time when it was fashionable to argue that state patronage of the arts was undesirable. It has become indispensable, and we shall need more of it. Publishers and even newspapers may come to need it. Meanwhile more and more is coming to depend on centralised planning. Is the Arts Council right to let about a sixth of its total grant of £17,300,000 go to Covent Garden Opera while only about 4 per cent goes directly to creative artists? Is the Council right to let its subsidy for London orchestras be divided between so many of them? George Solti has suggested we would be better off with only two large orchestras (apart from the BBC and the opera house orchestras) each having 120 players on contract and each with a permanent home. In the theatre, too, much depends on the relationship between the company and the building, and far too much money has been handed out under the Housing the Arts scheme without simultaneous planning for what is going to go on inside the buildings. This is a mistake which the Arts Council now recognises.

Originally, members of the Council were selected by the Chancellor of the Exchequer, and the Treasury was the government department with which it was most closely connected. A treasury officer sat with the Council as assessor. When Harold Wilson appointed Jennie Lee as Minister of State for Education and Science with a special responsibility for the Arts, the Council's direct link with the Treasury was replaced by one with the Department of Education and Science. Meanwhile, more was being spent on education, more universities had been created and the arts were coming to be regarded almost as something that could carry on where education left off, satisfying the intellectual appetites that had been whetted. Lord Goodman's speeches in the House of Lords imply a very suspect view of what culture is, but they were well calculated to foment enthusiasm for public spending on the arts:

> I believe that young people lack values, lack certainties, lack guidance; that they need something to turn to; and need it more desperately than they have needed it at any time in our history, certainly, at any time which I can recollect. I do not say that the Arts will furnish a total solution. I believe that once young people are captured for the Arts they are redeemed from many of the dangers which confront them at the moment and which have been occupying the attention of the Government in a completely unprofitable and destructive fashion. I believe that here we have constructive work to do which can be of inestimable value.

This is really not far from saying that more money should be spent on the arts as something to keep the younger generation out of mischief, but undoubtedly, Lord Goodman succeeded in increasing the prestige of the arts in government circles and in strengthening the tendency that had begun with the new alignment between the Arts Council and the Department of Education and Science. This is particularly important because the disparity between the amount of money spent on education and the relatively small sum made available for the arts is already being singled out as an anomaly, and it is possible that this kind of thinking will produce more and more public money for the Arts Council to distribute.

13 EQUITY AND DEMOCRACY

It is difficult to run a trade union democratically. During the ten years before it was suspended by the General Council of the TUC in July 1972 for registering under the Industrial Relations Act, Equity became very much more powerful than ever before, but it was the paid officials and the unpaid council who worked to make it more powerful, and it is they who wield the power they have achieved. The Council of Equity (unlike the Arts Council and its advisory panels) is elected, and though there has been more variation recently, the same council members tend to get elected year after year. In the 1972 elections there was 114 candidates, and members could vote for 45. All the candidates are proposed and seconded, but most of them are unknown to most of the voters: the tendency therefore is to vote for the best-known names.

Quite early in the fifties it was proposed that since the Council ought to be representative of the whole profession, it would be fairer to include on the voting paper a brief statement by each candidate, describing himself and the policies he would pursue if elected. The Council opposed this proposal, arguing that it would cost too much to print the extra details on the voting paper, and for years, although the idea was persistently canvassed, the Council's resistance continued – a resistance which is hard to explain unless council members sensed a threat to their own chances of being re-elected. When the proposal was finally adopted, it did seem to make an appreciable difference: names on the Council became less starry. The Theatre Section[1] of the Council for 1950–51 consisted of Felix Aylmer, Laurence Olivier, John Clements, Leslie Banks, Edith Evans, Harold

[1] The other sections are Ballet, Opera, Stage Managers and Variety Artists.

Warrender, Sybil Thorndike, Richard Attenborough, Margaretta Scott, Rosamund John, Marius Goring, Margaret Rawlings, Bruce Belfrage, Charles Farrell, Derrick de Marney, Laidman Browne, Jack Allen, Walter Fitzgerald, Hugh Burden, John Varley, John Fernald, Clifford Mollison, Raymond Huntley, Henry Oscar, Ralph Truman, Reginald Tate, Walter Hudd, Clive Morton, Peter Copley, André Morell and Hermione Gingold. The Council for 1972–73 consisted of Marius Goring, Ernest Clark, Peggy Ashcroft, Michael Denison, Kenneth More, Richard Briers, Kenneth McClellan, Hugh Manning, André Morell, Frederick Jaeger, Peter Honri, Milton Johns, Clive Morton, Trevor Baxter, Michael Boothe, Donald Sinden, Margaret Rawlings, Corin Redgrave, Howard Goorney, Andre Van Gysenhem, Nigel Patrick, Peter Bennett, Paul Eddington, Robert Flemyng, Richard Warner, Raymond Francis, Michael Hordern, Leslie Phillips, Richard Attenborough, Barbara Lott and Charles Farrell. One of the unsuccessful candidates was John Clements, whose managerial status seemed to weigh against him more than it had in the past. The council was still, obviously, much too full of well-known actors to be representative of a profession in which most members play supporting parts and are out of work 70 per cent of the time. The tendency to vote for performers one has seen and liked is inevitably very strong, and the system of inviting every member to vote for so many candidates loads the dice even more, because every voter who casts more than a single vote in each section is also voting against everyone he is voting for. This favours the stars. Most members do not want to waste any of their votes and use up about thirty of them on well-known names.

In fact only a very small proportion of Equity members exercise their democratic rights. With 18,409 full members in full benefit, the vote recorded in 1973 (which was the highest ever) was 3,541, while most of the recent annual general meetings have had attendances of between three and four hundred. Over three times as many members came to the two meetings on the Industrial Relations Bill, and nearly 5,000 replied to the questionnaire about earnings and employment which was circulated in March 1972.

Actors seem to dislike efforts to organise them. The way they work is more likely to promote competitive individualism than the formation of a common front. Theatres are not like factories where workers can be rounded up by shop stewards. It took a long time to unionise the profession. Long before the end of the nineteenth century it was clear that some form of organisation was necessary. As the old stock companies were breaking up, businessmen were eagerly cashing in on the new boom in touring, and companies of actors who had accepted jobs with unknown but reliable-looking managers sometimes found themselves abandoned in a rainy provincial town with no salary for the week's work and no money for the train-fare back to London. When there was no one to make employers pay rehearsal salaries, actors were liable to work hard for two or three weeks before finding out that their boss had been unable to raise enough money to get the show on. Or the show might open after four unpaid rehearsal weeks, only to be taken off after a couple of badly received performances. This happened in London in 1930 with a play called *A Business Marriage*, which had just two performances at the Court Theatre on 26 and 27 December.

The first Actors' Association was formed in 1891, with Henry Irving as its President, and in 1905, his son, H. B. Irving, who had studied Law at Oxford, was a founder of the Actors' Union. But neither at first recruited enough members to have much influence; though the Actors' Association eventually built up to a membership of 6,000. It was first suggested in 1906 that it ought to become a trade union which could pressure simultaneously to improve salary levels, working conditions and the status of its members. But many actors were violently opposed to the idea. In 1895 Irving had been the first actor to receive a knighthood. Surely it would stigmatise a profession which had only just become respectable if it formed itself into a trade union, and this did not happen until August 1918. Its first strike, which lasted about twenty-five minutes, occurred in King's Lynn during a tour of *When Knights Were Bold* in 1920. The actors, who were playing twice nightly with an additional Saturday matinée, refused to go on unless they were guaranteed extra pay for the matinee. Lionel

Barwood, the manager, capitulated and gave his personal guarantee in time for the curtain to go up late. The strike was inspired by the example of American Equity, which had been founded in 1912 and in 1919 called its first strike, which succeeded in improving conditions of working.

Equity itself – The British Actors' Equity Association – was formed in December 1929 by a unanimous decision at a mass meeting of members of the Actors' Association and the Stage Guild. Even then there was strong feeling that it should be a professional organisation rather than a trade union, and it was not until December 1940 that it was finally affiliated to the Trades Union Congress. Godfrey Tearle, who had been president for ten years, resigned in protest.

The situation here was also complicated by the continuing existence of the Stage Guild, which had been founded in 1925, and by 1930 had 2,697 members in the artists' section, and thirty-seven playwrights. Membership was also open to managers, and though there were only twenty-seven of them, their presence at meetings made it dangerous for men who needed work to speak up against current conditions of employment.

Like most unions, Equity had very few full-time officials to begin with. At first Alfred Wall, the Honorary General Secretary, had only one full-time assistant, and though actors were appointed as Equity Deputies in each company, it took a very long time to enrol a large membership. It was clear that the new union would never have any real power until almost every actor in the country joined. So long as non-members were willing to work for less money than members, Equity would be in no position to enforce its minimum rates. It was also essential to standardise contracts: while *ad hoc* agreements were drawn up for each engagement, employers could take advantage of the actor who was too eager for the job to study the clauses in small print. A great deal of litigation was going on, caused by breaches of contracts which had never been properly understood.

Efforts to create a closed shop produced a major dispute in 1934 during negotiations for the first standard contract, when the Society of West End Managers (which had been founded in 1908) baulked at the stipulation that 'the Artist shall be required to work only with members of the British Actors' Equity Association'. Equity won when eighty-six leading actors pledged themselves to refuse engagements which would deny their right to refuse to work with non-members. Without these stars, employers would have been powerless to go on operating as they were. But before giving in, they involved the Ministry of Labour in the dispute. In 1935, when a production of *Glamorous Night* was being prepared at the Theatre Royal, Drury Lane, the management was refusing to include a clause in the artists' contracts acknowledging Equity's right to a closed shop. Alfred Wall, who had previously been Secretary of the London Trade Council, had been present at the early actors' meetings as a representative of the trade union movement. He now decided that the right moment had come to challenge this most powerful management to a decisive battle. All Equity Members were instructed to refuse to sign contracts with the Theatre Royal. H. M. Tennent, who was then its Managing Director, and Walter Payne, President of the Society of West End Managers, reported the incident to the Ministry, asking for help. After meeting representatives of both sides, both separately and together, Frederick Leggett, the Principal Assistant Secretary to the Ministry, conceived the idea of a joint body to work for higher standards in conditions of employment and to stimulate a theatre which was currently being threatened by competition from the cinema. A major threat from outside usually helps to produce unity inside: Equity and the managerial associations now agreed to co-operate in forming the London Theatre Council. First on the list of objects was 'to secure the largest possible measure of co-operation between managers and artists for the safeguarding and development of the theatre as a part of the national life'. The other aims were to devise means of settling differences; to 'secure complete organisation of managers and artists'; maintain the level of conditions of employment; and to maintain standard forms of contracts.

A concealed form of union shop was introduced by arranging to keep a register of approved artists and approved managements. Members of Equity were automatically registered, and so were producers who were members of the Society of West End Managers, but all registered managers and artists must undertake to use the standard forms of contract that the London Theatre Council approved. The Minister of Labour appointed Lord Esher as Chairman, and he was given power to make recommendations whenever there was a dispute, and, if both sides agreed, to arbitrate. The standard contracts still bear his name. A couple of shady small managements immediately went out of business, and one big manager, C. B. Cochran, was so hostile to the sheme that he refused to register. When Equity members obeying their Council's instructions, reciprocated by refusing to sign his contracts, he threatened to cancel all his production plans. But eventually he came to terms and registered.

In 1942, the Provincial Theatre Council was formed on exactly the same lines, under the same Chairman, Lord Esher. Again there were two Joint Secretaries, one representing the managers, with the General Secretary of Equity as the other. Either council can require a management which has not established itself sufficiently to be accepted as a member of one of the approved organisations to deposit money equivalent to two weeks' salaries of the artists and stage management before going into rehearsal with a new production. Then if the management goes bankrupt or turns out to be unable to fulfil its commitments, the actors can at least be paid for two weeks' work. Since 1945 Equity has been careful never to waive the deposit requirement, though sometimes it has had to interrupt rehearsals, ordering the actors not to do any more work until the money is in the kitty. Deposits acquired in this way have often been used to save them from working unpaid.

Equity and the Arts Council are the two most powerful organisations controlling what happens inside our theatre, but they have very little in common except structurally. There is a parallel in the working relationships between the permanent staff, who are there every day, and the honorary councillors and panel members who are not. A newly elected member of Equity's Council, like a newly appointed member of the Arts Council or its Drama Panel, may leap enthusiastically into office with the intention of fighting for important changes. But in neither Equity nor the Arts Council is it easy to alter the way things are done: departures from continuity cause administrative difficulties, and in both organisations the permanent staff, who do the administrative work, have a vested interest in continuity. They also tend to stay for a very long time. Senior appointments are frequently made by promoting the next in rank. N. V. Linklater, who succeeded Joe Hodgkinson as Drama Director of the Arts Council, had been his Deputy Drama Director; while Gerald Croasdell, who succeeded Gordon Sandison as General Secretary of Equity, had been his Assistant General Secretary.

In fact Gerald Croasdell has less control over his council than most General Secretaries of trade unions. Most councils are smaller and meet less often. But, as in all committee-run institutions, committee members are not there when most of the practical decisions have to be taken. Although the General Secretary does not vote at Council meetings, his presence helps to constitute a quorum, so technically he is part of the Council. As the most seasoned campaigner, he always used to be regarded as an expert whose advice should be followed, and it still is largely followed in matters of strategy, though probably less now in matters of policy. When he is at odds with the rest of the Council, a vote is taken, and recent policy seems generally to have been determined mainly by a genuine consensus among the Council.

Most decisions about policy and methods are taken at the Council meetings which are normally held each month. There is also an Executive Committee of twenty-one members, selected each year by the Council from within itself, in order to have a smaller body which can work more smoothly and speedily. The officers of the union are automatically members of this committee; the other members are elected. It has no power to make policy decisions; it is there to carry out decisions made by the full Council. The Executive Committee used to meet three times a month, but recently, with greater pressure of work, the whole Council has been meeting more than once a month, and the Executive Committee therefore less frequently. In the year 1971–72 the Council had twenty-six meetings and the Executive Committee fifteen.

But, just as the membership meets too irregularly to control what the Council does, the Council and the Executive Committee can only broadly control what the paid officers do. Situations change from one day to the next, crises occur, decisions and actions have to be taken quickly. Sometimes there is time for telephone consultations with Council members; sometimes, because they are themselves busy performers, there is not. Although much depends on the voluntary work done by the Council, much also depends on how its policies are put into practice by the paid officials. The General Secretary's personality and attitudes play a large part in the formation of policy, and a larger one in its execution. In preparing to negotiate over salary levels, for instance, Gerald Croasdell believes more than Gordon Sandison did in canvassing the views of actors' agents. The Assistant General Secretary is also in a position of power as the activist responsible for seeing that the long-term policies are carried out. The present Assistant General Secretary, Peter Plouviez, who has been a Labour candidate in Quintin Hogg's constituency, is an effective public speaker and an expert on committee procedures, who can exert a powerful influence on the decisions that are taken. The Assistant Secretary is in charge of the day-to-day running of the union, and there are separate groups of Organisers for liaison with companies of members involved in theatre, in 'the mechanical media' and in variety. Then in each company an actor is still appointed as 'Equity Deputy', so whenever a member is working he can have immediate access to someone who is representative of Equity. It is also the responsibility of the Equity Deputy to see that rehearsals are not too long or the lunch hours too short.

Not that the General Secretary and the Assistant General Secretary can carry Equity in a direction in which the Council does not want it to go, but they are professionals in an activity in which professional actors can only be amateurs. A council member may in private hold very strong views which he finds it hard to bring out persuasively at a committee meeting, whereas a professional knows exactly how to influence the mood of a meeting or how to wait for the mood to change before introducing the point that matters most. There is a technique involved which has little to do with the technique of acting, though the emotions are involved and the sympathy of the audience, however small, can be won or lost by the performance. Actors can learn the techniques involved and some of them do learn very quickly. The Council members who are most influential at meetings are not necessarily those whose opinions, considered under different circumstances, would have the most appeal to other members.

At both large meetings and small ones the chairman is in a position from which the flow of feeling can be largely directed. The attitude he takes – explicitly or by implication – towards a speaker and his argument can influence the reaction of the whole meeting. Much depends on the order in which points are taken, how much departure there is from the agenda, who is allowed to speak, the order in which they speak and for how long. Anyone who thinks that the discussion about a resolution or an amendment has gone on for long enough can propose from the floor 'that the question be now put'. It is then up to the Chairman to decide whether he will accept this. If he does, and it is seconded, a vote must be taken immediately (provided that the speaker who moved the resolution has had a chance to reply to discussion). So the whole outcome can depend on the Chairman's reaction. There are also meetings at which the result can depend on timing: whether the hall has to be vacated by a particular time or whether the basic motion is put to the vote ten minutes earlier or later. Of course there are limits beyond which the chairman cannot manoeuvre the meeting, but these are quite wide.

There is also the possibility that an organised group can take advantage of procedural formalities to override the wishes of the majority about how time should be spent. This happened at the 1972 Annual General Meeting, when the discussion about the Industrial Relations Bill became a pretext for generalised political argument, which was so protracted that little time was left to go into the particular problems which most people must have come to discuss. Consequently an old idea was mooted again: of spreading Annual General Meetings over two days, devoting the first to specialised 'commissions' on the problems of different sectors of the profession, each member being free to attend the commission most relevant to his own problems, while the second day would be spent on receiving the commissions' reports in a plenary session, and voting on resolutions.

There is less continuity in the membership of Equity's Council than there is of the Arts Council, especially now that statements by candidates for election to the Council are issued with each voting paper. But there is a hard core of councillors who are steadily re-elected. Of the Theatre Section in the 1972–73 Council, eight members were already serving in 1956–57. This continuity also acts as brake on change, but since the end of the sixties there have been hopeful signs of growing interest in the affairs of Equity from a larger proportion of members. This pressures the Council to be more flexible. All through the fifties it had been adamantly hostile to the idea of controlled entry into the profession. The question had been regularly brought up at Annual General Meetings, but even after a working party had been appointed to investigate means of applying control, its recommendations were rejected by the Council. Eventually actors who were in favour of control were elected on to the Council, where they championed the idea, and finally achieved a majority.

The ultimate democratic procedure is a referendum involving the whole membership. This happens very rarely – perhaps once in twenty years – but it did happen over the question of registering under the Industrial Relations Act. After a prolonged battle about whether the interests of the profession were best served by accepting the Government's concession in allowing 'approved closed shops' or by obeying the TUC's instruction to de-register, the Council's initial decision was to obey the TUC, and in September 1971 Equity became a de-registered union. When the Industrial Relations Act's provision about closed shops came into force in February 1972, to remain off the register would have meant abandoning the closed shop. This could have made undercutting and exploitation as uncontrollable as they were in the early thirties, and the Council, by a majority of twenty-three votes to sixteen, decided to register and to have a referendum. Before the referendum had taken place, a Special Meeting was requisitioned with the signatures of 400 members, and a resolution condemning the Council's decision to register was defeated by 519 votes to 388. In the referendum 2,137 votes supported the decision, with 1,249 against. But the TUC had indicated that its suspension of Equity would be lifted if it de-registered again, and at the Annual

General Meeting in June 1973 it was decided to do this. The feelings of the majority may well have been influenced by the behaviour of the Department of Employment during the wage freeze. Equity's new West End agreement, concluded in October 1972, had been due for implementation in two phases, in November and January. Having informed the Society of West End Managers that it would be illegal to pay the higher rates from November, the Department of Employment was forced to admit that it had been misinterpreting the law, but tried to persuade both sides to continue with the old rates, and, after this attempt had failed, the Secretary of State issued an Order pegging salaries at the old rates. This remained in effect until the end of Phase One of the government's anti-inflation programme. The increases that should have taken effect from November were introduced at the end of February, and the January increases from the beginning of April.

When the Council decides that one of the existing contracts needs to be revised, a working party is formed consisting of one of the Organisers from the Theatre Group or the Mechanical Media Group and some actors whose experience is relevant. Some will be Council members, some not. When the working party is ready, it presents its proposals to the Council, which either accepts them as they are or modifies them. Notice is then given to the management or management association that Equity wants a revision of the contract, and the Council appoints a negotiating team, usually of six to ten people – Council members and paid officers – which will meet the management's negotiators. If the team arrives at an impasse, it can report back to the Council for instructions, but it has no authority to break off negotiations. Major decisions of that order always have to be made by the Council.

There are also, as in the Arts Council, sub-committees and working parties which go on holding regular meetings either over a limited period – perhaps six months, perhaps eighteen – or on a permanent basis, depending on whether the object is to study a particular problem and produce a report for the main Council, or to go on advising it about a particular sphere of activity. The Sub-Committee on the Mechanical Media is reporting on video-cassettes, films, radio and television whenever there are new developments which will affect conditions of employment, contract and fees or salaries. At the end of 1971, there were over a dozen Equity sub-committees meeting to discuss a mixture of subjects including agents, control of entry, employment and training, drama schools, coloured artists, casting directories, publications, stage managers and revision of Equity rules. There is a Sub-Committee of Extras, Walk-ons and Small Part artists. Representatives of this, together with two of the paid staff, recently met representatives of the BBC to discuss complaints about conditions of work, the stamping of insurance cards and so on. There are also separate committees dealing with Scotland, Wales, Northern Ireland and different areas of England.

The Finance and General Purposes Committee is one of the most important. It is a permanent committee under the chairmanship of the Honorary Treasurer, which deals with financial policy and with particular questions like subscriptions and the salaries paid to staff. None of these sub-committees can make decisions: they make recommendations, which the Council rarely accepts without modification. Sometimes the sub-committee is asked to reconsider certain points, and occasionally the Council rejects a recommendation altogether, as it did over the question of controlled entry.

The basic question of whether sub-committees could take over more of the decision-making is currently being discussed by the Rules Revision Committee. This sub-committee was appointed after the Council had become aware that the rules framed for a relatively small union, with members working mainly in live entertainment, were inadequate for a union which has to negotiate with large, high-powered industrial organisations like the BBC and commercial television companies. In the future, Equity will have increasingly to deal with international organisations marketing audio-visual cassettes. The Rules Revision Committee is also hoping to find a means of electing a council more representative of the profession as a whole. It has considered various forms of proportional representation based on skills and fields of work. Some members of the committee are arguing that since the Annual and Special General Meetings can never be representative of the membership as a whole, they should be replaced by some form of delegate conference. An executive body could be based on a structure of committees representing the different sectors of the profession. Others argue that the highest practicable form of democracy is already achieved through the sovereignty of the Annual General Meeting. In fact, though, the only decisions of an AGM which are binding on the Council are decisions about the revision of rules – and these have to be carried by a two-thirds majority. Otherwise the Council can overrule decisions taken by AGM, or a Special General Meeting. In 1954 there was a Special General Meeting at which the majority was in favour of imposing limitation of entry on repertory theatres. This decision was vetoed by the Council, and at the next AGM a demand was made for action to stop the Council's abuse of its power of veto. It still possesses this power, and the Council's decision can be overruled only by a referendum. To call a referendum, a petition has to be presented to the Council signed by a hundred full members in full benefit.

Even without using its veto, the Council can effectively delay the implementation of decisions taken by a vote at an Annual General Meeting. A situation can change so rapidly that an action is out of date before it is taken, and the Council, which has to get on with the job of running Equity's affairs, would have no time to canvass the feelings of the majority of the membership, even if the majority ever came to meetings or took part in postal ballots. At the 1971 Annual General Meeting 698 members came and 2,148 valid ballot papers were received. No means has yet been discovered of finding out what the majority wants.

The fact that Equity (unlike American Equity, which is concerned only with legitimate theatre) also represents variety artists, opera singers and ballet dancers also produces anomalies. A sword-swallower or a belly-dancer who is a full member qualifies for acting jobs in the theatre or films, while a student who has completed three years at drama school may be excluded because the rep which would have offered him his first job has already used up its annual quota of places for new members.

Equity is also involved in monitoring the number of engagements offered to foreign artists within Britain, and the length of time that a foreign company is allowed to play in a British theatre. Equity has no jurisdiction of its own: working permits are controlled by the Home Office. On receiving applications from producers who want to use foreign labour, it invites Equity to give its advice – which is not always taken. The producers have to make it clear whether the engagements they would like to offer are subject to a time-limit: with a fairly short one, Equity is more likely to be sympathetic. The American musical *Company* was allowed to open in the West End in 1972 with an all-American cast, but the management had undertaken that after the first three months of the run all but two leading parts would be recast, providing jobs for Equity members. When Equity opposes an application, the producer is at liberty to argue the case that no British artist could play the part so well. Equity is also concerned to protect British members who work abroad. And protection is often necessary.

There are two main obstacles to democracy within Equity. One is the difficulty of making contact between the members. It is hard enough to keep them informed of what is happening. So many members are out of work at any time that the majority will not be looking at the notice-boards in theatres, and circularising such a large membership at frequent intervals would be extremely expensive. The quarterly newsletter is useful, but provides only a small part of the contact that is needed. The other obstacle is that even if a means were devised – perhaps through some form of proportional representation – of making the Council more representative of the profession as a whole, the problem would still remain unsolved of how to get Council members together. An actor in fortnightly rep in the North of England cannot attend regular meetings in London.

But the trend is in the direction of more democratic thinking. The possibility is being discussed of forming area committees which would send delegates to central meetings. Meanwhile the Council, as it becomes slightly more representative, becomes slightly more flexible. Normally members of the Council are unable to speak at AGMs as individuals. Before the meeting the Council discusses every item on the agenda and decides whether it is for or against each motion. Council members who disagree with Council policy are required by the Standing Order to stay silent while that issue is discussed: in 1972 that Standing Order was suspended. Even if this does not become normal practice, at least a precedent has been created.

14 THE ACTOR'S AGENT

To have an agent is to have a kind of reassurance that you exist. ARTHUR MILLER

One of the agent's functions is to be a scapegoat for an actor's anger at being underemployed, and angry actors sometimes say that if agents were all abolished, the only difference it would make to the theatre is that actors would pocket all their earnings instead of 90 per cent. This might once have been almost true, but the industry and the profession have both grown so large and so complex that middlemen between employers and employees are indispensable. Directors and casting directors who try to get in touch with actors are liable to be delayed and frustrated by unanswered telephones, changes of address and landladies who forget to deliver messages; without agents, directors would also be inundated with persuasive letters and persistent telephone calls from actors trying to find out whether there were any jobs in the offing and to recommend themselves even when there were not. An agent is both a means of communication and a filter.

As a filter, agents are already becoming less effective than they were, because there are now so many of them.[1] In the early fifties, after the advent of commercial television had accelerated the decline of provincial touring and repertory, more and more actors based themselves on London, and the agency business boomed. As actors were coming to change jobs more frequently, they began to need agents more than when they had gone out on long provincial tours and signed long-term contracts with reps. The total amount of work available for actors was declining, but the amount of television work was roughly doubled, so the average rate of payment per job was substantially increased – which made it easier for an agent to earn

[1] See p. 38.

a good living. And because of their structure, the commercial television companies found them even more useful than the BBC had.

In BBC television, drama directors do the bulk of their casting individually, but each commercial company has its own casting department, and while most drama directors would have very clear ideas of who they want for leading parts, they would consider their casting director's suggestions for supporting parts and for leading parts if their first choices turn out to be unavailable. Casting directors were of course bombarded with approaches from individual actors – many had no agent and even more were not content to rely on an agent to sell them – but for the most part the filtering was effective. Today, though, agents have multiplied so much, that television casting departments have to be far more selective in dealing with them. So many of them ring up to promote their clients and to find out what casting is going on, that instead of relying on the agents to filter the actors, a casting director now has to subject the agents themselves to filtering. And he is now much more likely to be secretive about scripts he is working on, for fear that one agent will leak news to another about parts that are going to be cast, and that the telephones will be ringing more busily still.

This is a development which tilts the balance more than ever in favour of big agents who have a lot of star actors on their books. A theatrical producer or a television director who wants a star actress for his next play will be asked to send a script to the agent, who will read through it, looking also for parts which some of his other clients might be able to play. Not knowing how much the actress's decision will depend on her agent's advice, the producer or director may not feel he can risk offending him by refusing to interview or audition some of his other clients. Even when he does not get access to a script, a good agent will use the power that his stars give him to promote clients who are less in demand. The star actress may be busy on a film job that will last for six months, but each telephone inquiry about her can possibly be diverted into a chat about the other parts that are going.

The proliferation of agents and the consequent increase of competitiveness between them have made the most talented and the most photogenic drama students who are about to graduate more alert than ever before to the demand they will be in when they do. Agents come to see them in school productions and vie with each other to express a flattering interest in their work and in their future. Nor is it easy for drama school principals to advise students about which offers to accept. There are large international agencies like IFA (International Famous Artists) and London Management which have hundreds of clients and perhaps a dozen executives looking after them.

For the actor who joins an organisation like this, a very great deal depends on which executive is looking after him and whether the agency is structured in such a way that each executive looks after a certain number of clients, handling their engagements in all three media, or whether there are some executives dealing exclusively with theatre, some with television and some with films. In this case an individual actor would be in the hands of different people, some of whom would probably be more interested in him than others. One executive might be handling the television engagements of three hundred clients. With most of them, inevitably, he will feel little personal involvement, while the ones in whom he develops the greatest interest may find they are kept busy exclusively on television for three years at a stretch. The fact that none of the agency's executives would concern themselves with his overall development as an actor might look like a good reason for the drama school principal to advise him not to go to that agency, but while there are a great many small agencies, few of them are really good, and the good ones, who are in great demand, know that they can handle only a limited number of clients effectively, maintaining a personal interest and a personal relationship. Fifty years ago the profession was small enough for an agent to register every actor who walked into his office and to send several along for each job that came up. But today an agent does not need to have a good reputation in order to find he is being approached by far more actors than he can take. Even the student who rises to the top of a drama school may finally have to choose between one of the large agencies and one of the small ones which might not get all the necessary information or be able to exert all the necessary influence, and might not even make all the necessary effort. In any form of industrialisation the expansion of the system favours the larger unit.

It also favours commercial considerations against artistic ones. Some of the executives in the large agencies care genuinely about their clients' development as actors. But the company is probably owned by a still larger company with a diversity of interests that create a financial perspective in which the cultivation of an individual actor's talent can look very trivial. Some of the executives would probably approach their work quite differently if they were in business on their own, but they have to satisfy their directors and their directors' accountants – which may mean paying more attention to a client's current earnings than to his future potential. It has also happened that directives have been issued to stop executives from taking on actors who want to work outside London, and in some firms actors whose earnings fall below a stipulated level are told that another agent might be of more help to them.

Many pressures are combining to make it difficult for agents to send young clients out to get experience in rep. Even a part as desirable as Macbeth at a rep which pays as well as Birmingham may seem unattractive to an agent who thinks in terms of the journey he would be expected to make to see his client working. And valuable television offers might come in during the two months the actor is tied up at a salary of £60 a week, yielding only £6 a week in commission. At the same time, agents who really care about launching a beginner's career in the best way are handicapped by the casting agreements Equity has made with the Council of Regional Theatres. Each rep can offer only a small number of jobs each year to fledgeling actors, and usually the quota will be used up quite early in the year. The agents who have rep directors as clients are in the best position to put forward candidates for the few places they have to dispose of.

So actors are more than ever dependent on their agents for the launching of their careers. But even at the beginning, actors vary enormously in flexibility – some depend totally on their agent's advice, others listen to it without ever letting it deflect them from their own inclinations. Ideally an agent who realised that a client was taking no notice of his advice would no longer want to go on representing him, but in practice it hardly ever happens that the relationship breaks up for this reason, though of course there are all kinds of ways in which, consciously and unconsciously, an agent can influence a client's decisions. Just by the way he passes on information about an offer that has been received, he can make it sound interesting or unattractive, and, depending on how unscrupulous he is, he can censor the information or withhold it altogether. Every actor ought to be told about every telephone inquiry that is made for him, but he has no means of knowing whether his agent (who may be waiting for the interest a film director has been showing to harden into a definite offer) may be suppressing news about an offer of a leading part in a Fringe production of a new play. Sometimes an actor is so tired of being out of work that he is liable to commit himself to something very much less lucrative than his agent would think worth while.

It often happens that after being out of work for several successive months an actor receives three conflicting offers. It is an important and quite delicate part of an agent's function to juggle with them, keeping one potential employer waiting while another makes up his mind about which actor he wants for a part or waits for a decision from someone else he would prefer but may not get. Even if the agent tries to keep his client *au fait* with each step in each negotiation, it is his responsibility to keep the various balls in the air as long as necessary, and to decide when the moment has come to catch one and let the others fall to the ground.

Some agents put their clients under contract. Al Parker's contracts have mostly been for seven years, but an actor can usually leave earlier without much risk of being sued. Sometimes agents make their clients sign an annual contract which renews itself automatically unless either of them gives notice after ten months. Usually the actor wanting to go to another agent forgets to give notice in time and finds himself committed to stay on an extra year, at the end of which he may no longer want to leave. Many agents have no written agreement with their clients. Probably this is conducive to mutual trust, but it can be unfair when an agent works hard to get a five-picture contract for an actor who leaves him before any money has come in from the film company. The 10 per cent eventually goes to his new agent.

Inevitably, too, small agents frequently lose clients just as they are becoming successful. How much of their success they owe to the agents is uncertain, but gratitude is not usually going to hold them back from joining a firm which looks likely to be of more help on the international film market. Agents vary in their scrupulousness about stealing their rivals' clients, but generally, as the business has grown more competitive, it has grown more unscrupulous. In one of the big firms executives were instructed to concentrate more on taking established actors from other agents than on picking up promising beginners from drama schools. The more unscrupulous the agency business becomes, the more actors are pressurised – not necessarily directly – to opt for well-paid engagements. Not that commercial pressures are always towards type-casting or towards exploiting the image that an actor has already established. It was the result of an agent's suggestion that Frank Finlay was cast as Casanova in the television series about him, and it quite often happens that an agent is able to persuade a director or a producer to consider an actor for a part totally out of line with those he usually plays. This can be invaluable, not just for the actor's career but for his development. Or an agent may find he needs to persuade a client not to break too violently into new territory, or to wait for the right moment and the right opportunity to do so. An actress like Eileen Atkins, who builds up a very good reputation in the the theatre, is (and has been) well advised to turn down certain film offers. But it becomes harder for personal management of this calibre to survive as films and television become more international, encouraging the growth of large agencies with international contacts and affiliations and little interest in anything but big deals.

Some agents who have broken away from large organisations to set up in business on their own have done so partly for the sake of being able to have a more direct, more personal relationship with their clients. The fact of taking a percentage rather than earning a salary may then tend to make them more involved in artistic considerations, though it could make them more money-conscious than before.

Clearly the overheads of running a chic West End office are very high: rent, rates, a heavy telephone bill, heating, lighting, and the secretary's wages all have to be covered each week before the business begins to show a profit. Sometimes the big organisation will make a deal with an executive who wants to set himself up independently, and who will be taking away most of the clients he has been looking after. Usually he will undertake to pay 5 per cent of their earnings – 50 per cent of the commission – during his first year of business. This will make it very difficult for him to cover his costs that year, but no deterrent could be effective in stopping the splintering that goes on. Some agencies put elaborate clauses into their service agreements to protect themselves from losing executives and actors, but it is very hard to stop them by litigation, because a man cannot legally be barred from exercising his skills to earn a living, and a law court would always recognise that he is professionally an agent.

Many of the better agents have been actors themselves, but anyone can become an agent without any training or qualifications. The procedure is simply to advertise one's intention for three successive weeks in *The Stage*. If no objections are received, and if the prospective agent has an office address and no criminal record, the local authority will then automatically issue him with a licence on payment of a couple of guineas. The licence has to be renewed annually and the local authorities have legal powers to control agents' activities, but in practice there is little supervision, although the dishonest or financially unstable agent can easily take advantage of his clients.

Agents normally receive all their clients' fees and it is not even compulsory for the money to be kept in a separate account. If an actor, in his contract, signs over the payment for a job to his agent, who then spends the money on himself or his business, this legally constitutes a civil debt, not misappropriation. An agent who is short of cash and habitually pays over money to his actors six or eight weeks after he has received it can be living on it in the meantime. In fact the money legally constitutes part of the agency's assets until it is paid over. Equity has been campaigning for the law to be changed on this point, but so far without success. A lot of money has been lost by actors in this way. An agent can incur debts of £10,000 or £15,000 before the bank forecloses on his overdraft or creditors force a liquidation, and then the fees which have not yet been paid over to the actors who earned them become available for distribution to creditors – a category which may include the agency's directors and backers. The clients may not even know how much money is due to them: they sign their own contracts but depend on the agent to tell them what fees have come in for repeats of television plays.

At the moment there is nothing to stop an agent from becoming involved in management and production. He can set up his own production or invest in a show or buy shares in a theatrical management or sell out to one. A theatrical manager can provide the capital for an agent to set up in business, and his clients may never find out who his backer is. There may be no conflict of interests in practice, but an agent who is selling the services of his clients to his own backer is not in a good position to hold out for the highest salaries or the best terms. The directors of a commercial television network can have financial interests in agencies, and in 1972 there was still a television casting director who was also in business as an agent. It may be that he does not give priority to his own clients and that other television casting directors have no bias towards the agencies that belong to associated companies, but obviously it would be better if the temptation were not allowed to occur.

In 1964 the Guild of Independent Theatrical Representatives (GOITRE) was formed when a few agents collectively approached Equity to negotiate a standard agreement for putting actors under an exclusive contract. One of Equity's stipulations was that 10 per cent should be the maximum rate of commission, and another was that an agent who has a financial interest in a show in which one of his clients is to appear must tell him about it and charge no commission on that particular engagement. Both these conditions were accepted by the thirteen agents who joined GOITRE, but neither is enforceable on the agency business as a whole.

Relationships between companies can become so intricate that it becomes hard to know which personalities are involved, and how deeply. In 1946 Lew Grade, who was to become Deputy Chairman and Managing Director of ATV, formed the company Lew and

Leslie Grade Ltd together with his brother Leslie, and in 1960 they re-named it the Grade Organisation. In 1956 Lew Grade was a director of several companies including the Montague Lyon Agency and the Incorporated Television Programme Company. In 1960 he resigned as a director of the Grade Organisation but remained a shareholder and, the same year, the Organisation acquired nearly half the shares in London Management, and by 1967 all the shares. In 1962 Robin Fox, an agent active in film and theatre production, a member of the Council of the English Stage Company and a director of Robert Morley Productions, was appointed a director, and in 1963 the Organisation bought half of Harold Davison Ltd, including the Harold Davison Agency, which represented several of the leading pop groups and singers. In 1964 the shareholding was reorganised and shares issued to the directors and shareholders of London Management and London Artists.

This was the giant agency which had been created to take over the executives and clients of London's branch of MCA (the Music Corporation of America) when the American Trust law prevented it from continuing to trade both as a management and an agency. It had been the most important agency in London, representing more of the stars than any other. When it closed, some of its executives formed London Artists and in 1964 two of them, Laurence Evans and Olive Harding, joined the board of the Grade Organisation. When the Organisation became a public company in July 1964, London Artists, London Management and London Authors were among its subsidiaries, and two of its associated companies were Ivy Productions and Elstree Distributors. Ivy Productions was the film company which produced *The Servant, Sparrers Can't Sing, The Young Ones, Summer Holiday* and *Wonderful Life*. All the profits went to the Grade Organisation. Elstree Distributors was owned half by the Grade Organisation and half by the Associated British Picture Corporation.

Lew and Leslie Grade have another brother, Bernard Delfont, who has also been extremely active both as a producer and an agent. In 1965, for £100,000 and 230,000 shares (out of the total of 2,730,000), the Grade Organisation acquired the Bernard Delfont Management and Enterprises, the Bernard Delfont agency and their subsidiaries, which included Donmar Productions. The next year, the Organisation paid £1,500,000 and £500,000 worth of shares for the Shipman and King group of cinemas – thirty-two well-run cinemas mostly in monopoly situations in the south of England. The same year, 1966, the Organisation bought Tito Burns Productions, another big agency handling variety artists, and Bernard Delfont's other big company, Bernard Delfont Ltd. In 1967 it bought an important literary agency, Gregson & Wigan Ltd, which represented a number of leading screenwriters and playwrights. Later in the year, the Organisation was the object of a successful take-over bid by EMI (Electrical and Musical Industries) the giant company which had been formed in 1931 as result of the merger of two gramophone record companies, Columbia and HMV.

By the end of 1968 its subsidiaries included the Associated British Picture Corporation (ABPC) and London International, the agency which had been formed to incorporate London Artists, London Management, London Authors and Gregson & Wigan. While Lew (now Sir Lew) and Leslie Grade could exercise little influence on EMI policy, because their shareholdings in the company were small, Bernard Delfont went on to the Board of EMI, and a statement was made that 'The Grade Organisation will continue to operate as a separate entity'. After acquiring ABPC, of which Bernard Delfont became Chairman, EMI gave undertakings in March 1969 to give up voting control of Thames Television (though it continued to own nearly 50 per cent of the shares, and an EMI director, Lord Shawcross, became Chairman of Thames) and to sell off the theatrical and variety agencies acquired with the Grade Organisation. London International had already been sold by then. Most of the executives who had been working for London Artists combined in January 1969 to form a new company, the International Famous Agency Ltd, associated with the American company Ashley Famous. Laurence Evans, Robin Fox and Olive Harding were the three principal executives. Two of the other executives, Ros Chatto and Michael Linnit, have since left the organisation, separately, taking clients with them. They formed two separate companies (with the same telephone number) operating for a while in a house in New Bond

Street. Leslie Grade and Bernard Delfont remained joint managing directors of the Grade Organisation.

An interesting survey of London agents was made by Peter Lowman for a report published as an appendix to the Arts Council's *The Theatre Today* (1970). He took a sample of 649 appearances by actors in important parts in unsubsidised West End productions. He was able to ascertain who the agents were for 425 of these and found that 211 were handled by eleven agents, leaving 214 which were spread around eighty-one agents. The eleven agents were

London International	77 actor appearances
Plunket Greene	21
Fraser & Dunlop	20
Bryan Drew	14
Peter Crouch	14
Delfont-Grade Agency	13
William Morris Agency (UK)	12
London Management	11
Essanay	10
Richard Hatton	10
Herbert de Leon	10
	211

So 101 actor-appearances out of the 425 were handled by companies which had been formed or acquired by the Grade Organisation.

15 THE PLAYWRIGHT AND HIS AGENT

*The full-blown actors are merely the completed types
of secret actors who are called producers, backers,
directors, yes, playwrights ... The actor himself is
the lunacy in full profession – the lunacy which in
others is partially concealed.* ARTHUR MILLER

If the theatre can be compared to an organism, the playwright is the brain, the director the nervous system, and the actor the physique. None could survive without the other two. During earlier phases of the theatre's evolution, when there was no director as such, the function of directing the actors was assumed either by the playwright or the leading actor. The playwright's role is the most creative: director and actors are interpreters. The director can be an innovator in a more valuable way than an actor can – but if you consider the innovations which have made modern theatre what it is, we clearly owe more to playwrights like Ibsen, Chekhov, Strindberg, Shaw, Brecht, Genet, Beckett and Pinter, than to directors like Stanislavski, Reinhardt, Copeau, Meyerhold, Piscator, Grotowski and Brook, or to actors like Irving, Duse, Forbes Robertson, Jouvet and Gielgud. Actor–managers like Barrault, Gründgens and Olivier would have been less influential as producers if they had not also been stars, but it is not mainly by their acting technique that they have made a permanent contribution to theatre history, just as it is not mainly by his techniques as a director that Peter Hall has contributed, though he could not have been so influential as a director of a theatre if he had not also been a director of plays.

A theatre cannot be in a healthy state without a constant flow of good new plays: one of the main advantages our theatre had over the French, German and American theatres during the sixties was that our playwrights were producing more interesting work. But the system is not geared to encouraging the writer to work for the theatre, when he not only stands a far greater chance of selling his wares to television, but commands a better price for them without any risk of having the run curtailed by bad reviews or public apathy. There are a handful of playwrights (like David Storey) who can turn out a full-length stage play in less than a week, but for most writers it involves an investment of several months' work. Commissions in the theatre are rare and seldom involve a guarantee of production: most plays are written on spec, and there is nearly always a long delay before a production is arranged or before the point comes at which it is clear the play is never to be produced. Aspiring playwrights are not easily deterred, but it seems that less plays are being written now than in the late sixties. Most of the plays that used to arrive unsolicited in the offices of theatrical managers may have been very bad, but at least there were a lot of them.

The Writers' Guild of Great Britain, which protects the interests of film, television and radio writers, is affiliated to the TUC and negotiates corporate agreements which cover minimum fees and conditions of work. The League of Dramatists, an association formed within the Society of Authors to protect the interests of the playwright, can help him in a number of ways – drafting contracts or advising on contracts drafted by managements, collecting royalties, dealing with repertory and amateur rights and providing free legal advice. But it is not a trade union and it does not have the power of the Writers' Guild. It would be virtually impossible to unionise playwrights, which means it would be virtually impossible to standardise contracts. Consequently, the playwright is even more dependent than the actor is on his agent. Different agents will agree to different royalty scales, different advances, different apportionments of the subsidiary rights. They also vary in how hard they fight for their clients' rights and whether they can negotiate with managements from a position of strength. This depends partly on who their other clients are.

A playwright has seldom been able to earn as much as a leading actor. In Shakespeare's time, when even the cheapest actors were earning six shillings a week, a play would be sold outright for £10. In a fascinating essay on 'The Playwright and his Money'[1] Richard Findlater points out that Ben Jonson's total earnings as a playwright – less than £200 during twenty-three years of work – come to less than Neil Simon has averaged each month for the last ten years, even allowing for changes in money values.

Outright sales of plays for lump sums continued for over 200 years, but a primitive form of the royalty system was introduced at the beginning of the seventeenth century, the author being given the box-office takings of the third, sixth and ninth performances minus daily running costs. But there was no means of protecting the writer from dishonest managers, who falsified the figures or deducted losses incurred on other performances. By the end of the seventeenth century a playwright could make £140 from one play, as Southerne did from *The Fatal Marriage* in 1694, in addition to gifts from private patrons and fees for publication rights.

The Beggar's Opera was one of the biggest successes of the eighteenth century, but Gay, who was given the profits of only four out of the sixty-two nights it ran at Lincoln's Inn Fields, made less than £700. Everything depended on the manager, and the actor was far better placed for getting money out of him than the writer. Charles Macklin, who was a leading actor, was able to claim 20 per cent of the net receipts from some of the performances of his successful play *Love à la Mode*. In 1776, according to Garrick, a playwright could make up to £1,000, including money for publication rights. By the end of the century a new system had been introduced at Covent Garden and Drury Lane by which the playwright received £33 6s. 8d. for each of the first nine performances, then £100 if it reached twenty, and another £100 if it reached forty. It was very hard for a dramatist to average as much as £500 a year, while a star actor could make ten or even (like Kean) twenty times as much. So he could easily draw a playwright into becoming his satellite. Sir Thomas Talfourd wrote

[1] *Theatre Quarterly* No. 8. I am grateful to Mr Findlater for allowing me to read his article before it was printed, and in this chapter I am more indebted to it than to any other source.

for Macready, George Colman wrote mainly for Charles Mathews, while Kean and Kemble almost monopolised other writers.

Theatre outside London was growing, and by the middle of the nineteenth century, professional theatre was being enjoyed in over two hundred towns, but the playwright did not participate in the profits his plays made. As soon as a play was published, any company could legally produce it, and copyists could be bribed to provide country theatres with scripts of brand new London plays. It was an unauthorised performance of a play by James Robinson Planché that provoked him into agitating for reform of the copyright laws so that playwrights should be protected. Finally in 1833 the Dramatists' Copyright Act became law, but in spite of it, a great deal of piracy went on.

There was no international copyright governing performances until 1887; meanwhile the availability of French plays for the price of a translation depressed the native market. The Irish playwright, Dion Boucicault, scored his first big success with *London Assurance* (1841) which he sold for £300. A few years later a manager offered him £100 for a new play: why should he pay more when it would cost only £25 to commission a translation of a play that had already proved its audience appeal in Paris? Tom Taylor's play *Our American Cousin* had already been a success in New York (1858) before it was put on at the Haymarket in 1861, but he still made only £150 out of its London run, though it earned £20,000 for the management, and Edward Sothern's performance as the idiotic Lord Dundreary became so fashionable that long sidewhiskers like the ones he wore in the part came to be called 'dundrearies'.

Charles Kean gave G. W. Lovell £400 for *The Wife's Secret* (1848) and offered £1,600 for a play by Sheridan Knowles, author of *The Hunchback*, a play very popular with young actresses. But not many playwrights could expect more than £50 per act, and James Albery was paid only £3 a performance for *Two Roses* when it was produced at the Vaudeville in 1870 and the young Henry Irving (who had made his London début four years earlier) was scoring a big success as Digby Grant.

The most important turning point in the development of the playwright's earning power came when Boucicault managed to introduce sharing terms. This was either in 1860 or 1864. Professor Allardyce Nicoll supports Sir Francis Burnand's version of the story, which is that when Boucicault and his wife were playing the leading parts in the London production of *The Colleen Bawn* in 1860, having already made it into a success in New York, they feigned sickness in order to force the manager to give them better terms. Richard Findlater finds Townsend Walsh's story more plausible: that having failed to secure sharing terms when he made his first bid for them, Boucicault succeeded at the Princess's in 1864 with the production of *The Streets of London*, which he had adapted from a French melodrama, *The Poor of Paris*. He could now earn £400 a week as a playwright, while Tom Robertson, whose *Caste* was produced in 1867, was making £7 a week. Robertson's comedies, which altogether earned him about £6,000, are said to have made about £100,000 for the Bancroft management.

The outright sale of plays continued into the Edwardian period, but sharing terms came to be widely accepted during the eighties, and, as long London runs and long provincial tours became more common, the economics of playwriting changed. Royalties on a popular play could be as lucrative as royalties on a popular novel. In the eighteen sixties, according to Findlater, the Dramatic Authors' Society had less than sixty members, most of whom were adapting plays from the French. But by 1909 (the first year in which a playwright – Henry Arthur Jones – received a knighthood) there were 230 dramatists at work, including novelists like Arnold Bennett, John Galsworthy, Somerset Maugham and J. M. Barrie. By now the agent was playing an important role not only in selling plays but in bringing them into existence. In 1906, when Addison Bright, who had cheated his clients of many thousands of pounds, committed suicide, Barrie wrote that 'it was owing to his encouragement and zealous help more than to any other cause that novelists and poets have of late years produced plays'.

As the possibility emerged of selling the film rights of a play, the most successful playwrights became very rich indeed. The cinema has also provided a comfortable retreat for playwrights like Rattigan during periods when fashion has swung against them. The film rights of a play can sell for £50,000 or more, and if the author is given the job of writing the screenplay himself, his earnings can be colossal. Without rising to this level of earning power, the successful playwright can do extremely well for himself out of television, radio, and royalties on his published scripts. A few contemporary plays sell as many as 20,000 copies each year, and there are many which average 5,000 a year. Eighty thousand copies of *Serjeant Musgrave's Dance* have been sold and, in Britain alone, 500,000 of *A Man for All Seasons*.

There are a few exceptional playwrights like Arnold Wesker and Edward Bond, who owe their reputations to the Royal Court and have their plays produced all over the world, but make little or no money out of the West End. Only two of Wesker's plays have been produced there, one unsuccessfully, and none of Bond's. But for most of our playwrights it is hard to make money in the theatre unless their careers have been launched in the West End. The National and the RSC have not played a large part in establishing the reputations of new playwrights, though Tom Stoppard's was made by *Rosencrantz and Guildenstern Are Dead*, which had its professional première at the National, and David Mercer's reputation has been fortified by the RSC after being made by television and boosted by a West End production of *Ride a Cock Horse*.

Robert Bolt was a school teacher who wrote radio scripts until his agent, Margaret Ramsay, managed to interest the producer–director Frith Banbury and the Tennent management in *Flowering Cherry*, which they jointly presented, with Ralph Richardson starring and Banbury directing. It ran for eighteen months. Without the earnings from an uninterrupted run like this in the West End, Bolt could not have afforded to give up teaching. As he has said, the subsidised theatre could never have subsidised him into turning professional. Tennents and Banbury also jointly presented his play *The Tiger and the Horse* co-starring Michael and Vanessa Redgrave with Banbury again directing, and Tennents presented *A Man for All Seasons* with Paul Scofield starring.

Much depends on stars and on the determination of agent and manager to stick out for them even if it means a long wait, as it often does. When Margaret Ramsay sold Alan Ayckbourn's *Relatively Speaking* to Peter Bridge, 'he wanted two years to get Richard Briers and all those stars (Michael Hordern, Celia Johnson and Jennifer Hillary) and it *would not* have worked without stars.'[1] A powerful agent can have a huge degree of control over a playwright's fate – helping to develop the talent and the career, the reputation and the earning-power. The agent can make seminal suggestions about the writing of a play or about how to convert a radio script into a full-length stage play.

In Germany virtually every theatre has a Dramaturg – a sort of theatrical editor. In England the first equivalent position was created in 1963 when Kenneth Tynan was made Literary Manager of the National Theatre, and in 1971 Ronald Bryden was appointed Play Adviser of the RSC. Peter Hall took an even more important step in this direction when he appointed a Drama Professor, John Russell Brown, as an Associate Director of the National Theatre, with special responsibility for scripts. Television companies have script editors and story editors, but none of the reps or the West End producers employ anyone to do this very important job, though few writers can do as well without help as they could with help. How much help a playwright gets, then, depends entirely on chance. Some depend on a wife or a friend who gives useful or damaging advice. The agent, the producer and the director may all make suggestions. A good director needs to be a good editor, but it is quite possible to be a good agent or a good producer without being good at textual work. Playwriting is not taught academically and many of the playwrights who have emerged since the war have learned about theatre by working in it. But there may be potential playwrights who never acquire technical *savoir faire* because they never chance on the right adviser or the right agent. Even if the agent cannot spot what it is that stops a script from working, he should be able to recognise talent and to keep the young playwright's hopes alive until he comes up with a script that can engage the interest of a producer or director who will take over as midwife.

Once a script (with or without the agent's editorial help) is ready

[1] Margaret Ramsay interviewed in *New Theatre Magazine*, Vol. X No. 3.

to be seen, it is for the agent to decide where to offer it first – Royal Court or West End, Hampstead Theatre Club or regional rep. If it is to be in the West End, the agent must decide which management would be the best for this particular play. All the subsequent decisions about director, designer, style, stars and the size of the budget depend on this basic decision. The play's whole future may depend on its first production, and the agent can have a considerable degree of control not only over where it is produced but how. A play, like a baby, needs the most loving protection. Managements and directors often want cuts to be made: an established playwright can defend his own brainchild, but the beginner needs help from his agent, who will be in a very strong position if his other clients are sufficiently important for the producer to be nervous of losing his goodwill. If Margaret Ramsay had not defended them, the foot-kissing scene and Childie's speech about being forced to drink bathwater would probably have been cut from the original production of Frank Marcus's play *The Killing of Sister George* (1965), and, once cut, they might never have been reinstated.

It is hard to estimate how much influence an agent's powers of persuasion have in tilting the balance on a decision about whether or not a play should be staged. Sometimes it does seem to have made all the difference, as when George Devine was hesitating about Ann Jellicoe's play *The Knack* at the Royal Court. 'Why *not* do it?' said Margaret Ramsay, and it was done. There is a great deal of interest-juggling in the preliminary stages of setting up a play. Sometimes it is advantageous to get a star interested in a script before showing it to a management: it may then be a much more attractive proposition. Alternatively (or additionally) it can make a big difference if the interest of a well-known director can be secured. But once an actor or director has said yes to a script, there is a commitment to him, whether he buys an option or not. Perhaps he will never actually do it – in which case time is lost while he works on other projects. Perhaps he will finally do it, but using it as a vehicle for his own personality, destroying the balance of the play and ignoring or misunderstanding the writer's intentions. Perhaps he will do it well, helping to make the writer's reputation. But once the first commitment is made, whether to actor or director or management, everything else follows from that. The writer, even if he knows what he wants, will only be able to get it if he and his agent make the right decisions about who should be offered the script first. And then second, if the first person says no. And so on down the line of possibilities.

Here the agents who represent not only playwrights but actors and directors have a certain advantage: they can prepare a 'package' to offer to a management which may build the careers and the fortunes of several of their clients at the same time. Some actors' agents have opened literary departments partly for their own sake but partly in the hope of producing packages like this. This is not always an advantage for the writer. If his agent is a purely literary agent, there is the whole of the profession to choose director and actors from. An agent who also represents directors and actors is bound to consider his own clients first. It may be that the ideal director and the ideal leading actors are not among them, but it can also happen that the third best director and the fifteenth best leading lady are given first refusal of the script if the writer doesn't know better than to resist his agent's suggestion. Not that all agents would be biased to this extent in favour of their own clients, but it would be unnatural for them to be totally unbiased.

The playwright's agent can also help him through the difficult early phase of his career in which he is making so little money out of writing that he may give it up altogether. There are a few exceptional playwrights like Shelagh Delaney, Michael Hastings and Christopher Hampton who make their mark with plays they have written while still in their teens, but it usually takes a good playwright far longer than a good actor to break through. Joe Orton was living on the £2 10s. 0d. a week he had from National Assistance when he wrote *Entertaining Mr Sloane*: when he was killed, three years after its first production, his earnings from royalties were about £6,000 a year and the film rights of *Loot* had been sold for about £100,000. The five months West End run of *Entertaining Mr Sloane* made £2,500 for Orton, but by then he had been writing for over ten years. Edward Bond was given a Sunday night production at the Royal Court for one of his early plays, *The Pope's Wedding* (1962), but he was thirty before he had his first full-scale production, *Saved*, in 1965. David Mercer was living on his earnings as a supply teacher and on money borrowed from his agent while he was writing the unproduced stage plays that preceded his first television success, *Where the Difference Begins* (1961). He was in his late thirties when his first full-length stage play was produced. Peter Nichols was nearly forty when his first stage play *A Day in the Death of Joe Egg* was produced in 1967. There is no knowing how much talent is wasted when playwrights do not go on persevering for long enough. The agent can be all-important both in keeping a writer's hopes alive and in keeping him solvent, possibly by helping to sell his plays to the radio.

If the standard of our theatre is to be raised, new playwrights are more important than new buildings, but the problem of how the talented playwright is to survive between the ages of twenty and forty is being almost completely ignored by the Arts Council. Even if every agent were willing and able to act as a private patron, making loans to promising young clients who needed them, there would not be enough to go round. The state is the only patron with the funds to cope with the problem.

There is a great deal that is wrong with our theatre today but nothing is worse than the lack of provision for the talented playwright who is not yet successful. Neither the National nor the RSC is oriented towards the new playwright, the Royal Court is less of a writer's theatre than it was in its first ten years, and except in a few towns like Stoke-on-Trent the regional audience tends to stay away from new plays. There is a plethora of Fringe theatres where new work is done, but not profitably enough to make a living for the writer. There was one London writer who had a play staged at the Edinburgh Traverse but the theatre could not pay for him to go up to see it, and he would have been out of pocket on the production if he had bought himself a return railway ticket. This is not untypical, but a few Fringe companies are generous to writers. Paradise Foundry (which is Portable Theatre reconstituted) commissioned Snoo Wilson to write *Vampire* with a payment of £150, and gave him another £150 as an advance against royalties when he delivered the script, without even asking for any participation in the play's future earnings. This is exceptional, though. For the most part the playwright earns very little from Fringe productions, apart from grant money, and, as John Elsom has pointed out,[1] £100 does encourage a new playwright who wants to see his work performed, but it does not help the television playwright to go back to the theatre.

Unless he can write very quickly, the playwright is staking a lot of time on winning what is seldom more than a small reward. A 'try-out' at Hampstead Theatre Club or one of the smaller reps might bring an advance of only £50 (or £100 if the Arts Council is supporting the play) and this is likely to be all the writer will earn unless the production transfers. The theatre is normally given exclusive rights to the play for six months after the first night of the run, and it can claim a London option. It then makes a deal with the producer for a proportion of the box office gross and of his profits, plus a share of any earnings from television, film or radio during a stipulated period – probably two or three years. If the try-out theatre does not take a London option, it has a right to 1 per cent of the playwright's net box-office earnings and 5 per cent of his net television and film earnings from the script.

Only a small minority of the plays which are tried out have any subsequent life, and only a small minority even of the ones that reach the West End make much money for the playwright. Twenty thousand pounds may be spent on the production, but the usual advance to the author is only £200. It can be £100 or, if he is well known, as much as £500. This advance gives the management an exclusive option on the play for an agreed period – six months, nine months or a year. Sometimes the option has to be renewed while the manager and the director are trying to assemble the cast they want. Once there have been twenty-one consecutive performances in the West End, the manager normally retains the professional rights to the play for five years, as long as he presents at least fifty performances each year. Some managements also ask for control of the amateur rights. The playwright's share of the West End box office takings is usually on a sliding scale. Sometimes he receives 5 per cent until the production

[1] *Theatre Quarterly* Vol. III No. 11, July-September 1973

has covered its costs and then 10 per cent; sometimes it is 5 per cent of the first £1,000 of the weekly gross, 7½ per cent of the next £500 and 10 per cent of the remainder. This is negotiable too: he may get only 5 per cent of the first £2,000.

A long-running success in the West End will obviously be extremely lucrative, especially in a large theatre where up to £10,000 a week can be taken at the box-office. But this is not all: if a play is favourably received in the West End, it acquires prestige which creates a demand for it elsewhere. A play which has, say, an eight-week run in Shaftes-bury Avenue might well earn as much again from amateur rights, foreign rights, and publication royalties. Apart from the cinema, the biggest potential source of income is America. Since Peter Nichols's play *A Day in the Death of Joe Egg* was first staged in 1967, his total stage earnings (to the end of August 1972) were £52,724·97, and £19,624·42 of this money was made in the United States. The West End run produced £3,732·70 for him and he has earned £3,974·25 from rep, and £1,938·73 from amateur productions. Royalties on productions abroad (excluding the US) have come to £23,454·87, and he has earned £79,170·58 from the film, and £1,481·21 from the printed text.

Not many plays produce as much as this. Since 1958 Arnold Wesker (who also earns most of his money abroad) has fluctuated between about £9,000 and about £24,000 a year, averaging perhaps £15,000. The peak earnings were due to payments for two film-scripts which were never produced. His earnings for 1970–71 were roughly:

	UK	Abroad
theatre	800	2,207
amateurs	330	—
radio	67	500
television	40	2,050
publication rights	800	1,130
	2,037	5,887

A play does not need to be a smash hit in order to enjoy quite a profitable life after its London run. Hundreds of pounds can accrue from selling options on performance rights not only to France and Germany but to Holland, Italy, Austria, Poland, Yugoslavia, the Scandinavian countries and Japan. Then royalties can continue for years if they exceed the option money which is paid as a non-returnable advance.

It would be interesting to guess how many playwrights could earn enough out of theatre to survive, but the question is almost meaningless: successful playwrights – like successful actors – invariably earn more from outside the theatre than from inside it. A sixty-minute television play can earn anything from £270 to £1,250 according to the slot it goes into and the status of the writer. Again, overseas sales can multiply a writer's earnings. And since writing for the screen, like acting for the screen, involves different techniques, experience gained in one medium is that much less valuable for the other. There are a few writers, like William Trevor and John Mortimer, who sometimes convert short stories or radio plays first into television plays and then into stage plays. Pinter, too, has done this with radio plays. But it happens more often that a play written for the stage is adapted for one of the other media, and altogether the traffic between the media is not of much importance as a means of developing technical skill. Most playwrights would prefer to spend more time working for the theatre: like actors they go to the other media to balance their budgets. Edward Bond has earned a great deal more out of writing for the cinema than for the theatre, in spite of the number of productions his plays have received at theatres all over Germany. Charles Wood has made a considerable reputation as a playwright, but his only West End run was a brief one at the Vaudeville. He has made more out of television than the theatre, and still more out of the cinema. This does not make them all amateurs but it does make them all victims of a system in which the creative talents who are contributing most of all to the theatre are not earning most of their living from it.

16 DIRECTORS

To define is to limit, and it is difficult to define the scope of the director's work because there is almost no limit to it. He can create a show into which a script enters only secondarily, as with Joan Littlewood's *Oh What a Lovely War* and Peter Brook's *US*. Both shows had contributions from more than one writer – but the actors' improvisations, inspired and then edited by the director, provided so much of the substance and effect of both shows that no one talks of either as being 'by' the writers. A good director needs to be a good editor of the playwright's script, and sometimes he can use his editorial talent to concoct an evening in the theatre without any help from a playwright. Patrick Garland himself provided the script for *Brief Lives* (the one-man show in which he directed Roy Dotrice) by cleverly anthologising John Aubrey's biographical sketches of seventeenth-century notables into a montage which presented a portrait of Aubrey himself. John Barton's *The Hollow Crown* is an equally amusing and equally successful piece of compilation by a director, though it is not dramatised to the same extent.

The extent of a director's contribution to a new play is not always evident. John Barton's talent for theatrical editing was a factor in one of the RSC's biggest successes, *The Wars of the Roses* (1963). Here it is easy enough for anyone who is interested to compare the three parts of Shakespeare's *Henry VI* and his *Richard III* with John Barton's version (which contains some new lines). But with a new play only the author and the actors can possibly know the size of a director's contribution – and they will not always want to remember it. The director's work usually begins in an editorial way, but it is not merely a negative matter of cutting lines and sandpapering over-explicitness;

he may suggest new lines and ask the playwright for some material to develop a theme or a character, or to provide a better transition between two scenes or two moods. It can happen that the play is considerably deepened by the rewriting that ensues. Often the writer is not fully aware of his own play's potential.

Partnership is not a misleading word to describe the collaboration that is possible between a writer and a director, and in England today several of our leading playwrights have become involved in long-standing working relationships with directors. At the Royal Court David Storey's plays have nearly all been directed by Lindsay Anderson, Edward Bond's mostly by William Gaskill and John Osborne's by Anthony Page. Peter Nichols has been collaborating in the same sort of way with Michael Blakemore, as Arnold Wesker has with John Dexter. In fact, the pattern of close collaboration on a long term has become more prevalent than it was in the fifties or early sixties, though it did sometimes occur. Philip Wiseman directed all J. P. Donleavy's plays (*The Ginger Man, Fairy Tales of New York* and *A Singular Man*) and Joan Littlewood both Brendan Behan's (*The Quare Fellow* and *The Hostage*) contributing to construction and dialogue, as well as filling the plays out in rehearsal with *ad libs* and stage business.

Sometimes it is very hard to assess the relative importance of the director's pre-rehearsal contributions and of the work he does with the actors. John Dexter, for instance, has made suggestions to Arnold Wesker which have led to major changes in construction. After reading *The Kitchen*, which he directed in 1959, Dexter asked him to provide a quiet middle section, like a slow movement, to separate the two scenes of busy activity. Then, in rehearsal, Dexter built up the two climaxes in which the waitresses mill around the hotplates, shouting orders and collecting dishes from the cooks. Wesker wrote additional lines to fill out the shape the scenes were now acquiring. With *The Old Ones* (1972) Dexter's suggestions led to two major structural changes. The play was originally written as a series of almost unconnected scenes ending in a Jewish Friday night supper. Wanting a stronger framework to hold the scenes together, Dexter asked whether it was possible to start preparations for the meal from the beginning of the play. Wesker then thought of introducing a Jewish festival (*Succoth*) and rewrote the script with the characters preparing a ritual tabernacle (a *succah*) from the beginning. Originally the three youngsters in the play were all boys but, because Dexter (who directs a lot of opera) wanted the balancing sound of a young female voice, Wesker made one of them into a girl.

By the time he started rehearsals, therefore, Dexter had a very different script from the one he had originally read, but many more changes were effected before the first night. Some new lines and some ad libbing were introduced, but more change was produced by heavy cutting, and the balance was altered a good deal by a variety of devices to divide the audience's attention between several characters where a more straightforward reading of the script would have centred it on one. A revolving stage was used very cleverly to bring more characters into a scene than Wesker had envisaged, and a complex counterpoint was sometimes evolved by using singing or dancing as a background to speech or by using a tape-recorder to back speech or action. Dexter also introduced a theme to the play which Wesker had not intended. For Wesker the play is 'about old people, and incidentally they happen to be Jews'. They are 'concerned with growing old with dignity. And fight'.[1] The fact that they were Jews who did not believe in the Jewish religion had no particular significance for Wesker, but it was of great interest to Dexter, who made it one of the keynotes of a production which invested the play with much more suspense and resonance than it might otherwise have had.

With Peter Shaffer's *Equus*, which was premiered at the National in July 1973, Dexter again made an important contribution. The first draft that he read was concerned with narrating the events that culminated in a boy's putting out the eyes of six horses with a metal hook. The character of the analyst had barely started to emerge. Dexter asked him to dig into himself more deeply to find the man, and to reconstruct the play less naturalistically. As they went on working together on the script, the analyst became no less important than the boy. Treating the boy provokes a crisis in the man and, instead of merely working towards a climax in which the blinding of

[1] Interview in *The Times*, 5 August 1972.

the horses is re-enacted, the play also moves towards an outburst from the analyst in which he declares his envy of the Dionysiac freedom his patient has arrogated, and his disbelief in the methods he is using to 'cure' him.

Not only can a director have a big influence on a play's substance; often his influence is decisive over whether it is staged, and where. Some directors (like Tony Richardson, Frith Banbury and Allan Davis) enter directly into the management business, forming production companies of their own. By putting down maybe as little as fifty pounds, maybe a hundred or two, they can commission a play or an adaptation, or secure a six- or twelve-month option on a script they want to direct, producing it either on their own or, more likely, in association with a larger management. Directors without companies can also acquire scripts by commissioning or optioning, but what happens more often is that they start working with a playwright on a finished or half-finished script, suggesting cuts and revisions. There may be no formal or financial arrangement between them, but the writer feels morally committed to the director who has been helpful. If this director can then take the play to a management or a rep which invites him to direct it, everything proceeds smoothly, but it can happen that he submits it to someone who likes the play but not him, or that while he is still trying to set up a production, the writer receives an offer from a theatre which has a resident director who wants to do the play himself. The writer is then in the quandary of having to decide whether his main allegiance is to his brainchild or his collaborator.

Another area where the size of the director's contribution can never accurately be gauged is in the effect it has on an actor's performance. Here too the work is partly editorial. A creative actor will produce far more variations during a rehearsal period than can be used in a performance: the director must select the best, helping the actor to piece them into a coherent characterisation. It is more a matter of giving something back to the actor than of giving him something, but the actor can only give with confidence if he feels the director can take the right amount. The actor should feel free to go too far in rehearsal, confident that the director will stop him from going too far in performance. Every actor needs to feel he has the director's attention in rehearsal, for the director is the only audience, but some actors need more coaxing, more stimulation – provocation even – than others, and it can be a matter of feeding in ideas as well as confidence. Sometimes the actor has the impression of something being drawn out of him that he did not know he had. Often this has something to do with a libidinous or aggressive or ugly aspect of his personality at which he normally bridles. If a director knows how to release the normal inhibitions and free the actor from the normal anxieties about whether the audience will find him sympathetic, he can give him the sensation of discovering new areas of his own personality, and the possibility of using them for the first time is particularly exciting.

Directors vary in what they can give as much as actors vary in what they need. Some directors who get very good results in performance seem to be using the rehearsal period to give a performance themselves, ostentatiously dominating proceedings with a calculated cruelty, fastening on the vulnerability of the cast, bullying and making jokes, now at the expense of one actress, now another, inviting hostility but sidestepping rebellion by a hectoring paternalism mixed with good-humoured badinage. Collectively and individually the actors are being insulted, and there is an unmistakable masochism in the way they passively accept aggressiveness from a director they trust. He is treating them like children, but this in itself is reassuring: he will look after them as if they were children. Meanwhile they can even enjoy the performance he is giving at their expense. In the final performance they will be the active ones and he must be passive: meanwhile they will submit, go on being the audience for his jokes, his exhibitionism, certain that the process is leading towards an opening for theirs. During the actual performance, the director's power fades to nothing in the present tense, but the actors' responses and associations cannot slough off the experience of the last rehearsal weeks – they continue in the tracks he had laid down.

Though the director's power is enormous, frequently providing both the force that initiates and the force that shapes the production, financially his position is very insecure, unless he is employed by one of the large companies. Only a handful of full-time directors earn enough to survive as freelances. The median annual earnings of the directors who replied to the Equity questionnaire was only £1,352.

At the Hampstead Theatre Club, for instance, the fee for directing a play in 1972 was £100, and to do the job adequately it is necessary to devote at least ten weeks to it – a fortnight or more for preparatory work, three weeks for casting (which involves checking actors' availabilities, interviewing, discussing and persuading), four weeks of rehearsal, plus an incomplete week of dress rehearsals, technical runs-through, previews and sessions with the actors for notes. There is the hope, of course, that the production will transfer to the West End and that the director will then receive a larger fee, but most often it fails to transfer and he finds he has averaged £10 a week. Even if the play does transfer in his production, he will very likely be offered a lower fee than he would have got in a production created specially for the West End, on the grounds that most of his work has already been done.

In rep, both subsidised and commercial, directors are often paid less than £30 a week. At the National Theatre or in the West End there are a few directors who can command as much as £1,000 for a production fee, but £750 is more usual, though preparation and casting will probably not have taken less than five weeks' work and the rehearsal period at the National may stretch to ten or eleven weeks. In commercial productions it may be four weeks or even less. Of the really good directors there are few who would want to do more than four productions in a year (even assuming that the right offers were materialising at the right moment) so to earn a reasonable living is impossible without having a good income from royalties on plays already running. Peter Cotes, who directed *The Mousetrap* in 1952, has done very well out of it ever since, without even having to take rehearsals for changes of cast. Robert Chetwyn made money out of every one of the two thousand-odd performances that were given of *There's a Girl in My Soup*. In 1972 Ronald Eyre was participating in the gross box office takings of two big West End successes – *A Voyage Round My Father* and *London Assurance*. Clifford Williams, who

K

directed *Oh! Calcutta!* on Broadway, in London, and elsewhere, has made a lot of money out of percentages.

For the director, as for the playwright, the jackpots are extremely desirable, but there are a great many people competing for a very few, and often the married man with children and commitments cannot afford to go on freelancing when the offer of a regular job comes up, even if it means that more of his time would be taken up with running a theatre than with directing plays. The appointment of Oscar Lewenstein as Artistic Director of the Royal Court is a reminder that this is really more a managerial than an artistic job. To govern a theatre's policy, plan programmes, budget productions, argue with designers and stage managers when the budget is exceeded, negotiate actors' salaries, find last-minute replacements for productions that fall through, balance financial against artistic considerations, console actors who are unhappy, make emergency decisions when someone is ill, discuss angles on each play with the publicist and supervise everythings that happens – all this adds up to a totally different job from that of directing plays, and there are some good directors in regional theatres who spend less time directing than doing work which could be done equally well, if not better, by a theatrical manager. But at least the job provides a regular, though modest, salary and an opportunity to direct some of the time.

However, there are some good directors who would not make good artistic directors, and in any case there are not enough artistic directorships to go round, so how are the others to survive? There are not many companies like the RSC and the 69 Theatre Company in Manchester which employ more than one director permanently, unless it is in a junior position as an assistant director or to be in charge of a studio theatre or a 'theatre-in-education' team. Actor–directors (like Nigel Patrick) seem to be rarer in the younger generation, though there are a few, like Robin Phillips, who prefer directing but are willing to act when necessary. Several theatre directors (like Michael Elliott and Vivian Matalon) can also earn money by directing on television, and a few (like Lindsay Anderson) earn a lot from directing films. Ronald Eyre has been earning by introducing book programmes on the radio, and interviewing and writing for television.

Adapting a script for television would still bring in more money for him than directing a play at Stratford-on-Avon. Patrick Garland works for radio and television and cinema, as well as theatre, and organises Poetry International; Michael Bakewell, who directed Vanessa Redgrave in *Twelfth Night*, also runs a literary agency and organises events like the lectures and entertainments at the 1971 Book Bang. Many directors earn extra money by teaching at drama schools.

But, like acting and writing, it is a profession in which the casualty rate is very high. During the ten years after the war, two of the busiest and most intelligent directors in London were John Fernald and Michael MacOwan. In 1954 MacOwan gave up to become Principal of LAMDA, and in 1955 Fernald gave up to become Principal of RADA. The directors who were in the ascendant during the next ten years are not, mostly, in the ascendant now. A director like Peter Wood or Peter Coe can be in enormous demand for five successive years, then partially eclipsed for the next five, and then make a comeback. But there has been very little directorial continuity in the London theatre as a whole over the last twenty-five years, and what the RSC has achieved since 1962 is due more to continuity among its directors than among its actors – a point that gives some inkling of what our theatre could have lost by failing to make it easier for directors to survive. Of course new blood is always needed, but no tradition can be created or maintained without more continuity.

One of the injustices that make it unnecessarily hard for directors to earn a living is that legal copyright can be claimed only for written work. Some directors have done so much collaborative work on a script that the writer has agreed to make over a percentage of his earnings from it, but this happens seldom; normally a director earns money only out of his own production, even when he has contributed substantially towards finalising a script which will earn money for the author from productions all over England and America, perhaps all over the world. Even when a script is printed in an acting edition with stage directions copied from the prompt copy, the director earns nothing for devising the moves and the comedy business which constitute an important part of what the publisher is selling. Equity's Legal

Officer is currently investigating the possibility of enforcing copyright, but even if he succeeds, the copyright will remain indivisibly the author's except for stage directions of this sort. Nor can a director expect any kind of equivalent to a writer's royalties on casting ideas or on help given to actors. He may for instance stage a play which is subsequently made into a film with the same actors, using some of the ideas that he gave them, but whoever directs the film will not be called on to share either the credit or the profit.

Like actors, directors are at a disadvantage if an *ad hoc* agreement is made for each separate engagement. The need for a standard contract is obvious, but this can only be established through unionisation. Directors would be in a very much stronger position now if they had formed themselves into a trade union when the actors did. It was not until 1971 that a group of directors led by Gordon McDougall called a meeting in Manchester, after which the TUC was approached. Its reply was that it could not encourage the formation of new small unions – which meant that the only possibility of union representation for directors was through Equity. Though they had been eligible for membership of Equity, no attempt had been made to organise them collectively or to launch a recruiting campaign to make all the directors in the country join Equity. Even in September 1971, when an open meeting attended by fifty-six directors declared itself to be in favour of the idea, feeling on the Equity Council was divided. Wasn't a director sometimes an employer, otherwise always a representative of the employer, more inclined to identify with his interests than with those of the actors he was employing? But Peter Plouviez, the Assistant General Secretary, felt strongly that it would be in Equity's interests to represent directors, and the Council finally gave the scheme its support. A working party was then set up to inquire into the problems of directors, and two public meetings were called to which all professional directors were invited. There was a large majority in favour of Equity representation, but even with an intensive membership drive, it will take a long time to persuade all directors to join Equity, and it is only then that standard contracts can be enforced.

17 THE AUDIENCE AND ITS MOTIVES

Like most audiences they felt that, to some degree,
they owned the performing players. JOHN BERGER
in 'G'.

The urge to communicate with an audience must be integral to the
creation of any work of art from a painting to an oratorio, but drama
is the art in which the audience impinges most directly on the performance. The dancer, the singer, even the timpanist at the back of
the symphony orchestra is depressed by empty seats and boosted by
a full, enthusiastic house, but their performances are less liable to vary
than the actor's. However successfully he resists the temptation of
playing for sympathy or for laughs, the actor's rhythm is influenced –
even when there are no laughs – by his awareness of the speed at
which the audience is picking up the points, and by its attitude to the
material. He may be unable to overcome audience resistance but he
has to fight it. With an audience that is enjoying itself hugely he has
to fight himself: the inclination is to give it too much of what it
wants.

Audiences vary from night to night and from town to town.
Touring, even in a straightforward play like *Tea and Sympathy*, the
actor may find that his rhythm is quicker in Oxford than, say,
Cheltenham. He also finds that he reacts to an audience as to a single
entity. A sprinkling of amused young radicals makes little difference
to an audience that is predominantly elderly, conservative and easily
shocked. Ann Jellicoe maintains that 'there is no such thing as individual judgement in the theatre'.[1] Watching her play *The Knack* on its
pre-London tour, she was astonished to find how much her own
opinion of the play could be modified by the reactions of people

[1] *Some Unconscious Influences in the Theatre.* Cambridge, 1967.

sitting around her in the darkness of different theatres. At Cambridge the amusement of a mainly undergraduate audience convinced her that it was very funny. But at Bath, watching with a much older audience, she was uncomfortably sure that it was obscene. In London, sitting behind 'a large party of extremely sophisticated people', without at first realising that their reactions were influencing hers, she found the play innocent and childlike. How could she ever have thought it obscene? Of course she was watching a slightly different show, because the actors were also being affected by the varying responses, but the silent merging of individual reactions into a collective reaction is an important part of what goes on in an auditorium. Everyone is affected most by the people who are closest, and the collective reaction of the gallery may remain different from that of the stalls, but the pressure towards unification is a strong one, especially in comedy. A Marx Brothers film seems very much less funny on television (especially if you are watching it alone) than in a crowded cinema. And it is very hard to go on laughing at something that does not amuse the rest of the audience either in a cinema or a theatre. They are unintentionally pressuring you into thinking it is not so funny after all.

Group reactions are not always easy to anticipate. The lines that seem funniest to the actors rehearsing them are seldom those that get the biggest laughs, and a play which seems hilarious in the rehearsal room can fall quite flat in performance. Some playwrights, like David Mercer, have a gift for dialogue which on the page looks only mildly amusing but takes on a new comic dimension in the presence of an audience. It is when an audience is enjoying itself most that it is most able to act like yeast on both dialogue and performance as they bake in the open-fronted oven of the stage. Enjoyed in the darkness, this sense of collective potency is quite important, though no one would list it among his reasons for going to the theatre. Logical explanations of the audience's motives – like logical explanations of the actor's – tend to be incomplete. Plays can still be important talking points, and of course people do not want to be left out of conversations about a play that has become fashionable. This is one of the factors that make it fashionable. *Waiting for Godot, Look Back in Anger* and *The Care-*

taker were successful first because they corresponded to anxieties, frustrations, attitudes which were present in their potential audience, and then because – once the plays had brought these to the surface – they became pivotal points in a great deal that was written and said.

But more people go to the theatre to see actors than to see plays. A kind of collector's instinct seems to be at work, though no one understands quite how. Sex appeal is only one of many factors, and technical prowess has very little to do with popularity. The way in which an audience warms to the quietly reassuring clean-cut commonsensicality of Kenneth More's personality is quite different from the way it responds to a lovable eccentric like Robert Morley. The animal magnetism of Olivier is quite different from the overflowing humanity of Richardson or the nobility of Gielgud. Peter Cook and Dudley Moore broke the box-office record at the Cambridge in November 1972 because they make people laugh in a way that inspires a sort of love. With all stars, some sort of love is involved in the audience's identification, together with a feeling of ownership. The charisma builds up a large following of people who, like collectors, want to possess each of the chosen actor's performances as if it were something tangible. Star actors are liable to receive letters telling them off if a character they play is unsympathetic or unsuccessful – unworthy of a place in the collection. The middle-aged and elderly usually prefer the chosen star to go on looking as young as he was when they first saw him. He represents their youth, physically proving that the past is still alive in the present.

The words 'escapism' and 'entertainment' are used very loosely. Most musicals could be called escapist entertainments, in that instead of challenging the values we live by or holding up mirrors to contemporary reality, they comfort us with catchy music, attractive stage pictures, romantic sentiment, decorative girls and simple, appealing choreography. Most thrillers, farces and light comedies have equally few points of contact with the lives we are living. The experience of watching them is more of a distraction than a confrontation.

But most of the shows that are seen by large audiences are musicals, farces, light comedies and thrillers. In the twelve years 1960–71 and excluding these categories, only about forty shows in London received more than 250 performances, though *Boeing-Boeing* and *There's a Girl in My Soup* each had over two thousand. Of the more serious plays which passed the 250 mark, many were comedies and very few came critically to grips with the problems of being alive today. Many were set firmly in the past, whether historical costume plays like Robert Bolt's *A Man for All Seasons* and *Vivat! Vivat Regina!* or harking nostalgically back to more recent history, like *Right Honourable Gentleman*. Historical biographies had great audience appeal: *Portrait of a Queen* (about Victoria), *Ross* (about T. E. Lawrence), *The Miracle Worker* (about Helen Keller). There were also *Abelard and Heloise* and Roy Dotrice's one-man show based on Aubrey's *Brief Lives*. The successful revivals of Sheridan, Wilde, Shaw and Coward were glamorously nostalgic – *The Rivals* and *The School for Scandal; The Importance of Being Earnest* and *An Ideal Husband; You Never Can Tell;* and *Present Laughter*. There was a new Coward comedy *Sail Away* and an Ustinov comedy *Photo Finish*. There were several plays based on novels from earlier in the century – Frederick Rolfe's *Hadrian VII*, E. M. Forster's *A Passage to India* and *Where Angels Fear to Tread* and Henry James's *The Wings of the Dove*, and some on newer novels set earlier in the century, such as Muriel Spark's *The Prime of Miss Jean Brodie*. The two C. P. Snow novels to be dramatised successfully, *The Affair* and *The Masters*, were scarcely more modern, but there were two Iris Murdoch novels – *A Severed Head* and *The Italian Girl*. Only three Parisian successes were successful in London – two by Anouilh, *Poor Bitos* and *The Rehearsal*, and one by Félicien Marceau, *La Bonne Soupe*. The two other revivals were Pirandello's *Six Characters in Search of an Author* (with Sir Ralph Richardson) and T. S. Eliot's *The Cocktail Party* (with Sir Alec Guinness). Of the plays by new writers, three were successful because they combined high-pressure comedy with outrageous subject-matter: Orton's *Loot* (an embalmed corpse was humped about the stage and its false teeth were clicked like castanets), Frank Marcus's *The Killing of Sister George* (about lesbians) and Mart Crowley's *The Boys in the Band* (about homosexuals). Edward Albee's *Who's Afraid of Virginia Woolf?* was about two heterosexual couples, but it played the game of embarrassing the audience with its near-naked exposure of intimacy in the games the characters inflicted on each other. The other new plays to receive over 250 performances were Pinter's *The Caretaker*, Osborne's *Luther* (with Albert Finney) and *Inadmissible Evidence* (with Nicol Williamson), Peter Shaffer's *The Private Ear* and *The Public Eye* (with Kenneth Williams and Maggie Smith), Arnold Wesker's *Chips with Everything*, David Storey's *The Contractor*, Bill Naughton's *Spring and Port Wine*, Charles Dyer's *The Rattle of a Simple Man*, Keith Waterhouse's *Billy Liar* (with Albert Finney and later Tom Courtenay) and Alan Bennett's *40 Years On* (with Sir John Gielgud).

Except for the revivals, very few of these will have a permanent place in the history of drama, and very few indeed issue a challenging criticism of the way we live now. The Albee play, which does, gets away with it partly because of its deft use of the game-playing element. Very few plays of such high intellectual calibre succeed in the West End, and even with the much smaller audience that patronises the Royal Court and the National, game-playing playwrights (like Tom Stoppard) are more popular than playwrights who are critical of contemporary society in the way that Edward Bond is or E. A. Whitehead is in his frontal attack on working-class morality and the institution of monogamy in *Alpha-Beta*. Bond has said 'In western society morality is a form of violence and not, as it should be, of creativity. It is used to coerce people.' That he is writing his plays from this premise makes them unpalatable to a majority audience.

The plays that posterity considers to be important nearly always issue a disturbing challenge to social or sexual habits, or to conventional morality. They throw a new, clear and possibly harsh light on what is happening all round us. But the plays that appeal to the majority of that minority which goes to the theatre at all are rosy, cosy and reassuring. Happy endings imply that things always work out all right in the end, and the mirror images that the plays hold up to society and its institutions (including marriage) are always flattering. While the most popular television plays are seen by twenty million people and *The Mousetrap* has probably been seen by about three million – it has had over eight thousand performances in a theatre which seats 453 – *Waiting for Godot*, after a short run at the Arts Theatre Club, transferred to a 606-seat theatre, where it played for

226 performances. Assuming an average audience of 450, it would have been seen by just over 100,000 people. Even with subsequent revivals at the Royal Court, Stratford East, the Young Vic and in rep, it has probably not been seen in English theatres by more than 200,000 people. *Look Back in Anger* was a play which spoke much more directly to the young audience of the fifties, creating a character in which a whole generation seemed to see its own image and to hear its own tone of voice – or to remodel its image and adapt its tone to those of the character. But *Look Back in Anger* must have been seen by an even smaller audience. It was revived several times at the Royal Court and has been done in rep all over England, but never had a continuous run in the West End till 1960, and then only a brief one. *The Caretaker* had 444 performances, transferring after a month at the Arts to the Duchess, which has a capacity of 491, so assuming a 75 per cent average, it would have been seen by about 160,000 people. The film versions of both plays were seen by a larger audience.

The moods and the needs of an audience vary from town to town and from season to season. John Barton's production of *Troilus and Cressida* did not please the Stratford-on-Avon public when it was staged there in 1968, but when it came to the Aldwych the following year it was a great success because it tallied with the mood of the moment, endorsing it and encouraging it, in almost the same way that Jimmy Porter had both articulated and aggravated the mood of 1956. In 1969 at Stratford the RSC directors were surprised at the success of *Pericles* and *The Winter's Tale*, which are not usually popular, but as Terry Hands has put it,[1] 'the public seemed to be looking for optimism, for ideals asserted by positive affirmation, for happy endings.' The appetite for the same kind of strongly positive assertions may be seen behind the almost simultaneous success of *Godspell*, a musical based on the Gospel according to St Matthew, in 1971, and *Jesus Christ Superstar* in 1972. The audience as congregation.

Traditionally both tragedy and comedy are social statements. Schumaker's view[2] – which applies equally to Greek and Shakespearean tragedy – is that the audience's passive acquiescence in the

[1] Ronald Hayman, *Playback*. Davis-Poynter.
[2] W. Schumaker, *Literature and the Irrational*. Prentice Hall.

death of the hero is like the worshippers' passive participation in the sacrifice (divine or animal) celebrated by the priest. The audience at a tragedy is first made to feel like the guilty accomplice of the protagonist, who acts out its secret desires, disregarding taboos, throwing off the restrictions of the law and religion. But his death expiates the guilt. Health and harmony are restored to the social body represented in the play, while the audience, after having its criminal appetites vicariously indulged, enjoys having its normal habits of restraint vindicated by the spectacle of destruction which drives home the lesson that crime doesn't pay. The underlying message is always that the social and moral *status quo* must be preserved.

In nearly all comedy the characteristic happy ending brings the reconciliation of a group that represents in miniature the well-knit society. Sometimes the solitary misfit like Malvolio is expelled from the group or, like Bob Acres in *The Rivals*, gives up his claim to a wife, but the conflicts and confusion created by counter-pressures between private desires and public proprieties are all happily resolved – the implication being that they are always happily resolvable.

It is sometimes said that there are no shared values among the audiences of today. This is quite untrue. The morality of the Ten Commandments is the one that most people still live by, and an interesting book by the sociologist J. S. R. Goodlad[1] makes the point that the plays which become most popular both on television and in the theatre all supply reassurance about our morality and our society: the society is well organised and well able to defend its members against threats to their safety and happiness; the morality that holds it together is valid and just. Murder, stealing, adultery, covetousness and giving false evidence are the staple crimes, while the heroes are mostly professionals employed to protect society against its enemies – policemen, lawyers, detectives, secret agents, doctors.

According to Durkheim's *Elementary Forms of the Religious Life* (1912), the four main functions of ritual are to prepare the individual for life in society by promulgating the necessary self-discipline; to remind him of the traditions, values and beliefs that make up his social heritage; to create a feeling of social well-being; and to bring people

[1] *The Sociology of Popular Drama*. Heinemann.

together in a ceremony that celebrates social solidarity. Popular drama on both stage and television could be regarded as a ritual in the first three senses; popular theatre as a ritual in all four.

In Japan theatres contain shrines, and even in England being among an audience is not altogether unlike the feeling of being among a religious congregation. Possibly the need theatre satisfies is greater among people who are not members of trade unions, working men's clubs, supporters' clubs attached to football teams or other social units that provide a feeling of togetherness. Activity in amateur dramatics works not as an incentive to theatre-going but as an alternative. Amateur actors generally tend to patronise neither the professional theatre nor other amateur groups, while the audience for amateurs seems to overlap very little with the audience for professional theatre. Allegiance to the group is apparently more of a factor than interest in the drama. The football fans who dress up in the team's colours, arm themselves with rattles, travel miles to support the local team and try to pick fights with supporters of the rival team are showing a desperate need to side with one group against another. Today they have a more obvious affinity with the crowds who scream at pop concerts than with the more sedate audiences in theatres, but at one time theatre did cater for this social need. The eighteenth-century audience went to the theatre armed with whistles, rattles, catcalls and sometimes even wooden cudgels. Cliques would be organised to attack plays, and other cliques to defend them, and claques were organised to applaud. Allardyce Nicoll cites the case of a lawyer who won a big first night success for a play he wrote by having a hundred boys from his old schoool in the pit and boxes and about fifty 'young sprigs of the law' in the gallery to 'maintain a proper circulation of applause'. Whether or not payment was involved, members of cliques and claques had the satisfaction of providing the same sort of active and useful support as the football fans who shout and whirl rattles to egg on the home side.

The habit of applause which survives today is a vestige of a far more integral involvement in the performance. One of the earliest forms of drama was the tribal ritual in which the men danced in animal costumes to secure the gods' assistance in the hunt. The earliest evidence of clapping we have is a cave painting that shows Bushmen dressed up as animals, with sticks representing their forelegs. The dancers are surrounded by onlookers who are clapping – presumably in rhythm.

The Elizabethan audience did not listen, as we do, in silence. Sir Thomas More is known to have behaved like the on-stage spectators at the play of Pyramus and Thisbe in *A Midsummer Night's Dream*, interrupting and disputing at length with the actors. The noblemen who sat on the side of the stage were well placed to do this, and extempore battles of wit could be highly diverting for the other spectators, who must sometimes have felt almost as if the interruptor were on their side against the actors. Of course Shakespeare's audience must also have been capable of listening very attentively to the play, or he would never have written as he did. But apart from interruptions, there would be noise coming in through the open roof and chatter from inside. Attentiveness was no doubt patchy and one of the functions of the rhetoric must have been to make a bid for silence in the passages where it was most needed.

Spectators in the Restoration theatre were talkative and liable to be more interested in each other than in the play. Pepys's diaries contain evidence of the active social life that would be enjoyed all over an auditorium. When he went to see *The Maid's Tragedy* in 1667 he was distracted from the play by a conversation going on between a masked woman and a man who was dividing his time between trying to find out who she was and commenting loudly on the play and the actors' pronunciation. There seems to have been little group pressure on chatterers to keep their voices down. The playwright Wycherley had his first conversation with his future mistress, the Duchess of Cleveland, when he was in the pit and she was in the front row of the King's box. There were frequent duels. Sir Thomas Armstrong actually killed one Mr Scroop during a performance of *Macbeth*.

Audiences deteriorated further during the eighteenth century. In the Shakespearean and Restoration theatre verbal exchanges between actors and spectators had at least been witty; now there were coarser, more raucous interruptions. Apples, oranges and fireworks were thrown at the actors, and at the first night of *The Rivals* in 1775 Sir

Lucius O'Trigger, who was hit by an apple, stepped forward challengingly to demand 'By the powers, is it personal? Is it me or the matter?' But in 1841, when Macready tried to discipline the unruly intrusions that had become normal in certain parts of Drury Lane, he was attacked by the Press, which reflected the popular desire that the theatre should stay as it was. Obviously it was fulfilling a social function, but a manager could never dare to put on a play that might antagonise the pit or the gallery, and it was even dangerous to change the advertised programme. When this happened at the Haymarket, the irate Duke of Cumberland, who was in the Royal Box, did his best to incite the rest of the audience to pull down the theatre.

English audiences were subdued into a decorous silence between about 1828, when stalls began to replace the pit, and about 1880. The appearance of well-dressed women in the front rows of the stalls tended to silence the rowdies, who gradually took to patronising the music halls, which began to proliferate in the eighteen-fifties. Another important turning point was the abolition of the half-price system: when programmes lasted from six-thirty in the evening till midnight, people who arrived after nine o'clock were admitted for half price, which meant a noisy irruption of men from the pubs and women from the streets. But Charles Kean shortened the programme to one full-length play and a curtain-raiser, and then the Bancrofts started to present just one play in an evening. Altogether they did a great deal towards making the theatre more respectable. In 1865 when they reopened the disreputable old Queen's Theatre under a new name, the Prince of Wales, they redecorated it, putting down a carpet in the stalls. 'The action was symbolical,' Allardyce Nicoll comments. 'The old front rows of the severely benched pit were becoming refined.' The new decorum was not altogether welcome to the profession. In 1871 T. Purnell complained, 'The late dinner-hour of our day, combined with the increasing disposition of cultivated people to show no emotion is inimical to farce.'

The development of cinema-going was bound to militate against the habit of interaction between actor and audience, and the spread of television has encouraged the habit of chatting through dialogue, but without making people feel any less cut off from the action going on in front of them. Heckling, booing and hissing have died out almost completely. The first appearance of a favourite star is more likely to be applauded on tour than in London, and, unlike the French, we never clap at the end of a big speech. We even applaud an actor's exit less often than we used to. The role of the audience has been whittled down to laughter and to applause at the end of the act.

What then is the audience doing while it sits there undemonstratively? One of the pleasures of theatregoing is the pleasure of feeling strong waves of sympathy and repulsion without the possibility of any action ensuing from them. We are at the opposite extreme from the man who in the middle of a Chicago performance of *Othello* pulled out a revolver and shot Iago. We sit there in the safety of knowing we will not have to become involved in the conflict or to risk being rebuffed by the sexy actress. But it is pleasant to have a story unfolded in front of us and to empathise. The storyteller has had a place in every culture: the ancestry of the film and the television serial goes back to the troubadour, the ballad-singer, the serial novelist and the short story magazines. It also goes back to the medieval Church, which never had a monopoly on stories or drama, but would not have enjoyed the moral hegemony it did if it had not been able to grip the popular imagination with stories, plays and pictures that appeared to back up its dogmas and values.

Far too little audience research has been done, but it is obvious that the audience we get in the English theatre is not only unrepresentative of our society: it is unrepresentative even of the middle class. According to a survey made in the spring of 1965,[1] the median age of the British theatregoer was 31. Only 5·5 per cent of theatregoers were over sixty, though 16·6 per cent of the population was, and only 12 per cent of theatregoers were under twenty, though 30·8 per cent of the population was. Of the males in the audience 60·5 per cent came from the professional classes, which represent only 7·5 per cent of the population; 11·7 per cent were teachers, 19·1 per cent were in managerial positions, 15·9 per cent were clerical and sales staff, and only

[1] By the Twentieth Century Fund. Published in W. J. Baumol and W. G. Bowen, *The Performing Arts*. MIT Press, 1969.

4·6 per cent were blue-collar workers. Of the women in the audience, 58·8 per cent were from the professions, 22·8 per cent were teachers, 35 per cent did clerical work, 20·1 per cent were students, 16·2 per cent were housewives and only 1·9 per cent were saleswomen.

A depressing constant in English audience surveys is the high level of educational and occupational status. A survey of the audience at the Royal Court[1] indicated that about 40 per cent of those who were not still students were university graduates. And whereas the Elizabethan audience was predominantly male, the majority in our audiences is almost invariably female. When *Uncle Vanya* was performed at Sheffield Playhouse in 1965[2] over two-thirds of the audience was female, and though 33 per cent of the population (according to the National Distribution) are unskilled workers, only 2 per cent of the audience were; 18 per cent were in higher executive and professional positions (though only 3 per cent of the population were) and 32 per cent came from the 9 per cent of the population in middle management and lesser professional jobs; 39 per cent of the audience came from the 17 per cent of the population who were technicians, office workers or in lower managerial or semi-professional positions, while only 9 per cent of the audience came from that much larger category of the population (39 per cent) doing supervisory or skilled manual jobs. A survey of the audience at the Phoenix Theatre, Leicester, produced similar results. More evidence needs to be collected but generally a large section of the audience – often over 20 per cent – consists of students, and usually there are more young people of fifteen to twenty-five and middle-aged people of forty to sixty than young married couples or old people.

So, when many plays on television are seen by ten million people, and some are seen by twenty million, very few stage plays of any seriousness are seen by more than eighty or a hundred thousand people. Why does such a tiny percentage of the people who enjoy drama want the experience of going to the theatre?

A better-organised theatre would attract better audiences, but the

[1] In an M.A. thesis for the University of Essex by Peter Walton, 1967.
[2] The results of Peter Mann's audience survey are published in the *British Journal of Sociology*, Vol. XVIII No. 1 (1967).

main problem, in both theatre and audience, is disintegration. The young audience at the Young Vic hardly overlaps at all with the middle-aged audience for musicals at Drury Lane. The audience that came to the Royal Court when tickets were given away free for *Life Price*, and when the seats were taken out of the stalls and the prices reduced for the 'Come Together' Festival of Fringe events, has mostly stayed away ever since. The RSC has built up a fairly steady audience, but it seems to consist mainly of people who seldom go to either the West End or the Fringe. We have a split theatre and a number of separate audiences. Not that disintegration in the theatre can be remedied – or even discussed – except in a more general cultural context. The condition of our theatre is largely due to the condition of our language, our educational system, our attitude to leisure, the structure of our society. For the Jacobean audience, Cleopatra could be represented by a boy actor speaking superb poetry with rhythms, images and jokes that combined to build up an impression of a witty, sexy, spoilt, vulnerable woman. But to most of us today the name Cleopatra calls to mind Elizabeth Taylor in Technicolor.

We have become lazy. We know we are at the fag end of a civilisation, and so many easy gratifications are at our disposal that it seems pointless to make any imaginative effort. The situation is being exacerbated by bad cultural and educational planning, and though it could not be remedied by good planning, it could at least be improved. Children are still born with a natural creativity and a natural theatricality, but though theatre is now being given a more prominent place in education than ever before, few children go through the educational pipeline without having their imaginative faculties badly impaired.

If there is any hope of reversing the present trend, it is more likely to be through theatre than through any of the other arts. There are still pockets of vitality not only on the Fringe but in the subsidised reps and in the London theatre. It is still possible to put on a production without scenery in which a group of actors sit down in a lifeboat-shaped pattern on the bare boards of the stage and row with non-existent oars, and the audience not only pictures a lifeboat but enjoys the imaginative effort that it has to make. But costs will continue to rise, which means that theatre will become increasingly dependent on what the Arts Council does with the Government's subsidy and on whether local councils are willing to help more than they have.

How can we enlighten the planners? How can theatre be sold (or given away free) to the 98 per cent of the population who never go but would enjoy it if they did? And how can Fringe Theatre, Theatre-in-Education, subsidised theatre and 'commercial' theatres be brought closer together so that there is less rivalry and more interaction? The first step must be to understand the present situation. To understand it is to want to change it.

BIBLIOGRAPHY

(*Each book is listed under the number of the chapter which first draws on it for information*)

1

Winnicott, D. W. *Collected Papers: Through Paediatrics to Psychoanalysis.* Tavistock, 1958.

Winnicott, D. W. *Playing and Reality.* Tavistock, 1971.

Laing, Ronald. *The Divided Self.* Tavistock, 1960.

Laing, Ronald. *The Self and Others.* Tavistock, 1961.

Laing, Ronald and Esterson, Aaron. *Sanity, Madness and the Family.* Tavistock, 1964.

Sartre, Jean-Paul. *Saint Genet, Comédien et Martyr.* Gallimard, 1952. English translation: W. H. Allen, 1963.

Cole, Toby and Chinoy, Helen Crich (editors). *Actors on Acting.* Crown (New York), Revised Edition 1970.

2

Nicoll, Allardyce. *A History of Early Eighteenth Century Drama 1700–1750.* Camb. U.P., 1952.

Nicoll, Allardyce. *A History of Late Eighteenth Century Drama 1750–1800.* Camb. U.P., 1952.

Nicoll, Allardyce. *A History of Early Nineteenth Century Drama 1800–1850.* Camb. U.P., 1955.

Nicoll, Allardyce. *A History of Late Nineteenth Century Drama 1850–1900.* Camb. U.P., 1959.

Findlater, Richard. *The Player Kings.* Weidenfeld, 1971.

Richards, Kenneth and Thomson, Peter (editors). *Nineteenth Century Theatre.* Methuen, 1971.

Rowell, George (editor). *Victorian Dramatic Criticism.* Methuen, 1971.

Rowell, George. *The Victorian Theatre*. Oxford, 1956.
Bradbrook, M. C. *The Rise of the Common Player*. Chatto, 1962.

3

Burton, Hal (editor). *Great Acting*. BBC, 1967.
Rossiter, A. P. *English Drama from Early Times to the Elizabethans*. Hutchinson, 1950.
Wickham, Glynne. *Early English Stages 1300–1660*. Routledge, Vol. One, 1959; Vol. Two, Part One, 1963.

5

Granville-Barker, Harley. *The Exemplary Theatre*. Chatto, 1922.

6

Findlater, Richard. *The Unholy Trade*. Gollancz, 1952.
Goldman, William. *The Season*. Harcourt Brace, 1969.

7

Trilling, Lionel. *The Liberal Imagination*. Secker, 1951.

10

Elsom, John. *Theatre outside London*. Macmillan, 1971.

12

Williams, Raymond. *Culture and Society 1780–1950*. Chatto, 1958.
Harrod, R. F. *John Maynard Keynes*. Macmillan, 1951.

17

Jellicoe, Ann. *Some Unconscious Influences in the Theatre*. Camb. U.P., 1967.
Goodlad, J. S. R. *A Sociology of Popular Drama*. Heinemann Educational Books, 1971.
Schumaker, W. *Literature and the Irrational*. Prentice-Hall, 1960.
Baumol, W. J. and Bowen, W. G. *The Performing Arts*. MIT Press, 1969.

INDEX

AC/DC, 156
Actors' Association, 44
Actors' Company, 33, 179
Adelphi Theatre, 43, 60, 71
After Haggerty, 124
Albee, Edward, 94, 107, 157, 300, 301
Albery, Sir Bronson, 34
Albery, Donald, 72, 121, 124, 125, 132, 137
Albery Theatre (formerly New), 70, 72
Aldwych Theatre, 20, 67, 70, 79, 83, 89, 94, 102, 106–10, 124, 133, 139, 302
Alexander, Florence, 29; George, 29
Alfie, 168
Allio, René, 98
Almost Free Theatre, 75, 217, 218
Alpha Beta, 123, 159, 301
Alternative Theatre Company, 223
Ambassador's Theatre, 70
Ambiance Theatre, 216, 217, 219
Americah Hurrah, 122
Anderson, Lindsay, 111, 154, 155, 162, 163, 289, 294
Anouilh, Jean, 123, 300
Apollo Theatre, 59, 70, 116, 129
Arden, Jane, 34, 136
Arden, John, 24, 92, 151, 152, 154, 155, 157, 159, 168
Arrabal, Fernando, 93, 94, 184, 217
Arts Council, 7, 9, 31–3, 49–52, 55, 56, 67, 71, 73, 74, 78–80, 91, 95, 101, 102, 104, 105, 119, 120, 124, 125, 144, 145, 152, 161, 169–71, 177–81, 184–8, 191, 193, 194, 200, 202–5, 212–16, 222, 227–48, 249, 254–63 *passim*, 284, 285, 310

Arts Theatre, 71, 139, 217, 301, 302
Ashcroft, Peggy, 86, 87, 250
Atkins, Eileen, 133, 269
Aukin, David, 215
Ayckbourn, Alan, 196, 197, 281

Banbury, Frith, 130, 280, 291
Bancroft, Sir Squire and Marie Wilton, 62, 145, 279, 306
Barnes, Peter, 124, 156
Barrault, Jean-Louis, 137, 275
Barrow-in-Furness Theatre, 242
Barter, Nicholas, 235
Barton, John, 100, 107, 110–13, 288, 302
Basement Theatre, 222
Bates, Alan, 123, 134, 155
BBC, 51, 138, 141, 245
Beaumont, Hugh, 124
Beckett, Samuel, 32, 92, 121, 157, 184, 275
Behan, Brendan, 137, 289
Bennett, Alan, 116, 132, 301
Bennett, Arnold, 279
Bennett, Jill, 155
Bergman, Ingmar, 98
Bergman, Ingrid, 123
Berliner Ensemble, 62, 81, 82, 95, 97, 98, 121, 154, 214
Berman, Ed, 212, 216–19
Beyond the Fringe, 131
Bicat, Tony, 212
Billingham, Forum Theatre, 67, 187, 204, 240
Billy Liar, 137, 140, 301
Birmingham (including Alexandra Theatre), 67, 172, 174, 180, 185,

186, 188, 204, 206, 246; School of
Speech Training and Dramatic
Art, 44; Theatre School, 44
Birthday Party, The, 121, 138
Blakely, Colin, 81, 87, 155
Blakemore, Michael, 99, 129, 289
Blond, Neville, 138, 148
Boeing-Boeing, 122, 300
Bolt, Robert, 123, 280, 300
Bolton, Octagon Theatre, 49, 67,
182, 187, 190, 204
Bond, Edward, 150, 152, 154, 156,
158, 159n, 163, 280, 283, 287, 289,
301
Boucicault, Dion, 107, 124, 278, 279
Boys in the Band, The, 205, 300
Bradford Theatre, 175, 186
Brecht, Bertolt, 62, 63, 81, 84–6, 92,
97, 137, 148, 150, 151, 154, 157,
168, 239, 275
Brenton, Howard, 158, 160, 221, 225
Bridge, Peter, 281
Briers, Richard, 134, 250, 281
Brighton (including Theatre Royal),
67, 69, 172, 180; School of Music
and Drama, 44
Brighton Combination, 213
Bristol, 172, 204; Corporation, 125;
Hippodrome, 67, 177, 180; Little
Theatre, 186; Old Vic, 124, 177,
185, 188; Old Vic Theatre School,
44
British Drama League, 44
Bromley Theatre, 188
Brook, Peter, 65, 77, 100, 105, 111,
151, 275, 288
Brown, John Russell, 281
Browne, Coral, 97
Browne, Laidman, 250
Burton, Richard, 26, 27
Bury, John, 100
Butley, 134

Cadbury, Peter, 139, 245
Cambridge (including Theatre), 95,
175, 298, 299; Amateur Dramatic
Club, 54; Theatre Company, 179
Campbell, Ken, 160, 197, 213
Campton, David, 196, 197
Camus, Albert, 149, 168, 169

Canterbury Theatre, 204
Cards of Identity, 149, 150
Caretaker, The, 138, 169, 298, 301,
302
Central School of Speech and Drama,
44, 54
Changing Room, The, 122, 123, 132,
157
Chase Me Comrade, 205
Cheeseman, Peter, 36, 75, 182, 184,
190, 197, 240
Cheltenham, Opera House (Every-
man Theatre), 176, 204
Chester, Gateway Theatre, 67, 172,
187, 204
Chetwyn, Robert, 202, 293
Chichester Festival Theatre, 31, 59,
66, 80, 83, 123, 124
Chips with Everything, 202, 301
Christie, Agatha, 184, 189, 239
Church, Tony, 87
Clark, Ernest, 45, 250
Clark, Sir Kenneth, 230
Clements, Sir John, 31, 249, 250
Cochran, C. B., 141, 254
Cockpit Theatre, 215
Codron, Michael, 117, 121–4, 127,
128, 134, 136, 138, 139, 160, 202
Coe, Peter, 295
Colchester, Mercury Theatre, 182,
188, 189, 204
Coliseum Theatre, 70
Comedy Theatre, 70, 117, 219
Conduct Unbecoming, 117, 124, 125
Contractor, The, 301
Copeau, Jacques, 76, 275
Corona stage school, 54
Cotes, Peter, 293
Cottrell, Richard, 179
Council for the Encouragement of
Music and the Arts, 118, 119, 230,
231; *see also* Arts Council
Council of Repertory Theatres, 49
Courtenay, Tom, 301
Covent Garden, 23, 30, 70, 172, 277;
see also Royal Opera House
Coventry (including Belgrade Thea-
tre), 57, 157, 186, 188, 189, 198,
202–4, 246; Centre for Speech and
Drama, 44

Coward, Sir Noël, 24, 92, 116, 117, 124, 167, 183, 239, 300
Crawford, Dan and Joan, 222, 223
Cregan, David, 152, 155, 158, 159n, 160
Crewe Theatre, 204
Criterion Theatre, 68, 70–2, 134
Croasdell, Gerald, 255
Crucible, The, 150, 205

DALTA (Dramatic and Lyric Theatres Association), 179, 216, 233, 238
Daubeny, Peter, 103, 121
Davies, Elidir, 166
Davies, Sir Walford, 230
Day, Richard Digby, 200
Day in the Death of Joe Egg, A, 65, 284, 286
Dear Antoine, 123
Death of a Salesman, 197
Delaney, Shelagh, 137, 283
Delfont, Bernard, 122, 272–4
Dennis, Nigel, 149
Derby Theatre, 188, 204
Devils, The, 64
Devine, George, 24, 33, 63, 81, 86, 111, 136, 147–63 passim, 196, 282
Dews, Peter, 168, 185
Dexter, John, 81, 85, 98, 99, 157, 289, 290
Dirtiest Show in Town, The, 141
Dobie, Alan, 155
Don't Start without Me, 141
Donleavy, J. P., 289
Donnelly, Donal, 155
Dors, Diana, 155
Dotrice, Roy, 288, 300
Douglas Home, William, 116, 117, 127
Drama Centre, The, 44, 45
Drury Lane, Theatre Royal, 23, 30, 60, 61, 70, 74, 117, 128, 166, 172, 253, 277, 306, 309
Duchess Theatre, 71, 138, 302
Duffy, Maureen, 92, 93, 106, 152
Duke of York's Theatre, 70, 116
du Maurier, Daphne, 120
du Maurier, Sir Gerald, 27
Duncan, Ronald, 147, 148, 150
Dunlop, Frank, 99, 114, 168

Dyer, Charles, 94, 301

East 15 Acting School, 44, 45
Eccles, Lord, 194, 244, 246
Edinburgh, 26; Festival, 53, 129, 148, 179; King's Theatre, 180; Traverse Theatre and Workshop, 158, 160, 210, 211, 217, 225, 240, 241, 284
Eliot, T. S., 24, 151, 154, 300
Elliott, Michael, 36, 294
Embassy Theatre, 76, 209
England, Barry, 117, 124
English Stage Company, 34, 63, 121–4, 138, 147–64 passim, 238, 240, 246
Entertainer, The, 63, 153, 154
Entertaining Mr Sloane, 139, 205, 283
Equity, 9, 12, 33, 35, 36, 37n, 40, 44, 45, 47–52, 55, 56, 109, 134, 179, 180, 194, 207, 224, 249–63, 293, 295, 296; American Equity, 12, 38, 252, 261
Equus, 290
Esdaile, Alfred, 148
Esher, Lord, 254
Evans, Edith, 249
Evans, Laurence, 272, 273
Eveling, Stanley, 160, 225
Exeter, Northcott Theatre, 67, 87, 122, 187, 195, 204
Expresso Bongo, 136, 137
Eyen, Tom, 160
Eyre, Ronald, 97, 100, 293, 294

Farnham, Castle Theatre, 49, 183, 188, 199, 240
Fernald, John, 250, 295
Fiddler on the Roof, 122, 126
Fielding, Harold, 122, 123
Fielding, Henry, 168
Findlater, Richard, 277, 279
Finlay, Frank, 81, 87, 155, 269
Finney, Albert, 26, 27, 31, 34, 90, 137, 141, 163, 301
Flea in Her Ear, A, 89, 93
Flowering Cherry, 280
Forget-Me-Not-Lane, 117, 123, 126, 129
Fortune Theatre, 29, 128, 132
Fortune and Men's Eyes, 218

40 Years On, 116, 301
Foursome, The, 123, 127, 128, 159
Fox, Robin, 272, 273
Frisch, Max, 92, 157, 236
Frow, Gerald, 167
Fugard, Athol, 106, 160
Funny Thing Happened on the Way to the Forum, A, 122
Futz, 211

Gale, John, 122, 140
Garcia, Victor, 98
Garland, Patrick, 288, 295
Garrick, David, 24, 30, 42, 277
Garrick Theatre, 60, 70, 71, 127
Gaskill, William, 81, 85, 98, 99, 111, 152, 154–6, 162, 163, 215, 289
Gate Theatre Club, 208
Genet, Jean, 11, 149, 157, 163, 184, 275
George Jackson Black and White Minstrel Show, The, 220
Ghosts, 23, 117, 208
Gibson, Patrick, 244
Gielgud, Sir John, 26, 34, 84, 86, 90, 118–20, 148, 150, 156, 275, 299, 301
Gill, Peter, 160, 162
Glasgow, 129; Citizens' Theatre, 211; Close Theatre, 211; King's Theatre, 180; Unity Theatre, 148
Globe Theatre, 29, 59, 70, 128, 132
Godspell, 302
Going Home, 222
Good Woman of Setzuan, The, 150, 154
Goodman, Lord, 144, 193, 232, 233, 240, 244, 248
Grade, Leslie, 272–4; Lew, 271–3
Granville-Barker, Harley, 22, 91, 117, 150, 173
Gray, Simon, 117, 134
Great Yarmouth Theatre, 186
Greenwich Theatre, 66, 127, 129, 187
Grein, J. T., 23, 173
Griffiths, Trevor, 93, 106, 124
Grotowski, Jerzy, 76, 77, 150, 275
Guildford, School of Acting, 44; Yvonne Arnaud Theatre, 50, 113, 124, 183, 187–9, 201, 205, 238
Guildhall School of Music and Drama, 44

Guinness, Sir Alec, 15, 86, 90, 300
Guthrie, Sir Tyrone, 59, 90

'*H*', 93
Hadrian VII, 168, 169, 300
Haire, Wilson John, 160
Hales, Jonathan, 160, 161
Hall, Peter, 59, 66, 79–82, 84–7, 92, 99, 105–8, 111, 112, 151, 275, 281
Hall, Walter, 217, 222
Hall, Willis, 137, 157
Halliwell, David, 117, 127, 160, 217, 222, 225
Hampstead Theatre Club, 57, 64, 75, 79, 122, 127, 132, 282, 285, 293
Hampton, Christopher, 122, 123, 152, 156, 158, 283
Handke, Peter, 217
Hands, Terry, 100, 111, 112, 302
Harding, Olive, 272, 273
Hardwicke, Sir Cedric, 27
Hardwicke, Edward, 89
Hare, David, 64, 117, 122, 212, 220
Harewood, Lord, 148
Harrogate Theatre, 183, 204
Hastings, Michael, 151, 283
Haynes, Jim, 210–12, 217, 244
Haymarket Theatre, 30, 62, 70, 74, 118, 278, 306
Hays, Bill, 201
Hedley, Philip, 180
Henry, Victor, 160
Henslowe, Philip, 29
Her Majesty's Theatre, 58, 60, 70, 74, 118, 128
Herbert, Jocelyn, 163
Herbert, John, 218
High Wycombe Theatre, 188
Hillary, Jennifer, 281
Hitler Dances, 225, 226
Hobson, Harold, 138
Hobson's Choice, 91, 174
Hochhuth, Rolf, 31, 106
Hodgkinson, Joe, 255
Home, 123, 156
Hopkins, Anthony, 98
Hordern, Michael, 250, 281
Hornchurch Theatre, 183, 186, 188, 204

Horniman, Annie, 173
Hostage, The, 137, 289
Hotel in Amsterdam, 63, 155
Howard, Alan, 109
Howard, Trevor, 27
Howard and Wyndham, 176
Howarth, Donald, 123, 151, 155, 157, 158, 159n
Hull Theatre, 172, 175, 176
Hurwicz, Angelika, 85

Ibsen, Henrik, 117, 173, 208, 275
In Celebration, 155
In-Stage, 210
Inadmissible Evidence, 301
Independent Theatre, 117, 173
Inter-Action Trust, 212, 213, 216, 217, 219
Ionesco, Eugène, 137, 163
Ipswich Theatre, 172, 186, 188, 190, 204, 235
Irving, Sir Henry, 23, 26, 27, 61, 117, 251, 275; H. B., 251, 278
Italia Conti stage school, 54
Italian Girl, The, 124, 300

Jackson, Sir Barry, 174, 185
Jacobi, Derek, 109
James, Henry, 43, 58, 124, 151, 169, 300
Jeannetta Cochrane Theatre, 106, 212, 217
Jellicoe, Ann, 151, 152, 156, 157, 159, 282, 297
Jenkins, Hugh, 246
Jenkins, Warren, 198, 199, 202
Jesus Christ Superstar, 302
John Bull Puncture Repair Kit, 214
Johnson, Celia, 281
Johnstone, Keith, 152, 156, 159n, 160, 213
Jones, D. A. N., 120, 121
Jones, David, 100, 107, 111
Jones, Henry Arthur, 279
Jones, Dr. Thomas, 118, 230, 231
Jonson, Ben, 22, 29, 277
Joseph, Stephen, 190, 196, 197, 240

Joyce, James, 154, 169
Jumpers, 94

Kafka, Franz, 212, 220
Kean, Charles, 43, 61, 277, 278, 306
Keep, The, 149, 157
Kenny, Sean, 76
Kerr, Deborah, 123
Keynes, J. M., 227, 231
Killing of Sister George, The, 124, 282, 300
King, Philip, 239
King's Lynn Theatre, 251
Kitchen, The, 289
Knack, The, 153, 282, 297
Knights, L. C., 228, 229
Kulukundis, Eddie, 129, 130, 136

Laing, Ronald, 13, 14
Lambert, J. W., 237
Lancaster, Duke's Playhouse, 188
Lang, Robert, 89
Laughton, Charles, 27, 136
Lawrence, D. H., 154, 159n
Lay-by, 221
Leatherhead, Thorndike Theatre, 50, 67, 183, 188, 193, 195, 201
Lee, Jennie, 233, 244, 248
Leeds, 186, 201; Grand Theatre, 180; Playhouse, 188
Left-Handed Liberty, 168, 169
Leicester, 186, 188, 246; Phoenix Theatre, 67, 187, 308; Theatre Royal, 70
Leighton, Margaret, 86
Lennon, John, 92
Lessing, Doris, 149, 151, 169
Lewenstein, Oscar, 34, 124, 136, 137, 140, 147, 148, 153, 158, 162, 163, 294
Life Price, 155, 309
Lincoln, Theatre Royal, 50, 180, 182, 204, 235
Linklater, N. V., 255
Linnit and Dunfee, 120
Lister, Laurier, 201
Little Malcolm and His Struggle against the Eunuchs, 127, 160
Little Theatre Club, 217
Littler, Emile, 139, 245

Littlewood, Joan, 65, 78, 79, 100, 111, 137, 147, 182, 288, 289
Live Like Pigs, 159
Liverpool, 172, 174, 204, 206; Empire Theatre, 180; Royal Court Theatre, 180
Livings, Henry, 105, 117, 184
Lloyd George Knew My Father, 116, 117
Lock Up Your Daughters, 168
Logue, Christopher, 157, 159n
London Academy of Music and Dramatic Art (LAMDA), 44, 48, 295
London Assurance, 100, 107, 124, 278, 293
Long and the Short and the Tall, The, 137, 157
Long Day's Journey into Night, A, 94, 95
Look Back in Anger, 63, 150, 153, 154, 157, 298, 302
Loot, 202, 283, 300
Lowell, Robert, 168, 169
Luke, Peter, 168
Lulu, 124, 156
Luther, 34, 63, 137, 301
Lyceum Theatre, 60, 61, 128
Lyric Theatre, 70, 129
Lyric Theatre, Hammersmith, 70, 120

Macbeth, 119, 165, 305; Zulu version, 20
McCowen, Alec, 134
McDougall, Gordon, 296
McEwan, Geraldine, 89
McGrath, John, 36, 221, 225
McKellen, Ian, 179
Macmillan, Harold, 186
Macmillan, Lord, 118, 230
MacOwan, Michael, 295
Macready, W. C., 30, 278, 306
Macrune's Guevara, 93, 106
Magee, Patrick, 94
Man for All Seasons, A, 280, 300
Man Most Likely to . . . , The, 116, 205
Manchester, 172; Gaiety Theatre, 174; Library Theatre, 185, 193; Opera House, 180; Palace Theatre,

180; 69 Theatre Company, 124, 168, 204, 294; Stables Theatre, 106; University Theatre, 66, 187
Mankowicz, Wolf, 136, 137
Marat/Sade, 92, 100
Marcus, Frank, 124, 282, 300
Margate Theatre, 172
Marks, Alfred, 133
Marowitz, Charles, 55, 210, 212, 213, 216, 218–20, 246
Marshall, Norman, 209
Maugham, Somerset, 24, 124, 183, 279
May, Val, 125
Mayfair Theatre, 57
Meckler, Nancy, 211, 213, 215
Mercer, David, 64, 124, 280, 284, 298
Mercury Theatre, 216, 217
Mermaid Theatre, 8, 31, 57, 66, 67n, 68, 75, 79, 124, 127, 165–70, 189, 238
Michell, Keith, 122
Midland Theatre Company, 186
Miles, Sir Bernard, 31, 165–8, 189; Josephine, 167; Sally, 167
Miller, Arthur, 92, 128, 148, 150, 157, 205, 264, 275
Miller, Jonathan, 99
Milligan, Spike, 168
Miracle Worker, The, 300
Mitchell, Adrian, 93
Moore, Dudley, 299
More, Kenneth, 250, 299
Morley, Christopher, 100, 101, 189, 299
Morley, Robert, 299
Moro, Peter, 67
Mortimer, John, 93, 117, 123, 287
Mousetrap, The, 115, 116, 293, 301
Mrs Mouse Are You Within?, 124
Mulberry Bush, The, 149, 150
Murder in the Cathedral, 24
Murdoch, Iris, 124, 300
My Fair Lady, 116

National Association of Theatrical and Kine Employees (NATKE), 36, 128, 143
National Health, The, 93, 94
National Theatre, 8, 27, 31, 32, 34, 35, 43, 65, 66, 75, 78–114, 118, 121,

147, 156–8, 179, 190, 224, 237, 238, 246, 280, 281, 284, 290, 293, 301
Naughton, Bill, 168, 301
Neville, John, 188, 201, 223
New Lindsay Theatre, 76, 209
New London Theatre, 57, 69
Newcastle Playhouse, 198; Theatre Royal, 180
Nichols, Peter, 64, 65, 93, 117, 123, 284, 286, 289
No Sex Please We're British, 126, 140
Northampton Theatre, 50, 181
Northern College of Speech and Drama, 45
Norwich (including Theatre Royal), 172, 176, 180
Nottingham (including Playhouse Theatre), 49, 57, 67, 124, 129, 175, 186–9, 201, 239, 241; Royal Theatre, 186
Nunn, Trevor, 31, 100, 101, 106, 107, 110, 111
Nuttall, Jeff, 212

O'Casey, Sean, 107, 157, 168
O'Horgan, Tom, 211
O'Toole, Peter, 26–8, 137
Occupations, 106
Offending the Audience, 217
Oh! Calcutta!, 57, 116, 126, 141, 294
Oh What A Lovely War, 288
Old Boys, The, 169
Old Ones, The, 289
Old Vic Theatre, 7, 26, 60, 65, 70, 78–81, 91, 94–6, 99, 100, 106, 111, 119, 150, 158, 163, 237, 238
Oldham Theatre, 49, 205
Oliver, Peter, 215
Olivier, Laurence (Lord Olivier), 7, 26, 31, 80–2, 86, 87, 98, 99, 137, 154, 155, 166, 249, 299
Open Space Theatre, 55, 210, 218, 219
Orchard Theatre Company, 198
Orton, Joe, 24, 117, 139, 183, 202, 205, 283, 300
Osborne, John, 24, 34, 63, 92, 123, 124, 137, 150, 152–5, 158, 163, 184, 289, 301

Owen, Alun, 157
Owens, Rochelle, 211
Oxford, 175, 204, 239; New Theatre, 67, 177, 180; Playhouse Theatre, 113, 117, 179n; O.U.D.S., 54, 148

Page, Anthony, 111, 162, 163, 289
Palace Theatre, 31, 70, 74
Palladium Theatre, 70
Paradise Foundry, 33, 284
Parker, Al, 268
Parker, David, 223
Patrick, Nigel, 250, 294
People Show, The, 211–13, 215, 219
Philanthropist, The, 122, 123, 156, 158
Phillips, Leslie, 250
Phillips, Robin, 100, 133, 294
Piccadilly Theatre, 73, 145
Pilbrow, Richard, 131
Pilgrim Trust, 118
Pinter, Harold, 24, 32, 93, 99, 107, 117, 121, 138, 169, 183, 275, 287, 301
Pirandello, Luigi, 169, 184, 300
Plater, Alan, 36, 198
Plays for Rubber Go-Go Girls, 226
Plouviez, Peter, 256, 296
Plowright, Joan, 81, 87
Plummer, Christopher, 97
Pope's Wedding, The, 158, 283
Portable Theatre, 64, 212, 213, 220, 221, 225, 226
Portrait of a Queen, 124, 300
Present Laughter, 116, 300
Price, The, 128
Priestley, J. B., 24, 117, 124, 183
Prime of Miss Jean Brodie, The, 116, 300
Prince, Hal, 131
Prince Charles Theatre, 57
Prince of Wales Theatre, 58, 145, 306
Private Ear, The, and *The Public Eye*, 301
Prospect Theatre Company, 179
Proud, Frederick and Verity, 222
Purnell, Louise, 87
Pyjama Tops, 7, 121

Q Theatre, 209
Quare Fellow, The, 289

Queen's Theatre, 57, 68, 70, 118, 126, 135, 306
Quipu, 213, 217, 222, 225

Ramsay, Margaret, 280–2
Rattigan, Sir Terence, 24, 117, 239, 279
Rattle of a Simple Man, The, 301
Rayburn, Joyce, 116, 141, 205
Reckord, Barry, 152, 157, 159
Redman, Joyce, 81, 86
Redgrave, Corin, 250; Sir Michael, 81, 86, 90, 280; Vanessa, 280, 295
Rehearsal, The, 116, 300
Reinhardt, Max, 76, 275
Reluctant Peer, The, 116
Renaud, Madeleine, 155
Restoration of Arnold Middleton, The, 158
Rhinoceros, 137
Richardson, Ian, 87, 109
Richardson, Sir Ralph, 40, 86, 90, 156, 280, 299, 300
Richardson, Tony, 111, 115, 148, 153, 291
Richmond (Yorkshire) Theatre, 50, 172
Ride a Cock Horse, 280
Rigg, Diana, 122
Right Honourable Gentleman, The, 116, 300
Rites, 93, 106
Robert and Elizabeth, 116, 129
Robertson, Toby, 179
Rodway, Norman, 109
Rose Bruford College, 44, 45
Rosencrantz and Guildenstern Are Dead, 93, 280
Ross, 300
Rossiter, Leonard, 129
Roundhouse, 57, 65, 137, 214, 217
Rowland, Toby, 132
Royal Academy of Dramatic Art, 32, 42, 44, 45, 54, 295
Royal Court Theatre, 8, 24, 33, 34, 48, 63, 64, 70, 79, 81, 85, 111, 121–4, 127, 132, 136–8, 147–64, 173, 202, 209, 211, 215, 222, 246, 280, 282–4, 289, 294, 301, 302, 308, 309

Royal Hunt of the Sun, 93
Royal Opera House, Covent Garden, 60, 74, 144, 179, 238
Royal Shakespeare Company, 8, 12, 31, 32, 34, 35, 66, 78–114, 121, 124, 142, 147, 156, 157, 169, 179, 195, 202, 221, 224, 238, 280, 281, 284, 288, 294, 295, 302, 309; Barbican Theatre, 59, 66, 75; Stratford-on-Avon Theatre, 32, 59, 65, 79, 81, 83–5, 89, 100–2, 104, 106–10, 113, 119, 148, 295, 302
Royalty Theatre, 57, 126
Rudkin, David, 105, 106
Rutherford, Margaret, 120

Sadler's Wells Opera, 179, 238; Theatre, 60, 70
St James's Theatre, 28, 29, 70
St Martin's Theatre, 70
Saint's Day, 149
Salad Days, 124
Sandison, Gordon, 255
Sartre, Jean-Paul, 17, 120, 123, 149, 157
Saunders, James, 93, 117, 196, 234
Saunders, Peter, 74
Savages, 123
Saved, 156, 284
Saville Theatre, 129
Savoy Theatre, 116
Scala Theatre, 70
Schweyk in the Second World War, 168, 169
Scofield, Paul, 27, 34, 90, 94, 120, 136, 155, 280
Secretary Bird, The, 127, 140
Self Accusation, 217
Semi-Detached, 137
Sense of Detachment, A, 63
Serjeant Musgrave's Dance, 155, 280
7.84 Theatre Company, 221, 222
Severed Head, A, 124, 300
Shaffer, Peter, 92, 93, 290, 301
Shaw, George Bernard, 23, 32, 58, 117, 168, 173, 174, 275, 300
Shaw Theatre, 57, 75
Sheffield, 57, 183, 186, 205; Crucible Theatre, 188; Lyceum Theatre, 186; Playhouse Theatre, 198, 308

Shepard, Sam, 160, 211
Sherek, Henry, 120
Sherriff, R. C., 124, 168, 208
Showboat, 123
Silver Tassie, 107
Simmons, Pip, 212, 213, 215, 219, 220, 235
Simon, Neil, 277
Simpson, N. F., 151, 156, 157, 159n
Skyvers, 159
Slag, 122
Sleuth, 116, 126
Smith, Caroline, 199
Smith, Dodie, 116
Smith, Maggie, 81, 301
Soho Theatre, 213
Soyinka, Wole, 157, 159n
Sport of My Mad Mother, The, 159
Spring and Port Wine, 141, 301
Spurling, John, 92, 93, 106, 225
Stafford-Clark, Max, 211, 225
Stage Society, 32
Staircase, 94
Stanislavski, Konstantin, 27, 275
Stephens, Robert, 87, 98
Stirrings in Sheffield on Saturday Night, The, 198
Stoke-on-Trent (including Victoria Theatre), 12, 35, 75, 171, 183, 184, 196–8, 204, 205, 240, 241, 284
Stoll Theatre, 70, 132; Stoll Theatres (company), 129, 132
Stoppard, Tom, 77, 92–4, 218, 280, 301
Storey, David, 122, 123, 132, 154–8, 163, 276, 289, 301
Strand Theatre, 70
Stratford, Ontario, Theatre, 59
Strindberg, August, 106, 239, 275
Studio Theatre, 196
Sunderland, 26, 176
Sussex University, Gardner Centre, 187
Suzanna Andler, 133
Svoboda, Josef, 98
Swindon, Wyvern Theatre, 188

Taste of Honey, A, 137, 153
Tea and Sympathy, 297
Tearle, Godfrey, 252

Tennent management (H. M. Tennent), 34, 118–20, 124, 130, 133, 253, 280
Theatre Royal, Stratford East (and Theatre Workshop), 78, 79, 100, 137, 182, 302
Theatre Upstairs, 159–62
Theatregoround, 111–13, 195, 212, 235
Theatrical Managers' Association, 49
There's a Girl in My Soup, 117, 293, 300
Thomas, Gwyn, 149, 152, 157, 159n
Thorndike, Dame Sybil, 86, 250
Three Months Gone, 123, 155
Tiger and the Horse, The, 280
Time Present, 63, 155
Tiny Alice, 94, 100
Torch Theatre, 209
Tree, Beerbohm, 42, 58, 61, 117, 118
Trevor, William, 169, 222, 287
Trigon, The, 210
Tuckey, Anthony, 199
Turner, David, 137
Tynan, Kenneth, 31, 81, 86, 90–2, 98, 138, 151, 281
Typists, The, 210

US, 100, 288
Ustinov, Peter, 300

van Itallie, Jean-Claude, 122
Variety Artists' Federation, 40
Vaudeville Theatre, 71, 74, 278, 287
Vedrenne, John, 117, 150, 173
Vian, Boris, 105
Vivat! Vivat Regina!, 123, 124, 300
Voyage round My Father, A, 117, 123, 293

Waiting for Godot, 121, 298, 301
Wall, Alfred, 252, 253
Wallace, Hazel Vincent, 201
Warner, David, 85, 94
Wars of the Roses, The, 84, 85, 108, 113, 288
Watergate Theatre, 76, 209
Waterhouse, Keith, 301
Watford Theatre, 205

Webber Douglas Academy of Dramatic Art, 44
Wesker, Arnold, 150, 152, 154, 157, 158, 202, 280, 286, 289, 290, 301
West of Suez, 63, 123, 124
Westcliffe Theatre, 49
Westminster Theatre, 119
Wherehouse/La Mama, 211, 213
Whitby Lifeboat Disaster, The, 197
White, Michael, 122, 126, 136
Whitehall Theatre, 7, 121
Whitehead, E. A., 123, 127, 159, 160, 301
Whiting, John, 64, 149
Who's Afraid of Virginia Woolf?, 300
Wilkinson, Christopher, 226
William, David, 168
Williams, Clifford, 100, 293
Williams, Heathcote, 152, 156, 158, 159n
Williams, Hugh and Margaret, 116
Williams, Kenneth, 301

Williams, William Emrys, 230
Williamson, Nicol, 301
Wilson, Angus, 149
Wilson, Josephine, 167
Wilson, Snoo, 284
Windsor Theatre, 172, 234
Winnicott, Dr D. W., 11, 13, 19
Within Two Shadows, 160
Wolverhampton, Grand Theatre, 67
Wood, Charles, 64, 93, 117, 287
Wood, Peter, 151, 295
World of Paul Slickey, The, 63
Worth, Irene, 94
Wyndham's Theatre, 68, 70, 72, 143

Yavin, Naftali, 217
Yeats, W. B., 154, 174, 228
York Theatre, 172, 195, 200
Young Vic Theatre, 57, 94, 99

Zeffirelli, Franco, 98